PITT LATIN AMERICAN SERIES

Pitt Latin American Series
Cole Blasier, Editor
Selected Titles

Peru under García

An Opportunity Lost

John Crabtree
Latin American Editor
Oxford Analytica Ltd

University of Pittsburgh Press

Published in the U.S.A. by the University of Pittsburgh Press,
Pittsburgh, Pa. 15260

Published in Great Britain by The Macmillan Press Ltd

Copyright © 1992 by John Crabtree

Printed in Hong Kong

Library of Congress Cataloging-in-Publication Data

Crabtree, John
    Peru under García: an opportunity lost/John Crabtree.
      p. cm.—(Pitt Latin American series)
    Includes bibliographical references and index.
    ISBN 0–8229–1168–X
    1. Peru—Politics and government—1980– 2. Peru—Economic
conditions—1968– 3. García, Alan. I. Title. II. Series.
F3448.2.C73   1992
320.985—dc20   91–50755
                              CIP

For Isabel and Suzanna, and in memory of my father,
William (1905–91)

Contents

List of Tables and Figures

Tables

Figures

List of Maps

Preface

The military government of General Juan Velasco (1968–75) stimulated considerable interest in academic circles in the English-speaking world. This was because it highlighted the attempts of a poor, Third World country to change the pattern of its economic development and to introduce a series of radical social reforms. It also stood in contrast to the more conservative sort of military dictatorship which prevailed in much of Latin America at the time. Since then, the literature in English on Peru has been sparse. This is not because developments since the time of Velasco have been uninteresting or insignificant. The country has come to exemplify some of the worst effects of the Latin American debt crisis. It has given birth to one of the most singular guerrilla movements to have emerged in modern times: Sendero Luminoso. And, during the government of Alan García (1985–90) Peru defied the international financial community and evolved novel and heterodox methods to try to stabilise a highly inflationary economy.

The purpose of this book is to look at Peru in the 1980s, and in particular at the experience of the García government in the light of its ambitious goal to create a 'Perú diferente': to resolve some of the country's long-standing social, political and economic problems. It looks at both the achievements of García's first two years in office, and at the disappointments of the last three. It seeks to analyse both economic and political developments, and to see how these are interrelated. And it assesses the enormous difficulties that awaited García's successor, Alberto Fujimori, who took office in July 1990. In providing an overall view of the García administration, and one from an outsider, it is also hoped that it will make a contribution to the literature in Peru itself.

The book is divided into two parts. The first examines the situation which García inherited on coming to office and the first two years with the government's political and economic achievements; the second looks at the economic crisis of 1988 and its political and social consequences. Each part focuses on three separate themes: the economic context and the effects of policy; the political climate and in particular the relationship between government and political parties;

and finally the problem of political violence beyond the bounds of the formally established political system. The idea of this separation is not to isolate these elements but to let them stand side by side and to see how they affect one another. Indeed, the direction of policy and decision making cannot be properly understood without taking all three into account.

This work does not pretend to be the result of original research, although some of the material used is the author's own. It incorporates the views of recognised experts in different disciplines and fields of research, whose names appear in the acknowledgements. This book is thus the result of a collective research effort. The method of working was a little unusual, so in order to do full justice to those who collaborated, it is important to make this explicit. After an initial meeting in Lima, in July 1987, in which the framework was established, each contributor agreed to supply draft material on the understanding that the author would rewrite all of it into a more coherent whole. The idea was to avoid the discontinuities inherent in a book of essays, while at the same time letting the major themes stand on their own. Various of the contributors thereafter reviewed and commented on parts of the manuscript. But neither time nor finance permitted the writing of an 'agreed version'. Therefore, while any credit for this volume should be widely shared, the contributors are not responsible for its defects which the author accepts as his own.

The idea of writing an account of the García years in Peru first arose in 1986. It owes much to the initiative of Rosemary Thorp whose enthusiasm from the very start helped get the project off the ground. The original scheme, however, underwent several revisions. Not least this was because of the often unpredictable course of events in Peru itself. The bulk of the writing was done in the second half of 1989 and in the first few months of 1990, thereby taking into account the presidential elections of that year. The text was finally consigned to the publishers just as Alan García passed on the sash of office to Alberto Fujimori in July 1990.

Apart from acknowledging those who contributed to the text, special thanks need to go to the British Council and the Nuffield Foundation for timely financial assistance to cover essential costs; to the Economics Department of the Universidad Católica in Lima for providing me with space to work in, and to its head, Adolfo Figueroa, for his constant encouragement and advice; to the Instituto de Estudios Peruanos (IEP) and its director Efraín Gonzales for providing facilities and permitting the collaboration of a number of its researchers; and to José Augusto

Guilhon and José Alvaro Moisés at the Political Science Department of the University of Sao Paulo for giving me time and help in producing the final draft. I owe thanks to David Young at Oxford Analytica for allowing me to take time off from employment to write much of this book, and to Alan Angell and Malcolm Deas at St Antony's, who as well as providing moral support leant me their rooms in college while they were abroad. I am also indebted to those who read the text at different points and who made valuable criticisms, and in particular to Rosemary Thorp, Alan Angell, Adolfo Figueroa, Denis Sulmont, Guillermo Rochabrun, Felipe Portocarrero, Raúl Hopkins and Jonathan Cavanagh. A big debt of gratitude also goes to Elvira Ryan who typed much of the manuscript. Last, but by no means least, I want to acknowledge the help of Judith, my wife. Without her constant insistence and support this book would probably have never been started, and certainly never finished.

Oxford   JOHN CRABTREE

Acknowledgements[*]

Alberto Adrianzén	DESCO, Lima
Eduardo Ballón	DESCO, Lima
Eliana Chávez	CEDEP, Lima
Judith Cóndor Vidal	
Oscar Dancourt	Universidad Católica, Lima
Carlos Ivan Degregori	Instituto de Estudios Peruanos, Lima
Adolfo Figueroa	Universidad Católica, Lima
Alberto Giesecke	Instituto de Estudios Socio-económicos y Fomento al Desarollo
Romeo Grompone	Instituto de Estudios Peruanos, Lima
Narda Henríquez	Universidad Católica, Lima
Raúl Hopkins	Instituto de Estudios Peruanos, Lima
Sinesio López	Instituto de Democracia y Socialismo, Lima
Philip Mauceri	Cornell University
Andrew Nickson	Birmingham University
Liisa North	York University, Toronto
Fernando Rospigliosi	Instituto de Estudios Peruanos, Lima
Rosemary Thorp	St Antony's College, Oxford

[*]A list of those who kindly contributed in some way to this book.

List of Abbreviations

Adex	Asociación de Exportadores
ANP	Asamblea Nacional Popular
AP	Acción Popular
APRA	Alianza Popular Revolucionaria Americana
BCRP	Banco Central de Reserva del Perú
CADE	Conferencia Anual de Ejecutivos
CCP	Confederación Campesina del Perú
CGTP	Confederación General de Trabajadores del Perú
CITE	Confederación Intersectorial de Trabajadores Estatales
CNA	Confederación Nacional Agraria
Confiep	Confederación Intersectorial de las Empresas Privadas
Corah	Proyecto de Reducción del Cultivo de la Coca en el Alto Huallaga
CRF	Comando Rodrigo Franco
CTP	Confederación de Trabajadores del Perú
ECASA	Empresa Comercializadora de Arroz S.A.
ECLA	Economic Commission for Latin America
EGP	Ejército Guerrillero Popular
Enaco	Empresa Nacional Comercializadora de la Coca
ENCI	Empresa Nacional de Comercialización de Insumos
FEB	Federación de Empleados Bancarios
FOCEP	Frente Obrero, Campesino, Estudiantil y Popular
Fredemo	Frente Democrático
IDB	Inter-American Development Bank
Idesi	Instituto de Desarrollo del Sector Informal
IDS	Instituto de Democracia y Socialismo
IEP	Instituto de Estudios Peruanos
ILD	Instituto Libertad y Democracia
IMF	International Monetary Fund
INAP	Instituto Nacional de Administración Pública
INE	Instituto Nacional de Estadísticas
INP	Instituto Nacional de Planificación
IPAE	Instituto Peruano de Administración de Empresas
JNE	Jurado Nacional de Elecciones

MIR	Movimiento de Izquierda Revolucionaria
MRTA	Movimiento Revolucionario Túpac Amaru
PAD	Programa de Apoyo Directo
PAIT	Programa de Apoyo de Ingreso Temporal
PCP	Partido Comunista Peruano
PCR	Partido Comunista Revolucionario
PEAH	Programa Especial Alto Huallaga
PPC	Partido Popular Cristiano
PROEM	Programa de Empleo de Emergencia
PSR	Partido Socialista Revolucionario
PSR-ML	Partido Socialista Revolucionario – Marxista-Leninista
PUM	Partido Unificado Mariateguista
SAIS	Sociedad Agricola de Interés Social
Sinamos	Sistema Nacional de Movilización Social
SNI	Sociedad Nacional de Industrias
UDP	Unidad Democrática Popular
Umopar	Unidad Movil de Patrullaje Rural
UNIR	Unidad de Izquierda Revolucionaria

Peru

1 Introduction

The image of the 'beggar seated on a bench of gold' has often been used to exemplify the paradox of wealth and poverty in a country whose gold and silver in colonial times helped finance nascent European capitalism, but in which today poverty is more acute and widespread than in almost any country of Latin America. Lacking neither natural or human resources, Peruvians have been searching for the formula which ensures at once sustainable economic growth and the more equal distribution of wealth and power needed to establish a more stable economic and political system. The discovery of such a formula has long proved elusive.

Efforts to come to grips with Peru's problems have involved a wide variety of approaches, ranging from *laissez-faire* liberalism to comprehensive state intervention. Up until the 1960s Peru had an open economy geared primarily to the export of raw materials. The role of government was essentially passive: to provide the basic conditions of political stability so as to maintain export-led growth. But the problem was precisely that the model tended to benefit a small élite rather than the bulk of the population, and its failure to cater for rapid social change meant that it was inherently unstable. The political system failed to incorporate the majority of the population, who, by virtue of their increased levels of social organisation, came to represent an ever growing challenge to the political power of the élite.

Then, in 1968, a military coup brought to power a nationalist government committed to the modernisation of the country, its industrialisation, and to a programme of social reform aimed at redistributing income and wealth. Peru's military radicals, led by General Juan Velasco, were unusual in Latin America in seeing national security in reformist and developmental terms. Under the military government great emphasis was placed on the state assuming the central role in the promotion of the country's development. The state, it was thought, was a neutral force, independent of the main competing groups in society. Moreover, it was supposedly neither capitalist nor communist but Peruvian. Reliance on unfettered market forces was considered to encourage uneven development and exacerbate inequality. But the model was highly authoritarian, and even more exclusive than in the past: most of the Peruvian generals believed

1

that democratic institutions were incapable of engineering the social transformation required.

Under Velasco's successors, first under General Francisco Morales Bermúdez (who ousted Velasco in 1975) and then under the constitutional government of Fernando Belaúnde (1980–5), the pendulum swung back the other way. The role of the state in society was criticised for blunting private initiative and encouraging inefficiency and corruption. The system of constitutional government re-established in 1980 provided greater scope for popular participation than in the past, but the economic model adopted first by Morales Bermúdez and then Belaúnde did little to favour the interests of the poor majority. The 'structural adjustment' programmes adopted from 1976 onwards, under pressure from the international financial community, envisaged the return to a much more liberal approach with the emphasis on the market, not the state, as the most appropriate mechanism for the distribution of resources. But their impact tended to worsen rather than improve income distribution. Disillusioned with Belaúnde, in 1985 the Peruvian electorate looked for an alternative.

Alan García came to office promising a shift back towards the more statist approach. The market as the mechanism for successful development had again been found wanting. As under Velasco, more priority was given to state planning and economic intervention. But once again, as we shall see, the results were disappointing. The shortcomings of the García administration gave new impetus to the ideologues of the right, who, inspired by the apparent success of liberal economics elsewhere, campaigned for a radical assault on the power of the state. But, as the 1990 elections results were to show, there was widespread public scepticism as to whether the 'free economy' would be any more successful than in the past in resolving Peru's enduring social problems. Private profit, it seemed, was not the route to social equity.

The government of Alan García therefore tried to grapple with the deep-rooted problems inherited from the past within a democratic framework. The purpose of this book is to try to assess his government's performance in the light of these difficulties, and in the light of the shortcomings of his predecessors.

The task García faced was rendered more difficult in the context of the 1980s, with the effects of the debt crisis, the eruption of widespread political violence, and the expansion of the black economy prompted (amongst other things) by the boom in world demand for cocaine. Still, building on his electoral victory in 1985 and exploiting the divisions between his political opponants, García initially managed to elicit enormous public support for his reformist agenda. It provided an important opportunity to tackle Peru's structural problems in pursuit of a *'futuro diferente'*. But so as to understand the legacy of the past, we first turn to identifying these historical problems, which, while by no means unique to Peru, were all strands which combined to form in the Peruvian context a peculiarly intractable knot.

PATTERNS OF ECONOMIC AND SOCIAL DEVELOPMENT

One of the central problems of the Peruvian economy has been its failure to absorb the productive energies of a society which, between the 1940s and the 1970s, turned from being primarily rural to primarily urban. Traditionally, at least up until the 1960s, the most dynamic sectors of the economy were those geared towards supplying export markets. Indeed the characteristics of Peru's economic development from the time of Independence onwards had been shaped by the way the country was integrated into the world economy as a producer of raw materials to the industrialised economies.[1] In the mid-nineteenth century Peru became the world's major supplier of *guano*, a natural fertiliser produced from the deposits of sea bird droppings. During the twentieth century, following the collapse of *guano*, that integration was mainly through the mining and oil industries, though Peru was also an exporter of cotton, sugar and fishmeal. Compared with other Latin American countries, manufacturing was slow to develop, while traditional agriculture – undercapitalised and inefficiently organised – showed little dynamism. The most recent commodity boom is that of coca and cocaine.

Not only did the pattern of development make the Peruvian economy vulnerable to oscillations in the world price of notoriously volatile commodities – the 1929 crash, for instance, produced a period of severe economic dislocation – but also extractive industries tended to do little to help develop the economy as a whole. The economic spin-off effects of mining and oil production were limited, both in terms of the sort of investment and the amount of employment they generated. At any rate, the benefits tended to accrue to Lima rather than to the areas in which extraction took place.

The pattern of export-led growth at times had a perverse effect on the development of local industry. Periodic booms for specific commodities brought with them cycles of abundant foreign exchange which made it easy and cheap to import; and imported goods tended to compete with what nascent local industries produced.[2] The development of Peruvian industrial capitalism and entrepreneurial experience was also limited by the degree of foreign ownership in the country's more dynamic economic sectors, and by the economic advantages which foreign companies often managed to obtain. The US-owned Cerro de Pasco Corporation came to dominate the mining industry of the central *sierra*; the International Petroleum Corporation (IPC) gained control of the oil industry in the north; the Marcona Corporation extracted Peru's iron-ore reserves; and the Grace Corporation became a leading sugar exporter. Foreign capital also played a major role in the development of railways, communications and banking.

Thus, though the 'open' economy which prevailed up until the 1960s had advantages – over the long term it ensured an annual rate of growth of around 1 per cent per head at a time when population growth was rapid – it did not constitute a *development* model. It failed to provide for a more equitable distribution of the benefits of growth or do much to ensure employment for those who began to abandon agriculture and move to the cities. It did not help reduce the dichotomy between the traditional sector of the economy with its low productivity, and the more capital-intensive, often foreign-owned modern sector – a dichotomy sharpened by the strong geographical differentiation between the coast and the *sierra*. It did little to encourage a dynamic agricultural sector capable of feeding a fast-growing population without recourse to imports. It did not foster the growth of a strong and independent class of entrepreneurs capable of dynamising Peru's own capitalist development. And finally, it did not encourage the development of state institutions since the export model did not require an interventionist state in order to function.

But, after a prolonged period of economic growth in the late 1940s and 1950s, the pattern of export-led development itself was entering into difficulties by the 1960s. Up until that time increasing export supplies in response to periodic booms in world demand had come from 'horizontal' extension – incorporating new land in the case of agriculture, tapping new mining deposits or fishing more intensively. Up to this point Peru's main difficulties had stemmed more from the fluctuation of world demand than from its capacity to supply. By the 1960s, however, increasing supply required heavier investment than in the past, coupled with greater need for technology and more sophisticated entrepreneurial skills. Extension of the agricultural frontier (especially on the coast) involved costly irrigation schemes. The opening up of new mineral deposits necessitated new mining operations rather than the extension of old ones. The expansion of oil production meant developing new fields in the jungle rather than tapping existing coastal wells in the north. Finally, in the fishing industry exploitation began to run up against biological limits of supply. Economic development therefore called for a new model of accumulation to finance the investment required.[3]

Imbued with much of the development thinking emanating at the time from the UN Economic Commission for Latin America (ECLA), the Velasco government sought to address these deficiencies. The main thrust of economic policy was to promote import-substitutive industrialisation. This went hand in hand with the nationalisation of most of the key foreign-owned companies which had dominated the export sector; a fairly radical programme of land reform (designed to help push Peru's élite from agriculture into industry as well as to reduce inequality within rural areas); and the creation of a regionally integrated market for manufactured exports, the Andean Pact.

However, while such a model represented an important break with the past, it raised new difficulties and in some cases exacerbated other long-term problems. Though the Velasco government finally broke the political power of the old landed élite, reduced foreign participation and produced some redistribution of income in favour of wage earners, it failed to produce a private sector capable of spearheading industrial development. Nor did the agrarian reform do much to remove the inefficiencies which had plagued *latifundista* agriculture, while the government – concerned to ensure cheap food in the cities – prejudiced agricultural development by keeping prices low and resorting to imports.

The pattern of import-substitutive industrialisation that took place in the early 1970s in fact did little to break Peru's economic dependency on the more developed world. Not only were many of the manufacturing companies which established themselves subsidiaries of foreign companies, but most relied heavily on imported raw materials, inputs and machinery in order to produce. The amount of value-added generated in Peru was often small. For this reason industrial growth came to hinge crucially on the foreign exchange available to finance imports.

Nor, as we shall see, through its industrial development strategy did the military government do much to help reduce regional disparities. Despite awareness of the need for regional development, industrialisation was concentrated almost entirely on the coast, and in particular in

Lima. In fact the strategy probably made old regional imbalances even more pronounced: while the economy as a whole grew quite fast up until 1975, the economies of the least developed departments, especially those of the southern *sierra*, stagnated. Agriculture as a whole suffered from the recourse to importing food on a large scale.

But perhaps the most important deficiency of all was the failure to develop a sustainable model of accumulation to help finance the accelerated pace of development. Bereft of foreign investment and lacking a strong self-confident private sector or a local capital market, the state necessarily became the motor of development. But without a tax system able to provide an adequate local revenue base, the military government opted for the 'easy' way of paying for public investment by tapping the fast-developing Eurodollar market.

With the glut in recycled petrodollars caused by the 1972 OPEC oil price rise, it was cheap to borrow. With dollar inflation higher than international interest rates, it was a borrowers' market. To the bankers, Peru, with its own oil export potential (exaggerated at the time), seemed a fair bet. The result was a plethora of expensive but badly planned and poorly supervised public investment projects – most of them signally failing to generate the foreign exchange to repay the money borrowed. The consequence was a debt on which servicing obligations quickly outpaced the country's ability to pay. Peru's foreign debt increased sevenfold between 1970 and 1979, more than in many other heavily endebted countries of Latin America. Forced by the 1975–6 debt crisis into the hands of the International Monetary Fund (IMF), and under strong pressure from the banks, the military government of Morales Bermúdez found itself beating the retreat from Velasco's development strategy, but unsure as to what to put in its place.

The achievements and limitations of the Velasco period have to be set against the background of the profound changes in the nature of Peruvian society during these years, and specifically in the pattern of distribution within it. While overall the population of the country grew more rapidly than in many other countries of Latin America – an annual rate of 2.7 per cent between 1950 and 1985 – this growth was concentrated in the cities. In most rural areas, especially in the more backward, the population grew only slowly, if at all. Whereas in the 1940s six Peruvians out of every ten lived in rural areas, by the late 1980s it was only three out of every ten. Meanwhile, the population of Lima, the capital, doubled in the fifteen years between 1960 and 1975. Peru changed from a rural into an urban country.

The key to this dramatic change was the pattern of internal migration. This was, of course, a pattern paralleled by population movements in most other countries of Latin America. In a few cases, like Brazil, the scale of migration was even more pronounced than in Peru. As elsewhere, the dynamic of migration was determined by a combination of 'pull' and 'push' factors. Though rural poverty, the push factor, was of great importance, it was very often the more prosperous, younger and more mobile peasants who migrated. They were attracted by the pull of the city, the prospect of a better income and a better life. This meant that the negative effects of migration were compounded in the economies of the communities left behind, bereft of their more capable workforce.

The process of migration was accompanied and accelerated by the spread of education in the 1960s and 1970s. Primary education, especially in rural areas, expanded faster in Peru than most other countries of Latin America at the time. Though the numbers were much less, there was also a rapid increase in those participating in secondary and further education. The barriers between the city and the *campo* were broken down further by the development of road communications and the spread of the mass media.

In the cities, the consequence of migration was the development of the shanty town, as newcomers made their precarious homes on the fringes of existing urban areas. Around Lima, from the 1950s onwards, new squatter 'cities' began to appear on the hitherto uninhabited desert dunes, on land set aside for urban development or previously used for agriculture. Irrespective of lack of land titles, the squatter settlements on the urban periphery soon turned into more permanent forms of settlement, as bricks and mortar replaced panels of woven reed, cardboard and corrugated iron.

In employment terms, the corollary of this was the growth of what in the late 1960s and early 1970s was termed 'marginality', and in the 1980s renamed the 'informal sector'. The basic problem was that the supply of new workers into the labour market far outpaced the capacity of the economic system to provide jobs. Despite the growth of manufacturing industries in the 1970s, these did not absorb the available manpower. But the growth of the city itself led to the development of new types of employment. Migrants to the cities found it easier to enter into the service sector or into distribution and retail than into activities like manufacturing where wages were higher. Workers in the informal sector enjoyed little or no job security, received none of the benefits of social security, and (with few

exceptions) were outside the world of the trade union or the collectively agreed wage contract.

The term 'informal sector', however, covered a multitude of types of
employment, varying from the street-seller to small-scale 'informal'
factories providing inputs – usually very cheaply – to large industries in
the formal sector. In some industries indeed 'informal' firms undertook
the manufacture of technologically unsophisticated products or
components. In the main, however, economic units were small and
usually based around the family. Measurement of the size of Peru's
informal sector runs into obvious problems of definition and of how to
quantify those who work beyond the reach of official statistics
gatherers. What is clear is that the size of Peru's informal sector grew
very fast from the 1950s onwards, and the effects of recession in the
formal sector of the economy beginning in the mid-1970s contributed
significantly to its expansion. By the mid-1980s the informal sector is
thought to have accounted for around one third of the workforce, and
the black economy in Peru had become one of the largest of any
country in the whole of Latin America.[4]

One attempt at quantification of the scale of the changes in Peruvian
society in the 1960s, 1970s and 1980s has been undertaken by the
sociologist Joel Jurado, on the basis of census material and other
official statistics. His results show with striking clarity the shrinkage of
Peru's peasant population (especially the servile and communal
peasant forms) since 1960; the growing importance of medium-scale
farming; the growth of the urban informal sector; and the shift in the
structure of formal employment from blue-collar to white-collar
activities (Table 1.1). And, in as much as he links these findings to
the structure of national income distribution, Jurado underlines the
tendency towards a less equal rather than more equal distribution of
income.[5]

The important point here is that, despite the achievements of the
Velasco government (when real wages reached an all-time high), and
despite the process of urbanisation and *descampesinización*, Peru
remained one of the Latin American countries with the most unequal
patterns of income distribution, only slightly more equal than the
countries of Central America. According to a study carried out by
ECLA on the basis of data for the year 1970, roughly half the total
number of households in Peru were classified as being below the
poverty line, as defined by the income needed to acquire a minimal
basket of goods and services.[6] According to the same study, a quarter
of Peruvian households were beneath what was defined as the 'extreme

Table 1.1   Peru: occupational structure, 1961–88

	Percentage of the labour force			Participation in national income (%)[3]		
	1961	1981	1988[1]	1961	1981	1988[1]
1. Peasant	32	24	22	6	4	3
Servile	10	2	1			
Communal	15	10	8			
Land-owning	4	6	6			
Semi-peasant	3	6	7			
2. Small and medium landholders	2	6	8	3	6	7
3. Urban informal	15	19	22	13	14	12
Workshop	4	5	6			
Street sellers	5	10	12			
Services	6	4	4			
4. Wage earners	49	50	47	47	31	29
Blue collar (priv)	29	19	15			
Blue collar (pub)	3	5	5			
White collar (priv)	4	12	14			
White collar (pub)	7	10	10			
Domestic	6	4	3			
5. Employers	2	1	1	22	41	47
Total %	100	100	100	91[2]	96[2]	98[2]
Total (thousands)	2951	4753	7100			

[1] Estimates on the basis of official surveys

[2] The remainder is accounted for by net interest.

[3] Official figures on the share-out of national income provide only a rough guide.

Source: Joel Jurado; 'Protagonismo de las Clases Populares: Límites y Potencialidades en la Crisis' (mimeo) (Lima: IDS, 1989).

poverty' line, below which income was insufficient even to pay for a minimal amount of food. Of the ten countries included in the study, only Honduras had greater indices of poverty on both scores, and only Brazil had the same extreme poverty rating as Peru. Comparing these findings with figures for 1985–6, and using similar definitions, a more recent survey showed 57 per cent below the poverty line and 32 per cent below the extreme poverty line.[7] According to this newer study, just to return to 1970 levels of poverty would involve a massive transfer of 20 per cent of GDP to 60 per cent of the population.

Nor, as we have seen, did the pattern of development pursued by Velasco and other presidents before or since do much to alter the social disparities in Peru when analysed geographically. A study conducted by the central bank in the early 1980s illustrates very clearly the sharp differences between GDP per capita in the coastal departments (especially Lima) and those of the *sierra*. It shows how low GDP per capita correlated almost exactly with areas with the highest levels of illiteracy, with the highest levels of infant mortality and with lowest rates of life expectancy.[8] By almost all the key indicators the poorest part of Peru continued to be what used to be referred to disparagingly as the *mancha india*, the departments of Ayacucho, Apurímac, Huancavelica, Cuzco and Puno. Excluded from the benefits of any 'development strategy' adopted by successive governments – Velasco included – these departments received only a tiny fraction of both the public sector investment budget and overall government spending. The agrarian reform did not boost the poorest, least competitive or least capital intensive types of agriculture, and the poorer peasants were not among its chief beneficiaries.

Just as the social composition of Peru's population has undergone profound change over the last fifty years, so too has its ethnic and cultural profile. While in the 1930s and 1940s it was still possible to draw a fairly clear contrast between the largely indigenous populations of the *sierra* and the *mestizos* and *blancos* of the coast, the process of migration led to a blurring of the distinction. This is the argument, for instance, of both José Matos Mar[9] and Carlos Franco[10] who, building on work done in the 1960s, point to the phenomenon of *cholificación*. By this they mean the fusion of popular cultures – Andean and coastal – into a new urban culture – what is now called *chicha* culture – today a hallmark of the popular classes in Lima and other major urban centres.

But this fusion, the result of mass migration, has not led Peru to become a more homogeneous country either ethnically or culturally. Arguably it is even more heterogeneous than ever, with greater variety in the degrees of *mestizaje*. The majority of the population of Lima is constituted by first or second generation immigrants who preserve ties with their places of origin, despite the often large distances involved.

Cholificación has not led to the disappearance of racism or racial consciousness. Indeed, the direct contact between *cholos* and whites is more frequent, and therefore the prejudices are probably stronger. There is a strong sense of cultural frustration among migrants in Lima, especially among the young.[11] At the same time, the cultural gap between the urbanised *cholo* and the *indígena* who stays behind has also become greater. It is difficult to understand the acceptance and even support which Sendero Luminoso came to enjoy in the 1980s without first understanding the strong sense of ethnic and cultural marginalisation in the *sierra*. Indeed, in Peru, as elsewhere, a strong sense of ethnic identity has been one of the factors that has favoured rural insurgency.

The ethnic divide in Peru is greater than in most other countries Latin America. This is partly a result of the proportion of the total population, rural and urban, of indigenous descent. But it is also partly a result of the fact that in other countries with big indigenous populations, like Mexico and Bolivia, there were violent revolutions and social upheavals during the course of this century which upset the pre-existing social order and brought with them an upgrading of the role of *indígenas* in society and an improvement of their social status. In Peru, however, there has been less of a revaluation of *indígena* social status, and despite the achievements of the Velasco years, the extent of social mobility in racial terms has probably been less than in either Bolivia or Mexico. At least in these two countries *indigenismo* became an important element in revolutionary ideology. In Peru, with the brief exception of the reforms of the Velasco years (which ratified Quechua as an official second language and changed history teaching in schools to exalt the country's Incaic past), such changes tended to be fairly superficial.

The transformation of Peruvian society from the 1950s onwards thus did not take place *pari passu* with the development of the country's economic structure. When compared with elsewhere in Latin America, economic growth in Peru was sluggish. Moreover, it was highly uneven, benefiting urban rather than rural areas, the coast rather than the *sierra*. The pace of urbanisation and the spread of both education and the mass media brought with it new demands for greater equality in the distribution of the benefits of growth. It also brought forth new forms of social organisation pushing for change, and expectations of a better future. So while the size of the cake stayed the same (or grew only slowly) the numbers fighting for a bigger share of it increased rapidly.

PATTERNS OF POLITICAL DEVELOPMENT

How did this pattern of uneven development and the persistence of a large degree of social inequality affect Peru's political development? Perhaps the overriding characteristic of Peru's political development this century has been the elusive nature of democratic and participatory forms of government. Again, in relation to the rest of Latin America, democracy has been particularly difficult to achieve, even in its most formal sense. Table 1.2 indicates the succession of military or military-backed governments, interspersed by only brief periods of elected government, and then only governments elected on a very limited franchise. When Fernando Belaúnde handed the presidential sash on to Alan García in 1985, it was the first time for forty years that one elected president passed on executive office to another. The 1980s, therefore, represented a new departure in Peruvian politics – a decade of elected government – even though for many it was not a political system which they felt adequately articulated their interests.

Historically, it has proved difficult to establish even a minimal consensus in Peruvian politics. In part this is a function of the extent of social differentiation. Such consensus is more difficult to achieve in a country with wide extremes of wealth and poverty; and wealth is easier to redistribute in an economy with rapid and sustained growth. But it is also conditioned by a number of specifically political factors: successive challenges to the political system arising from popular mobilisation which proved difficult to absorb; the weakness of the main political parties as mechanisms to articulate popular pressure; and the failure of the state to respond to the challenge of distribution.

The process by which the mass of the population came to participate in the political system during the course of this century was not an easy one. Popular mobilisation encountered fierce repression as well as eventual accommodation or co-optation. It proved difficult to exert influence in a system that offered few democratic opportunities, just as it proved difficult for the political élite to manage the pressures from below.

There have been four key periods in which those who previously lacked a political voice became active participants. The masses first made an appearance as a political force in the presidential campaign of Guillermo Billinghurst. Then, as a result of the social change that took place in the early part of the century and in particular during the eleven-year Leguía dictatorship (1919-30), there was a further period of mass political participation in the late 1920s and early 1930s. During the Leguía period both the working class and middle class grew, but at the margins of the political system. The eruption of the masses into the political life of the country, triggered by the 1929 economic collapse, was through the emergence of two new parties: the Socialist Party (which later became the Communist Party) of José Carlos Mariátegui and the American Popular Revolutionary Alliance (APRA) of Víctor Raúl Haya de la Torre. Of the two, APRA quickly gained pre-eminence. Though partly due to Mariátegui's premature death, the speed of APRA's growth owed much to Haya's skill in interpreting and articulating popular ideology. While in other countries of Latin America social change and the crisis of the old oligarchical regimes of the 1930s led to forms of government which widened political participation, this was not the case in Peru. The Aprista challenge to the *status quo* was successfully resisted and for long periods the party was driven underground, its leaders exiled and its rank and file brutally repressed.[12] The failure of APRA, Peru's first genuinely mass-based party, to win power in the 1930s set back the process of political incorporation by at least a generation.

A third period of political mobilisation took place in the 1960s, largely as a result of the development of agricultural capitalism and the weakness of the old land-owning élite. The first Belaúnde government (1963–8) played a central role here. In an attempt to appeal to a wider public as the man capable of modernising the country, Belaúnde's political campaigns of 1962 and 1963 awakened expectations, especially in rural areas – so did the spread of public education and the mass media. The Belaúnde government witnessed one of the most extensive waves of peasant protest in Peru this century, with land seizure in the *sierra* on a large scale. Helping to orchestrate protest was a small, but radicalised 'new left', strong in the universities and encouraged by the 1959 Cuban revolution.

A fourth phase – to a certain extent an extension of the third – arose during the Velasco regime. As was the case with Belaúnde, Velasco awakened expectations but failed to satisfy them. The scale of reform, however, was much more ambitious than under Belaúnde. The Velasco government sought to defuse social tension through timely reform and to mobilise popular organisation behind it. To this end it set up institutions like Sinamos (the National System for Social Mobilisation) and its own trade unions. Sinamos helped provide an impetus for popular organisation, but then failed to satisfy the expectations it helped generate. Increasingly, both in the urban and rural context, the newly mobilised of the 1970s came under the influence of the Marxist

Table 1.2 Political regimes, 1930–85

Years	Head of State	Political orientation	Mode of acquiring power	Percentage voters in total population
1930–31	Interim governments	Centrist	*Coup d'état*	
1931–33	Col Luis M. Sánchez Cerro	Conservative/repressive; APRA persecuted	Free elections	6.83% (1931)
1933–39	Gen.Oscar Benavides	Conservative/repressive; APRA persecuted	*Coup d'état* following assassination of Sánchez Cerro by Aprista	
1939–45	Manuel Prado y Ugarteche	Conservative/lessening repression of APRA	Controlled elections	9.09% (1939)
1945–48	José Luis Bustamante y Rivero	Centrist with APRA support	Partly controlled elections[*]	10.66% (1963)
1948–56	Gen. Manuel A. Odría	Conservative/repressive; APRA persecuted	*Coup d'état*	
1956–62	Manuel Prado y Ugarteche	Conservative with APRA support	Partly controlled elections[*]	17.5% (1956)[**]
1962–63	Military junta	Moderately reformist	*Coup d'état*	

1963–68	Fernando Belaúnde Terry	Moderately reformist	Free elections	18.09% (1963)
1968–75	Gen. Juan Velasco Alvarado	Radical nationalist	*Coup d'état*	
1975–80	Gen. Francisco Morales Bermúdez	'Neo-liberal'	*Coup d'état*	28.05% (1978 Constituent Assembly)
1980–85	Fernando Belaúnde Terry (AP)	'Neo-liberal'	Free elections	34.79% (1980)
1985–90	Alan García Pérez (APRA)	Moderately reformist	Free elections	45.00% (1985)

* APRA was not permitted to present its own presidential candidate.
** Women gained the franchise in 1955.

left. Indeed, from the beginning of the 1970s onwards the left came to be widely seen as the only channel through which popular energies could transform the country. The Velasco period saw the rapid development of a left-wing presence in the popular movement in all its various aspects: among the urban shanty towns, among the peasant federations, and among organised labour in which APRA's previous commanding position had been whittled away. It was a highly radicalised left, in which Trotskyist and Maoist as well as new left currents gained substantial weight, openly challenging the military government for its 'fascist' and corporatist leanings. It was also highly ideological, challenging all aspects of the 'bourgeois' establishment, including the state. In an already highly politicised climate, frustration at the limits of military reformism and at the gap between the government's rhetoric and its actions bred radicalism, especially in areas where the effects of reform were slight. It was in part the conviction that social mobilisation was getting out of control – that the results were proving to be the opposite of those intended – which prompted more conservative officers to oust Velasco in 1975.

As the social programmes of Velasco were abandoned by Morales Bermúdez, the Marxist left – despite its fragmentation – gained further ground in articulating protest and mobilising anti-government sentiment in the popular movement as a whole. The national strikes of 1977 and 1978, involving the union movement, students, and shanty-town dwellers, probably represented the high point of left-wing ability to organise the mass movement in opposition to the *status quo*. But as the left came within the pale of parliamentary politics after 1980, it became involved within the established political system and less of a direct challenge to it.

The re-establishment of constitutional government in 1980 was of course an important point in the move towards a more participatory kind of political system. Not only did the 1979 constitution establish universal adult suffrage for the first time by abolishing all literacy qualifications, but the 1980 election brought parties with genuine popular backing within the political system. However, the degree of effective popular influence over government proved to be limited. There were large sectors of the population which felt excluded – or at best only marginally involved in it – and which had little confidence in its ability to represent their interests. This feeling of marginalisation was especially strong outside Lima, in those parts of the country by-passed by the process of development. Ayacucho, the birthplace of Sendero Luminoso, was a case in point.

The development of democratic institutions was also hampered by the failings of the political parties in representing the interests of specific groups within the political system. The frequency of military dictatorship this century is itself an indication of the weakness of the party system.[13] This weakness can be traced back to the early years of the century, when none of the country's traditional political parties survived. Peru, for instance, stands in contrast to countries like Colombia and Uruguay where traditional parties persisted and transformed themselves into parties with mass backing. Also, as a consequence of APRA's failure to impose itself in the 1930s, Peru stands in contrast to countries like Brazil, Argentina and Mexico which emerged with strong nationalist and populist political movements during these years. APRA's initially radical ideology and its penchant for militaristic conspiracies helped reinforce the axis between the oligarchy and the armed forces, and their determination to exclude APRA from the political sytem.[14]

The only other major party to emerge was Belaúnde's Acción Popular. For a brief period in the 1960s it seemed that Peru was moving towards a system of competitive two-party politics, with APRA and Acción Popular vying for popular support. But APRA's behaviour did much to sabotage the system. By using its presence in Congress where it allied with the most conservative forces to block the Belaúnde government's programme of mild social reform, it helped precipitate the 1968 coup and another twelve years of military rule.

An important feature of the development of popular political parties in Peru was their hierarchical, personalist and authoritarian nature. They did not evolve as democratic structures with leaders accountable to the rank and file or with high levels of popular participation in policy formulation.

The most extreme example of the authoritarian, top-downwards political party is APRA. Until his death in 1979 Haya was the absolute leader of the party. Though the way party structure evolved was affected by the experience of repression and the need to organise in clandestinity, Haya's approach to politics had always been authoritarian. As an exile in Europe in the 1920s he had been impressed by the rise of fascism, and the party he created on his return to Peru was highly hierarchical. A huge gulf separated the leaders and the led, the party's institutional bureaucracy in Lima and its mass following. There were no 'wings' or spectrum of views to be found in APRA, and the most important political value which Apristas were encouraged to respect by means of an effective system of party discipline, was unquestioning loyalty. At the grass roots Aprismo was more a religion than an ordinary political movement. It was held together by faith that Haya would eventually lead the party – and Peru – to acheive a new, less exploitative kind of society.[15]

Personalism and politics 'from the top downwards' also was a feature of Acción Popular in the 1950s and 1960s, though not quite to the extremes inherent in Aprismo. Acción Popular was the personal political vehicle of Fernando Belaúnde. Like Haya, Belaúnde stood above the rest of the party's main leaders; he was the source of decision-making and party doctrine. At the same time, however, Acción Popular never developed the same system of discipline; nor did it generate the same sort of 'religious' fervour. Though Belaúnde enjoyed support in rural areas through some of his government's more populist measures, Acción Popular was more a party which appealed to a critical, less accepting, middle-class clientele.

Authoritarianism in politics reached its peak in Peru during the Velasco regime – ironically because the political parties had proved ineffectual in bringing about the sort of changes which the radical generals of the late 1960s thought were needed to prevent a social explosion. The Velasco government sought to replace the political parties as intermediaries between the people and the state by means of corporatist experiments like Sinamos. There was, however, an inevitable confusion as to what the functions of such institutions were supposed to be: channels of representation for grass roots feeling or rather mechanisms of social control from above. Irrespective of the aims, the result was a wave of radicalised social pressure which it became increasingly difficult to satisfy.

The growth of left-wing parties during the 1970s, in response to the frustrations that arose as a result of the military government, also revealed authoritarian features. This in part came from their Leninist concept of the party and the commitment of most of them to armed struggle. But it also arose from a personalist political tradition. Despite attempts throughout the 1980s to make leadership on the left more responsive to grass roots opinion, the achievements were only modest. In the public mind at least, parties continued to be associated with their leader figures, the 'line' more often coming from the top rather than from below.

So, as Peru returned to constitutional government in the 1980s, an authoritarian/personalist tradition persisted. The danger for democracy consisted in the extent to which the country's political 'class' – wider than it had been in the past but still fairly exclusive – really represented the interests and aspirations of those it purported to represent.

Finally, the third aspect of the Peruvian political system which requires emphasis is the lack of effectiveness of the state in mediating social conflict and ensuring at least a minimal amount of redistribution in favour of those with least resources. Despite its size and theoretical powers, the Peruvian state has not been noted for its success on either score.

The development of state institutions has not followed an even path. The original export-led model, as we have seen, did not require a sophisticated, interventionist state; and up until the 1960s the public sector was small in Peru compared with many other countries of Latin America. The size of the state began to grow rapidly during Belaúnde's first administration, but it mushroomed under Velasco. From 1968 to 1975 the social reforms enacted, the nationalisation of key industries and the rationalisation of others all led to a proliferation of agencies within the public administration and to the creation of new public companies both big and small. Within the conception of a pattern of development that was neither communist nor capitalist, the state played a central role as an independent entity within the political and social system, planning, financing and executing programmes aimed at developing the country, and at the same time engineering changes to ensure a more ordered distribution of the benefits of growth.

What were the main deficiencies of the state in Peru as it evolved from the Velasco period onwards? First, the pattern of bureaucratic development was excessively centralised on Lima. Irrespective of its stated intention of trying to improve the integration of the country, the military government in administrative terms increased the gulf between the capital and *provincias* by centralising control of all state agencies in the capital. The institutions of the state at the local level, especially in rural areas, did not receive the same attention as at the centre where large sums were spent, for instance, on extravagant office building to enhance the prestige of the bureaucracy. More seriously, decision-making was also concentrated in Lima, exacerbating regional and local antagonisms against the centre. This political centralisation was further enhanced by the weakness of local government in Peru. The first municipal election took place in 1963. From 1968 to 1980 local government had little meaning. Only after 1980 did local politics emerge once again, with municipal elections in 1980, 1983, 1986 and 1989. But though local politics gained considerable importance, the independence of local government continued to be circumscribed by dependence on central government for funds.

Secondly, the state emerged from the military government as a structure particularly susceptible to clientelism, corruption and inefficiency. Such defects have been magnified because of the fall in public sector wages during the 1980s and the failure to provide adequate training facilities to improve levels of competence and commitment among state employees. Patterns of corruption and clientelism are, of course, difficult to document, but the Peruvian state – especially those sectors of it with which the public has most direct contact – has an unenviable reputation for both. The treatment which individuals receive often appears to depend crucially on their ability to pay to swing decisions in their favour, or on their political contacts higher up the bureaucracy. The result is widespread cynicism in relation to the real autonomy of the state, and whether it can ever really work in the interests of those without money or political influence.

Thirdly, and related to this, is the lack of any real democratic control over the state. The problems of corruption and inefficiency have been aggravated by the autonomy and unaccountability of the more powerful state institutions and the absence of effective controls against malpractice. Major public companies like Petroperu operate with a large degree of independence from other departments of central government. The military enjoys even greater autonomy, an autonomy which it jealously guards. In these circumstances it is sometimes difficult for a president, especially a civilian one, to exert effective control over the functioning of the state as a whole.

It is even more difficult for the Congress to do so, even though one of its functions is supposed to be that of overseeing (*fiscalización*) the operation of the government and the rest of the state sector. The 1979 constitution increased the powers and responsibilities of the executive branch *vis-à-vis* the legislature, precisely to prevent the sort of clash between the two powers which helped bring down the first Belaúnde government in 1968. The independence of the legislature has been further circumscribed by the fact that during the 1980s the party in power enjoyed an effective majority in Congress, even though at times the legislative branch was able to flex its muscles and show a degree of independence.[16]

At the local level, where the party in office was not necessarily the same as that in Lima, there has been rather more by way of attempts by elected local government to exert some control over state functionaries. And where local mayors, for instance, enjoy widespread popular support, directly elected representatives have been able to force government-appointed officials to take local concerns into account in making decisions.

One of the paradoxes of Peru, indeed, is the distance between the pretensions of the state – the formal powers and responsibilities of president, government and public sector – and the weakness of these institutions in practice. One of the lessons learnt from the experiment in military reformism was that grandiose programmes of economic and social reform were in fact as good as the mechanisms which existed to put them into effect.

Peru thus entered the 1980s facing many problems which twelve years of military rule had failed to resolve. But of the various challenges, three major ones predominated, each closely related to the others. The first was how to achieve a more dynamic economic performance than in the past, capable of helping to absorb the effects of social change and modernisation and of satisfying people's expectations of a better future. Economic growth, in turn, hinged on tapping new sources of capital to finance development and on creating new markets both at home and abroad for the goods and services produced. Given limitations on the availability of foreign exchange, this meant prioritising those parts of the economy like agriculture, in which expansion did not require importing large amounts of raw materials, machinery or other inputs. The second challenge was how to combine growth while altering the pattern of distribution within society to promote greater equality. Without more equality of income it would be more difficult to create domestic markets to underpin growth. Also without greater equality, in the long run it would be difficult to achieve the sort of political stability needed to provide the foundations for economic development to take place. But was it possible to create greater social equality while at the same time relying on the private sector, the pinnacle of the pyramid of income distribution, as the key source of capital investment? Was it possible to redistribute – and in Peru any redistribution would have to be radical to have any real effect – without causing a political reaction from the private sector which would undermine political stability? The third challenge was how to consolidate a participatory democracy in which the size of the gulf between the state and the majority of the people was reduced. It was an urgent priority, for instance, probably clearer in retrospect than at the time, to attack the degree of political alienation characteristic of most of the country outside the capital. It was urgent to create new channels for popular participation in government at various levels, and thereby create an institutional basis for absorbing popular pressure. But how was this to be done in the context of limited resources and often intense competition for them? Indeed, was it possible to democratise further without risking a political breakdown? Or was a political breakdown of the existing order the *quid pro quo* for real change to take place in Peru?

The experience of the García government was to highlight many of these dilemmas as it set out to tackle some of Peru's more long-standing problems.

Part I

The Upswing, 1985–7

2 Economic Policy: Playing by New Rules

THE INHERITANCE

It was with high hopes and a sense of mission that members of President Belaúnde's economic team took up their jobs in 1980. Many of them had returned to Peru, like Belaúnde himself, from the United States. There, typically, they had worked in universities, corporations or in the IMF, World Bank or other multilateral financial agencies. Their aims on returning to Peru were to liberalise the economy. They sought to promote the private sector and to reduce the economic role of the state which had grown so during the military government; to increase the degree of competitiveness within the domestic economy and in foreign trade; to promote foreign investment as a motor of longer-term growth; and to reorient investment priorities generally towards export-led growth rather than import-substitutive industrialisation. They thus sought to modify in a very fundamental way the nationalistic and statist development strategy adopted by the military government of General Velasco.

The confidence of the new team, led by Manuel Ulloa (who combined the role of prime minister and of economy and finance minister), was boosted by Peru's economic 'miracle' in 1978 and 1979. Faced with a balance of payments crisis in 1975 and 1976, the Morales Bermúdez government had been forced by its foreign creditors and the IMF to introduce economic stabilisation policies, reversing many of the policies of the Velasco years. By 1979 Peru's external accounts had improved significantly and the trade balance had turned strongly positive. Having been previously blacklisted by the international financial community, the country was held up as proof of the beneficial effects of adjustment policies. In fact much of the improvement stemmed from the dramatic effect on exports caused by two major projects – the Cuajone copper mine and the northern Peru oil pipeline – coming on stream in 1977. These were projects initiated by the Velasco government itself, but delayed.

Whereas ministers under Morales Bermúdez were forced to undertake stabilisation measures because of the balance of payments crisis, their pragmatic approach gave way to a more ideological one under Ulloa and his team. The economic recovery of 1979–80 gave the new government an important margin for manoeuvre, which it sought to use to liberalise the economy. One of the most striking aspects of the new policy was to reduce the level of protection enjoyed by Peruvian industry by removing import prohibitions and reducing tariffs. It thereby sought to make Peruvian manufactured goods more competitive and to reduce inflation by allowing cheap imports to substitute for relatively expensive Peruvian-made goods. The government also sought to make the financial system more competitive, to sell off state companies, and to liberalise labour markets by getting rid of job stability, profit sharing and the labour communities, reforms introduced by the Velasco government.

This liberalising agenda for the longer term was, however, knocked off course with the return of balance of payments problems in 1981 and 1982. The Peruvian 'miracle' proved a very transient phenomenon. Low commodity prices hit the value of exports, especially copper, silver, lead and coffee. At the same time, the Belaúnde government's efforts to liberalise trade and reduce protective barriers led to a surge in imports. The level of imports in 1981 was almost double what it had been in 1979. As a result a $1.7 billion trade surplus in 1979 gave way to a $553 million deficit in 1981 and a $429 million deficit in 1982.

An important element of the Ulloa strategy was to make use of Peru's improved credit rating to finance development projects and the current account deficit through new loans. The new government initially received enthusiastic support in Washington at the World Bank which not only increased its own lending but encouraged commercial banks to do so too. Project spending increased rapidly in the first two years, helping to satisfy President Belaúnde's appetite for public works programmes. It was further to boost Peru's credit rating that Ulloa, in 1981, went so far as to make a substantial debt repayment of $377 million ahead of time. Then, just when exports were falling and imports rapidly increasing, the supply of commercial loans dried up in the wake of the Mexican debt default of August 1982.

From 1982 onwards Peru once again found itself obliged to submit to an IMF adjustment programme. In June 1982, it entered into a three-year Extended Fund Facility arrangement, whose aim was to stabilise the economy by way of a contraction of domestic demand. As is customary, the programme adopted involved a steady depreciation of the exchange rate, increases in the tariffs charged by public sector companies, the reduction and in some cases elimination of subsidies, the tightening of monetary policy and the imposition of strict curbs on government spending. The cornerstone was the reduction of the fiscal deficit, considered by the Fund to be the main motor of inflation. But reducing the deficit also proved to be the target which was hardest to achieve.

The resignation of Manuel Ulloa in December 1982 and his replacement by Carlos Rodríguez Pastor, a vice president of one of Peru's larger creditor banks, Wells Fargo, led to a renegotiation of Peru's terms with the IMF and the pursuit of targets with even more single-minded vigour. The year 1983 proved to be particularly difficult. The return to recession was aggravated by the climatological effects of the Niño phenomenon: widespread flooding in the north; drought in the south and the severe reduction in fishing catches all along the coast. The result was an extreme form of a problem familiar since 1975: 'stagflation', a combination of economic stagnation and high price inflation. In 1983, the average rate of inflation doubled to 111 per cent, while the economy contracted a full 12.2 per cent, a recession unparallelled in Peru at least since the 1930s. There was negative growth in all sectors of the economy, but manufacturing and construction were hardest hit by the collapse in domestic demand.

The longer-term policy goals which Ulloa and his team had espoused at the outset thus gave way once again to short-term, emergency-style economic management. The notion of planning was, in any case, downgraded by the Belaúnde government. It relegated the National Planning Institute (INP), which had played a prominent role under Velasco, to the administrative sidelines. Much of the Economy and Finance Ministry's time and energies went into negotiation with creditors, and trying to keep within IMF targets. The goals of longer-term development strategy were largely sacrificed for short-term fiscal austerity, with the public sector investment programme taking the brunt of cuts in public spending. Existing projects were stretched out (often a false economy), and new ones put on ice. But perhaps most importantly, it became increasingly clear that in the Peruvian case, conventional orthodox tools were not achieving either lower inflation or the greater macroeconomic stability needed for a resumption of growth. In fact the opposite seemed to be the case: orthodox policies were having perverse effects. With Peru's dependence on imports (not least food imports) devaluation spurred inflation while the competitiveness of exports was only marginally enhanced. The raising of the domestic price of petrol to reduce the fiscal deficit pushed up prices.

The attempt to keep interest rates higher than inflation also forced up prices as producers passed on higher financial costs to the consumer.

Inflation, it seemed, was driven in the short run more by costs than by the fiscal deficit. The adoption of orthodox measures contributed to a deterioration of government revenue by inducing recession and thus undermining the yield from taxes on income, profits, sales and trade. Also, up until 1984, when the Belaúnde government fell behind on interest payments on the foreign debt, a large portion of government spending was being channelled into debt repayment, making the deficit still harder to control. Indeed, given the size of spending on the debt and public sector imports, a large part of government spending had no bearing at all on domestic demand (Table 2.1).

One effect which stabilisation policies *did* have, however, was to revive the trade surplus. This was not achieved through increasing exports – up until 1985 exports hovered at just over $3 billion a year (lower than in 1979–80) – but through the dramatic contraction of imports. These fell from $3.7 billion in 1982 to as low as $1.8 billion in 1985. Without new loans coming in, orthodox policies proved effective in correcting the balance of payments.

Alarmed by the scale of the recession and the swing of public opinion to the left. Belaúnde sought to intervene more directly in economic policy. The Marxist Izquierda Unida (IU) won the municipality of Lima from the ruling Acción Popular (AP) in November 1983, while APRA during 1984 became favourites to win the 1985 elections. In December 1983, Belaúnde dismissed Rodríguez Pastor. Thereafter the inconsistencies in policy making became ever more evident. Though macroeconomic policy was in theory tied to the pursuit of IMF targets, Belaúnde sought to achieve economic reactivation in advance of the 1985 elections. As a result, the terms of a new agreement with the IMF in 1984 were violated almost before it was formally signed. Three finance ministers came and went in the last sixteen months of the administration, and by August 1984 the Peruvian government opted to buy time by suspending interest payments on the commercial debt.

Though orthodox policies helped improve Peru's balance of payments in the short term, they had negative effects of longer-term significance.

First, they resulted in a sharp fall in real living standards. Per capita income fell from the equivalent of $1232 in 1980 to $1055 in 1985. Real wages, which had risen slightly in 1981 and 1982, recovering from a precipitous fall with the 1976–7 stabilisation measures, proceeded to

Table 2.1   The Belaúnde government, 1980–5: economic indicators
(percentage growth rates)

	GDP Growth	Consumption	Investment	Exports	Imports	Inflation
1980	4.7	6.0	45.0	−11.6	36.4	59.2
1981	5.5	3.3	23.8	0.2	18.7	75.4
1982	0.0	1.4	−8.8	11.6	1.5	64.5
1983	−12.2	−4.4	−39.1	−11.6	−25.6	111.1
1984	5.1	2.3	−8.1	5.3	−19.5	110.2

Source: Central Bank.

tumble again in 1983 and 1984. Similarly, unemployment rose as the result of recession. Some 7 per cent of the workforce were officially qualified as unemployed in 1982, compared with almost 11 per cent in 1984. Unemployment and 'underemployment' in the official figures rose from just under 50 per cent to 54 per cent, with only 35 per cent of the workforce having adequate employment in 1984. The rise in unemployment, the lowering of subsidies on basic foods, and cuts in government spending in areas such as health and education hit the poor particularly hard.[1] The wealthier sectors of society, meanwhile, found it easier to mitigate the effects of inflation on income, through non-payment of taxes, dollarisation of their financial assets, and, especially in 1983 and 1984, through capital flight.

The crisis also hit investment (see Table 2.1). The deteriorating business environment after 1982 provided no incentive for the private sector to invest, while the higher cost of credit provided a further disincentive. Gross private investment in the economy fell from 21.2 per cent of GDP in 1982 to 12.2 per cent in 1985. Meanwhile, enforced austerity in the public sector led to a decline in public investment from 8.4 per cent of GDP to 6.3 per cent in 1985. At the same time, direct foreign investment which totalled $67 million dollars in 1981 slumped to $9 million by 1985.

A third effect of the crisis was what can loosely be described as the strengthening of defence mechanisms among the population as a whole. Collectively, this made it harder for the government to administer the economy effectively by the conventional tools. One such defence mechanism was dollarisation as those holding financial assets sought to protect their value in face of accelerating inflation and low real domestic interest rates. The pace of dollarisation during the Belaúnde period was rapid. At the end of 1981 30 per cent of deposits in the banking system were denominated in foreign currency; by the end of 1984 the figure was 49 per cent. In the labour market the main defence mechanism was the growth of the black or informal economy. Contraction of employment in the formal sector of the economy during the Belaúnde government, especially after 1982, meant rapid growth in the informal urban economy, where wages tended to be low, and other benefits, like access to social security, non-existent. The faster growth of the informal economy in relation to the formal did nothing to improve the government's tax income and made it more difficult to administer other types of economic policy like price controls.

A specific aspect of 'informality' requires separate mention: the coca/cocaine industry. In response mainly to demand in the United States, coca/cocaine became probably the fastest growing industry in Peru during the Belaúnde years. Acreages (mainly in the north-eastern Alto Huallaga valley) expanded rapidly (see p. 115). The numbers who came to depend directly or indirectly on coca agriculture and processing increased substantially, as did the amounts of money involved. The effects of recession from 1982 to 1985 made coca agriculture and *narcotráfico* an increasingly attractive proposition, albeit at the margins of the law, and stimulated rapid migration into the main producing areas.

By the time it reached 1985, the Belaúnde administration appeared to have lost its way. It had shed the liberalising impetus with which it had begun. Nor was there much to show for the reforming zeal of Ulloa's team of the first two years. The role of the state in the economy had not been reduced in any fundamental way; and though attempts to sell off public companies had consumed considerable time and energy, privatisation had been minimal. Partly as a result of hostility from organised labour, liberalisation of the labour market had had only limited effects. Even the policy of trade liberalisation had to be abandoned in favour of more protection to local industries as average tariffs by late 1983 were raised well above than their 1980 level. At the same time there was a growing perception, encouraged by the opposition on the left, that the methods of crisis management advocated by the IMF were not only failing to stabilise the economy, but were making stabilisation ever harder to achieve.

The political shift to the left during the last two years of the Belaúnde government, largely in response to the increasing unpopularity of the government's economic policies, thus helped focus attention on the search for alternatives.

THE 'HETERODOX' ALTERNATIVE

Whichever party had won the 1985 presidential elections would have had to examine alternatives to the sort of prescriptions which had guided economic policy for most of the Belaúnde period. The twin problems of debt and the effects of IMF stabilisation policies were at the top of the political agenda. Far from stabilising the economy, these policies seemed to do the opposite by inducing both inflation and recession.

García's first policy speech to Congress on 28 July 1985 was a response to the public mood. Since in some ways it was a more radical statement than APRA's election manifesto or even that of the Izquierda Unida, it served to boost expectations of a 'new beginning' in economic policy. It represented an alternative to what had gone before. The position on debt – limiting debt service payments to 10 per cent of exports – will probably be the part of the speech that will be best remembered, especially outside Peru. However, the speech attacked the IMF and orthodoxy, making it clear that Peru would no longer seek the mediation of the Fund in its dealings with its creditors.

Soon after García's speech to Congress, in the first week in August, the new government presented a much more detailed policy package. As well as announcing the psychological move of bringing in a new currency, the inti (which involved knocking three zeros off the highly devalued sol), the package focused on the freezing of key prices in the economy. Following an initial 12 per cent devaluation, the exchange rate against the dollar was to be a fixed one. Also, after an 18 per cent across-the-board wage increase and a 25 per cent increase in domestic fuel prices, prices and wages were to be frozen. Finally, interest rates were to be reduced in nominal terms in line with the fall in the inflation rate. In many respects the government's emergency economic plan bore more than just a passing resemblance to Argentina's Austral Plan, enacted six weeks earlier. It included, for instance, a number of essential price rises as the prelude to a freeze. But unlike the Argentine plan, which was conceived and born in the context of negotiations with the IMF and which finally received IMF backing, the Peruvian variant – like Brazil's Cruzado Plan the following year – was born in a spirit of defiance towards the international financial community.[2]

The Peruvian 'heterodox' position[3] was based on two fundamental but closely linked principles. The first was that normal debt payment, involving the export of large capital surpluses, was inconsistent with growth. The experience of Latin America since the Mexican crisis of 1982 had shown that the large trade surpluses required to service the debt could only be created by contracting imports. The value of exports was determined largely by factors beyond the influence of individual countries. But growth could not take place with imports falling. This was particularly the case of countries like Peru whose industrial output was highly dependent on imported inputs and raw materials. Since the renegotiation of debt payments depended on IMF policy conditionality being observed, and since the IMF's programmes had recessionary effects, the only alternative was not to negotiate but to limit such debt payments. What was saved in debt servicing could be used to pay for continued imports.

The second principle was that inflation in Peru was not the consequence of excess demand in the economy stimulated by too much public spending. For the Fund, budget deficits tended to be the standard explanation for inflation, and all stabilisation packages stressed the need to reduce such deficits. The existence of a large amount of idle capacity in Peruvian industry was itself indicative of the fact that excess demand was not a problem. While Peru had suffered the worst recession in living memory in 1983, inflation had accelerated, not fallen. The architects of heterodoxy stressed that the explanations for inflation were to be found on the 'cost' side. They stressed the effects of constant devaluation on retail prices; the impact of persistent increases in the prices charged by state companies (particularly the price of fuel); and the consequences of ever higher interest rates on companies' costs. In regard to the fiscal deficit, some went so far as to argue that it could actually be anti-inflationary and that in the short run using public spending to boost consumption reduced the unit costs of those producing to meet that demand.[4]

More specifically, the heterodox model rested on a series of assumptions derived from the above. One such assumption was that in the Peruvian situation non-payment of debt was the only way to provide the leeway to embark on reactivation without provoking an immediate balance of payment crisis. With its high dependence on imports, growth in Peru would lead inevitably to balance of payments difficulties, sucking in imports and possibly even diverting exports by making it more profitable for exporters to offload production on the domestic market. Not only would reduced debt payment mean less government revenue having to be syphoned off to pay creditors, but that a higher level of imports could be tolerated. The fairly healthy state of foreign reserves of $868 million in July 1985 helped.

A second assumption was that underused capacity would provide a margin to reactivate the economy through increasing real wages without creating new inflationary pressures. It also gave a breathing space to get a longer-term plan into operation in which to mobilise investment funds and to expand fixed capacity.

A third assumption was that reactivation, especially when coupled to lower debt payments, would lead to an improvement in the country's fiscal accounts by way of a higher yield on taxes on income, consumption and imports. This would mean less pressure to print money in order to finance the budget deficit.

Taking what they saw as being the vicious circles of recession and inflation generated by the orthodox experience, Peru's advocates of heterodoxy considered it possible to turn vice into virtue by turning orthodox policies on their head. If it was true that certain prices in the economy were of such decisive importance, then controlling them (or even freezing them) could have positive effects, especially in the short term. This meant that it would be possible to control expectations which heterodox economists tended to stress as being the crucial factor in making inflation in countries like Peru so difficult to eliminate.

Heterodox thinking, however, took time to develop, and it did so in reaction to concrete economic problems rather than as the result of following a preconceived blueprint. When Alan García became president there were no such blueprints available. APRA's own policy document, worked out by Conaplan (an APRA think-tank) in advance of the 1985 elections, was not considered worthy of publication. Conscious of the need to break with past policy, the government appears to have found some inspiration in the Izquierda Unida's *Plan de Gobierno*. This was drafted in 1984–5 under the guidance of the prominent Catholic University economist, Javier Iguíñiz, and set out to provide a set of alternatives to orthodoxy. But perhaps the most direct influence on the emergency economic plan was the Austral Plan itself. President Raúl Alfonsín's visit to Lima in July came at a particularly significant moment, and had a strong influence on García's decision on how to proceed.

The important point here is that Peruvian heterodoxy evolved in an improvised fashion in response to immediate pressures. This was to prove to be one of its weaknesses. It did not involve the careful and measured synchronisation or harmonisation of different aspects of economic policy – notably between wage, fiscal and monetary policy within an overall pattern of objectives. Indeed, the degree to which wage expansion would lead to growth appears to have been largely unforeseen by those in charge of economic policy at the outset. Nor did policy involve the meshing of short-term emergency measures with longer-term policies of structural reform.

The immediate effects of the government's heterodox package bore out some of the assumptions on which it was based. The rate of inflation, the most politically visible economic indicator, fell sharply. The monthly rate, which had risen as high as 12.2 per cent in April 1985, and which had settled back into the 10–12 per cent range in May, June, July and into August, fell in September to 3.5 per cent, in October to 3 per cent and in November to 2.7 per cent. While the notion of a price freeze had aroused considerable scepticism owing to the difficulties of policing a freeze in a country with such a large informal sector, the reduction in inflation was a striking achievement, even though Peru never came near to the zero rates of inflation temporarily recorded in Brazil the following year in the wake of the Cruzado Plan.

The effect of the programme on economic reactivation took longer to become evident. The initial impact on production was less notable. It was not until the second quarter of 1986 that there were sudden leaps in GDP, when, encouraged by the success of the initial package, the government sought to take further steps to boost real incomes. Real family income in Lima increased by 25 per cent between July 1985 and October 1986.

In sectoral terms, growth naturally was concentrated in those areas of the economy most responsive to increases in domestic demand: in manufacturing, construction and (to a lesser extent) in agriculture. By contrast, production levels in the sectors geared primarily to export, like mining and fishing, proved relatively stagnant. The size of the 1986 boom – over 10 per cent growth overall – came as a surprise to the policy-makers responsible (Table 2.2). Advance estimates had to be constantly revised upwards as the year went on and as new figures came in. It turned out to be Peru's best single year since the time of President Odría and the export-led boom of the early 1950s during and after the Korean War. In comparative terms, Peru's growth performance outshone the whole of the rest of Latin America. Inevitably, it was cited as what could be achieved by playing by new rules.

Another result of the government's policy was the preference of the public to hold their money in intis rather than in dollars. With the exchange rate frozen, it was no longer so attractive to hold dollars, and with lower inflation there was less need for such hedges. In June 1985, 57 per cent of total liquidity in the Peruvian banking system was

Table 2.2   The Garcia government, 1985–7: economic indicators
(% growth rates)

	GDP Growth	Consumption	Investment	Exports	Imports	Average annual inflation
1985	1.5	3.2	− 14.9	3.5	− 7.7	163.4
1986	10.1	10.8	54.9	− 13.4	23.8	77.9
1987	7.8	10.7	11.4	− 4.8	10.6	85.8

Source: Central Bank.

denominated in foreign currency; by the end of 1986 only 13 per cent was, and the proportion continued to fall during the first few months of 1987. One reason for this was that the government maintained a restrictive monetary policy, limiting credit to the private sector. Firms were thus forced to finance the working capital needed as a result of expansion by selling their dollar-denominated holdings to the central bank, helping thereby to boost dollar reserves. De-dollarisation was further encouraged by the 1985 decision to suspend the system whereby Peruvians held dollar-denominated certificates of deposit within the Peruvian banking system.

The growth in consumer demand did not cause an immediate rise in prices, though towards the end of 1985 shortages, particularly of food, began to appear. Inflation remained remarkably stable throughout the year, even though slightly above the average monthly rate during the last four months of 1985. During 1986 inflation varied between a minimum of 4 per cent (August and again in October) and a maximum of 5.3 per cent (March). But by the end of the year it became obvious that though prices were being kept down, it was at the cost of overvaluation of the inti and growing deficits in public sector companies whose costs rose faster than the prices they charged the public. Already, by the second half of 1986, the warning lights were beginning to flash concerning the problems that lay ahead.

First, a point which heterodox economists tended to downplay, was that reactivation was not leading to an improved fiscal situation through higher tax revenues, as was supposed to happen. Though in 1985 the public sector deficit was down to 2.7 per cent of GDP, the lowest since 1979, in 1986 it increased again to 5.1 per cent of GDP. This was not because of an increase in spending. In fact, despite the impression given of a free-spending populist administration, total public sector spending (current and capital) fell from 49 per cent of GDP in 1985 to 29 per cent in 1986. Total current income, however, also fell – from 46 per cent of GDP in 1985 down to 33 per cent in 1986 (see pp. 59–62). The government faced a dilemma between the short-term needs to provide incentives to specific economic groups and to keep public sector prices from rising, and the more long-term objective of achieving adequate financing for the state.

Secondly, by the end of 1986, the imminent problem of production reaching the limits of capacity in the economy, made it urgent to find ways of getting new investment going. In turn this highlighted the need for a credible strategy of accumulation. With no substantial new investment coming from abroad and with no significant new loans entering the economy, the government shifted its focus towards the Peruvian private sector as the most important source of funds for investment. How Alan García sought to court Peru's main economic groups around a plan for collaboration between the private and public sector is described below (see pp. 84–7). Here it is worth stressing that the government's strategy for investment was not well mapped out in advance; nor was it put into practice speedily once García took office. Indeed, it was not until July 1986, a full year after he became president, that he had his first top-level meeting with eminent private business-men to coordinate and develop joint investment plans.

The third main area in which the cracks in the model became clearly visible by late 1986 was in Peru's external accounts. In 1985, the trade surplus was nearly $1.2 billion, the highest since 1979, and an important factor in the build up of reserves. This, as we have seen, was due primarily to the depression of imports to as low as $1.8 billion, less than half their 1981 and 1982 level. Exports in 1985 were just under $3 billion, also their lowest since the 1970s. But as the reactivation fed through, imports rose. By the third quarter of 1986 the trade surplus had vanished. The quarterly import totals for 1986 show the rate of acceleration: $450 million in the first quarter, $625 million in the second, $707 million in the third and $814 million in the fourth. Given the fall in commodity prices for many of Peru's key primary exports, total exports were also down to just over $2.5 billion in 1986. Over the year as a whole Peru had a small trade deficit of $65 million. The breakdown of imports once again highlights the close relationship between the level of activity in the economy and the demand for imports. Consumer goods rose from $129 million in 1985 to $378 million in 1986; inputs from $824 million to $1242 million, and capital goods (proportionately less) from $558 million to $761 million. Food imports, a direct response to higher real wages (classified partly under consumer goods, partly under inputs), nearly doubled from $204 million to $386 million.

With debt repayments in 1985 and 1986 well in excess of the government's own 10 per cent limit, and with net debt flows becoming increasingly negative in the year, the balance of payments situation showed rapid deterioration as 1986 progressed. There were particularly large losses of foreign reserves in the second and last quarters: $268 million and $311 million respectively. Between March and December net international reserves in the banking system fell from $1.45 billion to $870 million, even though at the end of the year net reserves were still roughly equivalent to four months worth of imports, hardly a balance of payments crisis in itself. Though it is hard to put values on the illegal 'balance of payments', cocaine exports certainly helped the situation. Cocaine exports from Peru are thought to have brought in around $700 million–$1 billion a year at this stage, a key element in the foreign exchange equation, and one which made it easier to stabilise the parallel market for the dollar.

Finally, another problem symptomatic of a loss of confidence in the government's ability to sustain its economic model, was the increase in the price of the dollar on the parallel market. For its first sixteen months in office the government had managed to stabilise the free dollar market, partly by successfully reducing demand for dollars. At the end of August 1985, following the initial 12 per cent devaluation, the free exchange rate had settled at just over 17 intis to the dollar. It only passed the 18 inti level fourteen months later in October 1986, finishing the year at 20 to the dollar. The gap between the official dollar and the parallel dollar up until October 1986 varied between 24.5 per cent and 27 per cent. However, with fears about a coming balance of payments crisis coupled to the loss of reserves in late 1986, the differential began to grow. At the end of 1986 it stood at 43 per cent. In the first half of 1987 the parallel dollar went from 20 intis to 40 intis to the dollar, and the differential between this and the official rate widened to over 100 per cent. It thus became clear that the central bank was no longer able to control the dollar market. And, with reserves becoming increasingly scarce, it became ever more important for businessmen and others to acquire dollars. The rise in the price of the dollar was rapidly becoming a self-fulfilling prophecy.

The first half of 1987 represented a crucial moment for the government to take stock of the situation and to introduce adjustments to the heterodox model in order to avoid predictable difficulties in the future. As the year began, monthly inflation was still below 5 per cent, the government's political standing in the country was still strong, and though foreign reserves were down the government did not yet have a balance of payments crisis on its hands. But confidence about the future was beginning to wane. The majority of Lima's economic soothsayers were agreed that balance of payments difficulties, coupled with lack of investment, would cause a new crisis unless correctives were adopted.

For its part, the government believed confidently that it could get through 1987 – even 1988 – before serious problems arose. Officials geared policy towards another year of rapid expansion of the economy. Increasingly, however, the government began to feel the constraints – domestic and external – under which it was operating. It found itself trying to reconcile competing objectives: rectifying worsening external imbalances, remedying the problem of deteriorating public sector finances, and getting the private sector to invest, all within the context of keeping inflation down and production up. Already, by the end of 1986, the government found itself being forced to abandon important elements of its original heterodox plan. It started to try to curb wage rises, for instance, and to resort to devaluation of the inti. The problem was, however, that these tended to be *ad hoc* measures rather than parts of a planned transition from short-term stabilisation to a longer-term strategy of sustainable growth.

The main thrust of policy in the first half of 1987 was to get private sector investment flowing into industry on the basis of the political agreements reached between Alan García and the representatives of the key economic groups. However, the government's policy towards private business was itself erratic. Faced with the dilemma of appealing to the business sector and trying to get it to contribute more to the costs of the state through higher taxes, policy lurched uncertainly between these two objectives. For instance, in early 1987 the government introduced a compulsory bond scheme under which companies were obliged to buy bonds worth up to 30 per cent of their pre-tax profits in 1986. The scheme was greeted with howls of protest from representatives of the private sector who saw it as a confiscatory tax introduced without prior consultation; they took little notice of official assurances that the money would be ploughed back into the private sector through a state-sponsored investment programme. While the government had doubts about the sincerity of private sector promises to invest, threats of compulsion quickly sapped business confidence.

Inconsistent and sometimes arbitrary behaviour did not help. Having incurred the fury of private business over the bond scheme, the government proceeded to backtrack, allowing some and finally all Peruvian companies off the hook.

By the middle of 1987, then, there were unmistakable signs of the difficulties that lay ahead. Flagging confidence, especially in the private sector, as to the government's ability to sustain its overall policy made the situation worse. Dollar speculation appeared once again. And just when a steady hand was most needed in managing the economy, political rivalries at the highest level – between García and the economy and finance minister Luis Alva Castro – led to Alva's resignation in June 1987 (see p. 92). It was in this context that the president was planning to regain the initiative with his most daring move yet: the nationalisation of the country's private banking system.

DEBT POLICY

The issue of debt was a central one in the 1985 election campaign. All Peru's major parties agreed in their manifestos that the foreign debt could not continue to be paid as scheduled. The tone varied somewhat, with the Izquierda Unida arguing for a selective moratorium through to the right-wing Partido Popular Cristiano (PPC) which sought a more conciliatory, negotiated but long-term settlement with creditors. APRA's position had been to limit debt service payments to 20 per cent of annual exports.

On taking office, in 1985 Alan García decided to turn Peru's difficult debt situation to his advantage by assuming a radical stance. In his address to Congress on 28 July he made his famous declaration that he would be limiting debt servicing to the equivalent of 10 per cent of annual exports. The announcement – a specific commitment in a speech otherwise full of generalities – took public opinion by surprise. The strong position on the debt issue helped boost the new president's already high popularity. At last, it seemed, a president of Peru was standing up for Peruvian interests rather than those of the country's foreign bankers. But the debt stand also had an economic as well as a political logic. The idea of limiting debt repayments, and thereby stemming the outflow of foreign reserves, formed an integral part of the heterodox formula. The hard currency saved was to be used to protect reserves, to help stabilise local currency markets and to pay for the imports which would be needed to sustain a policy of growth.

In the rest of the world, the commitment to limit payments in this way caused a considerable stir. For the first time, a heavily indebted country was unilaterally limiting debt payment to its own perceived capacity to pay. Even more significantly, a debtor country was elevating non-payment to a central plank of economic policy. In common with other Latin American governments before it – notably Nicaragua and Bolivia – Peru under Belaúnde had decided it could not pay interest payments; but it had done so quietly, not challenging the banks openly or trying to turn the whole question of the debt into a major international issue. Though García did not explicitly call on other Third World countries to copy Peru, preferring just to advocate coordination with other Latin American countries through the Cartagena Agreement, it was quite clear from this and later speeches that he wanted to give leadership on the debt issue.[5] The seriousness with which his challenge was taken at the time was revealed by the speed at which the US authorities came up with proposals to relieve the burden of debt of those countries which stayed within the rules; the so-called Baker Plan, unveiled in October 1985 at the Seoul meeting of the IMF and the World Bank.

At the same time as deliberately politicising the debt question internationally, the actual wording of García's statement was cautious. It was not that Peru was reneging on its debt obligations; García said that the Peruvian government accepted the responsibility to pay and would do so as and when economic circumstances permitted. He also accepted responsibility for the poor use to which loans had been put by previous governments. There was not, at least at this stage, to be any discrimination between loans contracted by, for instance, the military governments between 1968 and 1980. Also the Peruvian position stood out in marked contrast to the more radical one adopted by Fidel Castro, who, at just this time, was calling on Latin American governments to stop paying altogether. Furthermore, as García announced it, the Peruvian '10 per cent' was, in the first instance, a temporary measure to last for his first twelve months in office. García repeated a number of times his government's willingness to negotiate or 'dialogue' with creditors with the sole proviso that negotiations would be direct and not under the auspices of the IMF.

Also, as became clear during García's first year at the helm, the '10 per cent' limit, though sounding specific, offered ample room for manoeuvre based on the definitions that were applied. It was left unclear at the outset whether the '10 per cent' was to include repayments on the private sector's foreign debts. Would it include short-term or trade-related debt, or just medium- and long-term obligations? What about debt payments being made in kind rather than in cash? And did 'exports' mean merchandise exports only or rather exports of goods and services?

As time passed it became clear that '10 per cent' was interpreted very narrowly, allowing for more rather than less debt to be paid. It transpired that it referred to public sector medium- and long-term debt only. By 1986 it became clear that barter deals were being left out of the equation (since 1983 an important form of repayment for debts to the Soviet Union and other eastern bloc countries). Then it slipped out that debt payments to other Latin American governments and specifically Latin American multilateral lenders were being left out of the calculation as well, while the percentage referred to goods and services, not just goods.

Nor was it made clear in García's speech to Congress what criteria would be used to decide – within the 10 per cent limit – whom among the creditors would get what sort of priority. This was subsequently made more explicit: those who would be repaid first would be those who continued to lend more than they were repaid. It was appreciated early on that what mattered from a balance of payments point of view was more the net inflow or outflow of capital rather than repayments *per se*. Peru had to ensure that net flows were positive. In fact a rough and ready order of priority suggested itself naturally. At the top of the list came the multilateral lenders, given the increased scale of lending from this source (especially from the World Bank) since 1980, and the number of loans contracted but not fully disbursed. The IMF, however, was not to be included here. Next came creditor governments followed by the commercial banks, suppliers and then, last of all, the IMF. The last three, it could be assumed, would at best receive only very small amounts.

In practice, however, repayment policy operated on a rather more *ad hoc* basis. Payments to specific creditors tended to be made at the eleventh hour to avoid reprisals. In April 1986, for instance, $35 million was paid to the IMF to avoid Peru being declared 'ineligible' for further Fund lending. Similarly, on a number of occasions last-minute payments were made to the US government under the threat of the Hickenlooper and other amendments being invoked. The banks also received a 'symbolic' $17.7 million in 1986 as Peru tried to keep renegotiation talks on the rails.

The pattern of debt repayment and disbursements in 1986, the first full year of the García administration, as between different types of creditors, is illustrated in Table 2.3. The figures refer only to public sector debt, and of that only to medium- and long-term obligations.

Table 2.3   Debt repayments and flows, 1986

	I US$ Service Payments	II Disbursements	III Difference (II-I)
Commercial banks	27.8	—	– 27.8
Latin American governments	68.6	35.2	– 33.4
Eastern bloc governments*	88.7	27.8	– 60.9
OECD governments	48.4	140.4	+ 92.0
Other governments	—	0.4	+ 0.4
Multilateral organisations	228.9	160.1	– 68.8
Suppliers	21.3	11.3	– 10.0
Others/various	24.8	—	– 24.8
Total	508.5	375.2	– 133.3

* includes payments in kind.
Source: Ministry of Economy and Finance, quoted in *The Peru Report*, August 1987.

Taking the strictest definition possible (that used by the government, excluding from the equation private, short-term, payments in kind, and payments to Latin American governments, multilaterals and suppliers), the percentage for 1985 was still 13.6 per cent and 13 per cent in 1986. Using a rather looser definition and including public, private and central bank debt (medium and long term, not short) as a percentage of exports (FOB), the ratios were 38.9 per cent and 34.7 per cent respectively.

Not only did García therefore fail to keep within his own limits, but Peru failed to achieve a positive net inflow from any major source in

1986, except with government-to-government official lending. This positive figure, however, is attributable almost entirely to inflows from the countries in the European Community. With the United States, for instance, the flow was negative. Debt payment in the first year of García's government was not much less than in the last year of Belaúnde's.

How did Peru's creditors react to García's debt position? During the last year of the Belaúnde government, the bankers' response to non-payment of interest had been tempered by the prospect of elections and the fear that a hostile reaction would only have served to give the advantage to those arguing for a more radical position on the debt. For the banks it was more prudent to wait and see who would win. Also, like Bolivia before it, Peru was clearly incapable of meeting its debt payments as scheduled, and the terms for rescheduling could only be negotiated with a new administration.

García's aggressive posture quickly killed off any residual goodwill among bankers. In October 1985, Peruvian debt held by US banks was declared 'value impaired', forcing creditors to set aside increased provisions on their Peruvian exposure. Partly because of the forbearance of the US authorities, this had been narrowly avoided during the last year of Belaúnde. Not only did it further reduce the possibility of new lending, but it gave a further knock to Peru's international credit rating.

But rather than adopt a confrontational position by opting for retaliations against Peru, the commercial banks decided to wait and see. The banks' steering committee, chaired by Citibank, threatened intermittently to dissolve the committee leaving it up to individual banks to choose the most appropriate method of getting their money back. But this involved risks too. It could lead to the breakdown of creditor solidarity by encouraging individual banks to do bilateral deals, something which in the longer run might actually strengthen Peru's bargaining capacity and weaken that of the banks. Relations with commercial banks deteriorated as the size of the arrears increased – $630 million by September 1986 – and as Peru demanded unrealistic terms for any long-term rescheduling arrangement. The bankers' mood was not improved when they saw Peru making full payment on its foreign debt to the Soviet Union and eastern European countries under payment-in-goods schemes. By the beginning of 1987, some banks – at the margin of the steering committee – were looking to make similar deals, notably First Interstate of California and Britain's Midland Bank.

Relations with multilateral lenders also quickly turned sour. The IMF's decision in August 1986 to declare Peru 'ineligible' for further Fund lending followed a steady build-up in arrears, and Peru's failure to comply with earlier promises to begin clearing the arrears. The negative effect was not so much on future Fund lending – Alan García had been specific enough in 1985 that he would not seek it – but on the institutional attitudes of other multilateral lenders, especially the World Bank and the Inter-American Development Bank (IDB). The World Bank made its attitude to heterodoxy quite clear in its review of Peruvian public spending policy produced at the end of 1986. But even by the end of 1985 it was giving heavy hints about its views on the García government by its decision not to replace the Bank's representative in Lima. The IMF's decision on Peru's ineligibility accelerated the deterioration in relations, and coincided with a slow-down in the disbursal of World Bank funds for project lending. In 1986, however, the net flow of funds was still positive in Peru's favour – disbursals of $135 million as against repayments of $115 million. But by early 1987 the net flow turned negative. Peru stopped paying, and – consequently – in May the Bank stopped disbursements.

Aware that his government was not keeping within its own self-imposed '10 per cent' limit, and that the net outflow was increasing rather than the reverse, García's response was to try to stick more rigidly to the limit and for Peru to pay still less. He was convinced that private sector debt repayments – extremely high in 1986 by historical standards – were being used as a channel for capital flight. The result was that in his Independence Day speech on 28 July 1986, the anniversary of his '10 per cent' policy, he announced the inclusion of the private sector debt in the '10 per cent' limit, and the blocking of profit remittances by the subsidiaries of multinationals in Peru. As 1986 drew on, García's position became even more uncompromising. A version of the country's Medium-term Development Plan, personally revised and modified by García prior to publication in December 1986, even called for debt payments in kind and payments to Latin American countries and financial institutions to be included within the '10 per cent'.

A new debt position was formalised at the beginning of 1987 with only 'new' debt (debt disbursed since August 1985) being serviced punctually. Old debt was to be serviced according to capacity to pay, within the '10 per cent' formula, and only in as much as the outflow of foreign exchange did not threaten the official 6 per cent growth target for 1987. The amount available would be distributed among creditors according to what was owed, but only once refinancing agreements were in place.[6] This meant that commercial banks would get nothing.

The situation by mid-1987 was, therefore, one of trench warfare, with each side refusing to negotiate. There was occasional sniping on either side, but no retreat. If anything, positions were becoming rhetorically harder, making future concessions more difficult to achieve. Peru had failed to swing other major debtor countries behind its stand. The only countries to announce similar-sounding policies were Nigeria and Brazil, but in neither case did these amount to permanent or long-lasting policies. At the same time, Peru continued to pay in excess of its own limit, though the low value of total exports in 1986 and 1987 made it harder to keep within the '10 per cent' limit. More importantly for the balance of payments, the net flows of debt continued to be negative after 1985 as the rate of disbursements of new lending also fell. In this setting the strategy of Peru's creditors was to ignore Peru in the hope that the coming balance of payments crisis would force García to the negotiating table. Meanwhile, the arrears on the debt continued to build up.

HETERODOXY AND INCOME DISTRIBUTION

No Peruvian president ever – with the possible exception of General Velasco – gave such prominence as García in his appeals to the public for the need for a fundamental shift in the country's distribution of income. The importance of reducing the inequalities in Peruvian income distribution was a central theme in both his campaign speeches and in those made after he took office as president.[7] The promise of a radical shift in income distribution in favour of the poor was a major reason for his popularity. It was not just idealism or the desire to swing support behind APRA and himself that made García take up the issue of distribution. It came also from a belief that unless there was some narrowing of the gap between the haves and have-nots in Peruvian society, neither social peace nor democratic political stability could be guaranteed. The growth of rural and urban violence in the five years before he came to office lent some credibility to this view.

The unequal nature of the distribution in family income in 1985–6 is summed up in Table 2.4. The size of the problem is indicated by the fact that the poorest 40 per cent received less than 12 per cent of family income, while the richest 10 per cent received more than three times that amount.

Table 2.4   Distribution of family income, 1985–6 (percentages)

Households	Rural Peru	Urban Peru	Country as a whole
Poorest 10%	1.32	0.62	0.45
10%	3.05	3.21	2.63
10%	4.05	4.22	3.68
10%	5.58	5.22	4.90
10%	6.34	6.40	5.96
10%	7.72	7.90	7.31
10%	10.01	9.76	9.15
10%	12.05	12.45	11.88
10%	13.80	16.14	16.77
Richest 10%	36.08	34.08	37.27

Source: National Statistics Institute (INE), *Encuesta Nacional sobre Medición de Niveles de Vida*, Lima (1985–6).

The problem was how to set about redistributive policies in a peculiarly difficult environment. In the first place, Peru's élite had never been conspicuous for its willingness to promote redistribution to its own detriment, always adept at evading governments' attempts to tax it. Also, it was a small élite – the peak of a pinnacle of a very broad-based income pyramid. Then, largely as a result of the debt crisis, the inflow of foreign savings which helped finance Velasco's reforms was no longer at Peru's disposal. Rather the reverse was true with net outflow of capital from 1983 onwards, compounded by private capital flight. In addition, while there was little excess to distribute, the means to distribute it was also lacking. Peru's public administration, as we shall see (see p. 58 passim), the vehicle for any reform, was notoriously inefficient and corrupt. Finally, with APRA lacking a strong organised presence among the poorest in Peru – these sectors tending to be more the social base of the opposition Izquierda Unida – there was a political problem of how to guarantee genuine participation in the share-out of the benefits of redistribution.

The goal of redistribution was one of central importance to the architects of heterodoxy. Inspired by the ECLA school of economic thought of the 1960s and early 1970s, they were convinced that national development would continue to be stultified in the long term by the lack of an internal market to act as a spur to production. Redistribution also meant tackling poverty, especially among the poorest: the *campesinos* of the *sierra*, and the urban poor often of recent peasant origin. It therefore involved trying to overcome the old contradiction in Peruvian agricultural/food policy of using low agricultural incomes to guarantee cheap food in the cities. Any strategy to reduce poverty levels involved two essential components: first, measures to induce self-sustaining growth in the economy; and second, redistributive measures like programmes targeted at specific social groups to increase their income share. Describing the aims of the National Development Plan (1986–90), the National Planning Institute (INP) argued that

the main objective [of the plan] is to improve the quality of life of the population, giving special attention to the inhabitants of rural areas of the *trapecio andino*, to the peasants of the *sierra* and to the marginal inhabitants of the cities. Accordingly, the short-term strategy has to be distributive. The main measures include the growth of wages in relation to inflation, a fiscal policy geared to favouring popular consumption, the promotion of development funds aimed at the peasantry and urban marginal sectors, and – most important of all – a policy of relative prices which favours peasants and informal workers.[8]

In evaluating the results of distributive policies, it is important to bear in mind the scale of the problem. As we have seen, Adolfo Figueroa has argued that if what was wanted was to close the poverty gap, it would have involved a transfer of 20 per cent of national income to 60 per cent of the population. In the case of Peru, where the poverty gap is among the biggest anywhere in Latin America, redistributive policies would have to be conducted on a scale probably hitherto unknown among developing countries.[9]

One of the major difficulties in evaluating the results achieved during the first part of the APRA government is the poor quality of the statistical information available, especially the data concerning wealth and income. The most complete set of data is to be found in the census, even though there are doubts about the reliability of information on income and consequently living standards. The last census was in 1981, and the next was due in 1991 with final results probably not emerging in published form until 1993 or 1994. This forces us to rely either on national accounts (not a reliable guide given the size of Peru's black economy) or figures which emerge as a result of special surveys conducted both by government agencies and private groups.

The available information does point to the growth in incomes *across the board* in 1986 and 1987 as a result of economic reactivation. Income per capita having risen slightly (2.4 per cent) in 1984, declined (– 1.1 per cent) in 1985, and then grew rapidly in 1986 and 1987 (7.3 per cent and 5.1 per cent respectively) according to the National Statistics Institute (INE). GDP per capita in 1987 was at its highest level since 1982.

The indicators show that from the end of 1985 until well into 1987 'urban' Peru underwent a mini-boom which went a long way to restoring income and employment levels reached earlier in the decade. The boom benefited both the formal and the informal sectors.

The main motor of reactivation was the policy to allow real wages in the 'modern' or 'formal' sector of the economy to rise, and thereby boost effective demand. Reactivation did not stem from higher external demand, which in most export sectors was depressed in 1986 and 1987, with the notable exception of cocaine. With drugs the employment effects tended to be confined to coca-producing areas, though in these they were very substantial indeed. The government's strategy was that the increased output resulting from extra domestic demand would boost employment – and thereby incomes – thus creating a virtuous circle. The method of achieving economic reactivation, therefore, was primarily through the formal sector of the economy, the sector where government policy had most direct impact. But as well as using macroeconomic policy to this end, the government also introduced a series of programmes designed to help boost incomes in the informal sector of the economy. These generally had less impact in terms of reactivation and redistribution.

Wage statistics for 1985–7 underline the reversal in the overall trend since the mid-1970s. As inflation fell in 1985 and stayed relatively low in 1986, real wages grew fast in the formal sector of the economy. The real average wage increase in 1986 was 9 per cent, considerably more than had been anticipated at the outset. The pattern varied from one sector to another, with some sectors achieving real increases well in excess of this average, and others hardly increasing their incomes at all. Those who did best were the unionised workforce with collectively negotiated work contracts. The wages of unionised workers grew by 24 per cent in 1986, according to Labour Ministry figures, while central government employees saw their wages rise by only 4 per cent (Table 2.5). The minimum wage only increased by just over 3 per cent, to the relative detriment of many non-unionised workers in the private sector and workers in the informal sector whose wages were guided by minimum wage rates.

Table 2.5   Wages index* for greater Lima, 1985–7 (1979 = 100)

| | A | B | C | D | | % Increase | | |
| | Private sector | | Central govt. | Minimum wage | A | B | C | D |
	White collar	Blue collar						
1985	85.5	64.3	58.9	67.9	−7.8	−13.7	−20.4	−10.7
1986	105.1	84.7	61.3	70.2	24.8	33.3	4.1	3.8
1987	108.8	90.8	69.4	75.7	4.8	9.6	13.2	7.8

* Annual averages.
Source: Labour Ministry, published by the National Statistics Institute (INE) in its *Compendio Estadístico* 1989–90, Lima, 1990.

Turning to the figures for employment, the rate of open unemployment in greater Lima (basically an urban phenomenon) fell from 8.9 per cent of the workforce in 1984, to 5.4 per cent in 1986 and 4.8 per cent in 1987. Underemployment – a misnomer since those who make up this category are the poorly paid who often have not just one occupation but several – fell from 42.7 per cent of the workforce in 1986 to as low as 35 per cent in 1987. Therefore, those officially classified as being 'adequately employed' – basically those in the formal sector of the economy – increased in relation to the total workforce from 54.3 per cent in 1984, to 60.3 per cent in 1987. In relation to the previous tendency for employment to stagnate and even to fall sharply (i.e. 1982–4), this represented an important recovery. The data suggest that the increase was particularly strong among manufacturing companies. In these there was a 12 per cent increase in employment during the first eighteen months of the García government. The rate of growth was still appreciable, but not so fast, in the trade and services sectors of the economy, as the figures in Table 2.6 show.

In the informal sector, there is little doubt that the expansion in domestic demand had a double effect in reversing previous tendencies. First, the expansion in the 'modern' sector, notably in manufacture and particularly in construction, led to the absorption of previously

Table 2.6   Employment index* for greater Lima by economic sectors
(1979 = 100)

	A Manufacture	B Trade	C Services	% Increase A	% Increase B	C
1984	86.1	91.8	104.9	– 10.5	– 8.5	– 1.9
1985	85.0	90.4	105.9	– 1.3	– 1.5	1.0
1986	90.1	93.3	108.1	6.0	3.2	2.1
1987	97.7	95.9	110.7	8.4	2.8	2.4

* Annual Averages.
Source: Labour Ministry, published by the National Statistics Institute (INE)
in its Compendio Estadístico 1989–90, Lima, 1990.

informal workers into the formal sector. This was no doubt encouraged by the PROEM scheme which made it easier for firms to take on
labour without granting workers rights of job stability. Secondly, it led
to the generation of higher income in the informal sector, as demand
for its goods and services picked up too. Many small firms in the
informal sector, especially those involved in manufacturing services,
were highly dependent on the formal sector, orienting their sales
almost entirely in this direction. Examples include the shoe and
clothing industries where 'modern' factories bought in work from
small, labour-intensive workshops in the informal sector.

Two points need to be addressed here. First, the term 'informal'
sector conceals a great deal of heterogeneity, both in terms of the
structure of employment and in terms of income levels. Commercial
activities predominate. Retailing, for instance, accounts for almost half
of total employment, while manufacturing is less than 20 per cent.[10]
The range of income also varies widely from those in absolute poverty
to those capable of modest saving. The revival in demand for basic
consumer goods, for instance, considerably improved incomes at the
poorer end of the scale among street sellers and ambulantes, as well as
those involved in larger-scale, manufacturing enterprise.

A second point is that there was a shift in the sex ratio within the
informal sector as a result of economic reactivation: the percentage of
men employed in the informal sector went down, while in the formal
sector it increased. At the same time (1985–6), the percentage of
women working in the formal sector went down, while in the informal
sector it went up (Table 2.7). This suggests that as men tended to move
into the formal sector as a result of greater employment opportunities,

more women took their places in the informal sector. The shift also reflects the effects of the government's special temporary employment programme, PAIT, which concentrated its efforts in providing employment to women rather than men.

Table 2.7 Workforce in formal and informal sectors by sex, 1984–6 (percentages)

	Male 1985 1986		Female 1985 1986		Total 1985 1986	
Formal sector	58	61	52	46	56	55
Informal sector	42	39	48	54	44	45

Source: Eliana Chávez, 'Políticas de Reactivación y Ajuste y sus Efectos en el Empleo', mimeo, 1988, on the basis of Labour Ministry surveys.

The general picture as it emerges is that the reactivation of the economy benefited first and foremost workers in the formal sector of the economy. It was primarily through allowing wages to rise in real terms that the government sought to launch its growth strategy. Within the formal sector income levels rose fastest for unionised workers in the private sector rather than for public employees. Probably those who did best were those working in sectors like manufacturing and construction, the main beneficiaries of increased domestic demand. If this is correct, then the main beneficiaries of the government's macroeconomic policy were not those whom García originally set as targets of redistributive policy, but sectors which he himself had defined as being relatively privileged (see p. 74).

This is, of course, not to say that the informal sector did not benefit, even the poorest within it. The expansion of demand also brought with it increased demand for the goods and services produced in the informal sector. The state of the informal sector is to a large extent determined by that of the formal sector, and indeed family incomes are frequently derived from a combination of both sources. Furthermore, as more men moved into the formal economy and more women and youngsters entered the labour force in the informal sector, family income was supplemented.[11]

Beyond the effects of overall macroeconomic policy on the urban informal sector, the government launched three specific programmes designed to increase employment and to generate income among the underemployed: PROEM, PAIT and IDESI.

The main objective of PROEM was to make it easier for firms to take on new employees by allowing them to by-pass the laws of job stability, first introduced under Velasco and then subsequently modified under Belaúnde. PROEM was set up in July 1986, initially for a period of two years, but was extended when that period came to an end. Most of the workers who were taken on during the period of expansion in 1986–7 were employed under the auspices of PROEM. The programme reached a peak in August 1987, by which time 42 000 workers had been taken on. Nearly 80 per cent of the jobs created under the PROEM scheme were in Lima, and nearly three-quarters of them in the larger manufacturing companies. The main benefit of the PROEM programme was that it encouraged a significant number of younger people to come into the labour market and to gain some work experience. However, it encouraged a two-tier structure of wages whereby many of the new employees were paid well below average market rates. And, as was to become clear by 1988, most of those who were taken on under the scheme were summarily dismissed when the economic upturn ended.

The PAIT was the government's most important programme to be aimed directly at alleviating urban poverty. Though it ended up more an employment programme, it was initially conceived of as an income subsidy to the poorest of the poor via temporary communal improvements programmes in urban shanty-town neighbourhoods. The programme was initiated in October 1985, and between then and July 1986 it involved between 27 000 and 35 000 people, offering temporary three-month periods of employment. It was successful in providing a limited income – a minimum wage – to those who otherwise would have remained outside the labour market. It was also popular in that it provided work in areas where employment opportunities were minimal. At its height, towards the end of 1986, the PAIT scheme involved 150 000 people, both in Lima and in the main urban centres of the provinces in programmes such as painting public buildings, planting trees, street cleaning and rubbish removal from Lima's beaches.

One of the limitations of PAIT was its failure to generate genuine employment, and even at its height it involved no more than 2.5 per cent of the workforce. It provided little by way of training to increase the skills of those involved and to make them better placed to get access to longer-term employment. Most of the schemes did little to promote skill-formation. When the three months of employment ended, the majority of PAIT workers had no option but to apply for another three months. A large percentage of those involved – mainly women – thus gained little but a desire for paid employment. Many of the construction schemes started were not finished. Finally, apart from its economic function, the PAIT scheme had a clear political purpose to rally popular support for APRA at the local level (see pp. 75–6).

The third programme introduced explicitly to assist the informal sector was IDESI. Its objective was to increase the flow of credit to small-scale entrepreneurs in the slum districts of Lima and other cities, where traditionally the only credit available was at usurious rates of interest. IDESI itself was an intermediary between the financial system and informal entrepreneurs, channelling small loans to workers in groups, whose collective credit rating was geared to the repayment by the groups' individual members. The system worked well initially as prompt repayment was the norm, and the government was enthusiastic in expanding it rapidly. By the end of 1988, for instance, IDESI had extended credits to some 62 000 beneficiaries and was meeting an important need in the informal sector where credit was either unavailable or available on prohibitive terms. While it provided small informal sector businesses with some know-how on use of the banking system, it failed to provide such other key aspects of business practice as how to conduct pricing in an inflationary economy, how to undertake more effective marketing, and how to maximise value-added. All too often money went to street traders for them to buy produce, sell it at a slight profit and then repay the loan. Moreover, like other government programmes, its effectiveness was largely overwhelmed when the economic boom ended and the agonising slump of 1988–9 set in.

So far as rural Peru went, agriculture had an important role to play in Alan García's original scheme of things. In a country in which more than 80 per cent of the rural population is in the lowest income stratum, any policy to redistribute income inevitably involves resolving some of the problems of agriculture. But another common theme in many of García's speeches before and after taking office was the need for Peruvians to learn to be more self-sufficient (*'aprendamos a vivir con lo nuestro'*). Applied to agriculture this meant reversing previous governments' policies of importing to meet largely urban demand. The two objectives therefore dove-tailed: reducing dependence on imports not only helped save scarce foreign exchange; it also provided the necessary stimulus to domestic agriculture which had been so lacking since the upheavals of the agrarian reform in the 1970s. And within agriculture the priority was to go to the small-scale peasant producer, thereby helping to reduce the social inequality which seemed to engender rural violence.

However, in 1985 these ambitious objectives were not matched by an operational plan involving specific policy goals for either the short or the longer term. The first six months saw little action from the Ministry of Agriculture and valuable time was lost. It was only after February 1986 when a new minister was appointed, Remigio Morales Bermúdez, son of the former president, that a clearer and more specific set of policies began to emerge.

On the one hand, the government sought to stabilise and improve the prices paid to producers; on the other, to reduce producers' costs and thereby increase their margins. To deal with the first of these a special government fund was created to subsidise agricultural products, the Agricultural Reactivation and Food Security Fund with 3 billion intis earmarked for 1986. The purpose of the fund was to provide guaranteed prices to producers while ensuring continued supplies of cheap food to urban consumers. Significantly, some 80 per cent of the money was destined for a handful of crops – rice, milk, hard yellow maize and sugar prominent among them. All of these crops were important in terms of the structure of urban food demand, but they were not, typically, those produced by the small-scale farmer and the Andean peasant to whom García wanted to transfer income and opportunities. So as to reduce the costs of production to farmers, the government introduced subsidies which reduced the price of fertiliser, but again, this was mainly to the benefit of coastal producers.

More importantly, the government substantially increased the flow of low-interest loans to agricultural producers. Between 1985 and 1987 the loans extended by the Banco Agrario went up from 0.88% of GDP to 1.76%, or in dollar terms from $124 million to $495 million. The benefits of low-cost finance to agriculture tended to be more evenly dispersed than the programme of subsidies, reaching a wider range of producers. Credit to potato farmers, for instance, grew by 120 per cent in real terms; credit to maize farmers by 154 per cent, to producers of beans by 127 per cent and to wheat farmers by 88 per cent. It did not mean, however, a radical switch in the traditional pattern of credit allocation in favour of poor, small-scale producers in the *sierra*. While large sums were devoted to expanding rural credit, much of it continued to be channelled to those farmers with more resources, those best placed to repay. These producers tended to be more integrated into the market economy rather than on the periphery of it. Though more credit than before went to small-scale agriculture in the *sierra*, only some 6 per cent of producers in the *sierra* had access to credit and technical assistance. The absence of a programme to extend rural technology reduced any long-term benefits that might have accrued. And, despite government promises to prioritise agriculture in Ayacucho and surrounding districts in the militarised emergency zone, the presence of Sendero made it especially difficult to distribute resources in this department. Peasant communities did, however, benefit from government cash hand-outs, resources which the communities often put to good use but which did not fit into a coherent plan of resource allocation, and which again did not go hand-in-hand with any strategy of back-up. This had more to do with buying political support than promoting community development in a systematic way.[12]

The other important element of policy was that of '*concertación*' with the peasant communities, of which the *rimanacuys* became the main expression. The *rimanacuys* were meetings organised in 1986 by the INP bringing together the representatives of peasant communities in what were supposed to be fora for dialogue with the government, personified by the president of the republic. Though not in itself a mechanism for the transfer of funds, it was an important innovation, indicating recognition at the highest level of the importance of the communities. The *rimanacuys*, however, provided the potential for more systematic coordination in the distribution of resources in agriculture. Unfortunately, it proved to be only a short-lived experiment in social communication, and was used more to project the political personality of Alan García than to take systematic account of problems facing peasant communities. It was an initiative which awakened expectations which it failed to satisfy.

The APRA government thus took some important steps to give agriculture a higher priority than previous governments by increasing the flow of funds it was prepared to push into the sector. However, the big improvement which took place in rural incomes during the course of the first eighteen months of the new government had more to do with the boom in the demand for food in the cities than with the efficacy of sectoral programmes, significant though these may have been. The best indicator of this was the variation in price for basic staple goods as demand accelerated faster than supply during 1986. For instance, the price of potatoes to producers rose by 93 per cent in real terms, and those of beans by 68 per cent. Neither of these two products were covered by the Agricultural Reactivation Fund, and for those products that were, market prices tended to be above the government's guaranteed price level. Demand for non-subsidised food (tubers, green vegetables, fruit and beans) rose by 44 per cent in the course of 1986. In response to higher demand, value of output grew by 4.0 per cent in real terms, compared with a yearly average growth rate for 1975–85 of just 1.4 per cent.

Those who appear to have benefited most were those more integrated into the market economy as suppliers of basic foodstuffs to the cities. The main sources of food for urban areas were the irrigated valleys of the coast, the jungle valleys (*ceja de selva*) and the most fertile regions of the *sierra* like the Mantaro valley in Junín. These were the regions which absorbed much of the subsidised credit and fertiliser made available. The response from the more capitalised sectors of agriculture was notable: demand for tractors, for instance, trebled between 1985 and 1986 and sales of fertiliser (more than 70 per cent of it to coastal agriculture) doubled in 1986.[13] Agroindustrial interests also profited as urban demand increased for products like vegetable oil and flour, while producers of chickens and eggs (more of an industrial than agricultural activity) saw business flourish. At the same time, though the increase in demand for food also benefited peasant agriculture, notably with the sharp rise in prices for crops like potato, this had little to do with the Agriculture Ministry's price support schemes. Most peasant farmers in the highlands did not profit from access to government subsidies. It is probable that the combination of higher wages paid in more commercially oriented agriculture – notably coca but food crops too – in combination with political violence in the poorest parts of the *sierra*, accelerated the process of migration within rural Peru, especially from Ayacucho and surrounding departments.

One of the major weaknesses of the APRA government's rural strategy was the slow speed at which it developed policies and programmes to tackle the main problems. When economic conditions improved in 1986 in response to the demand-led boom for food, there were no well thought out programmes in place to help the producer get maximum benefit, through facilitating a wider availability of inputs, broadening the scope of agricultural extension, or improving the diffusion of technologies. It was not until March 1988 that the Ministry of Agriculture unveiled its much-vaunted 'master plan' for backward agriculture, the Plan Sierra. The Plan Sierra envisaged the spending of $640 million over five years in a multifaceted programme to benefit 2000 communities with an estimated population of 2.5 million. It was an ambitious scheme bringing together a variety of different programmes to 'modernise' *campesino* agriculture. But it came two and a half years too late. The macroeconomic environment of 1988 was one of deep crisis, one of extreme instability, and not one conducive to successful agricultural development. The government's own horizons by that time were not six years into the future, but survival from one day to the next.

Poor coordination at the level of policy-making is again clearly revealed by the way in which the government – despite the rhetoric of '*vivir con lo nuestro*' – found itself obliged to increase food imports as the only way to ensure supply without shortages to the cities. Afraid of such shortages, the government in 1986 found itself having to import a wide variety of agricultural products including sugar, rice and even potatoes, in which in normal years Peru was self-sufficient. The import bill for the country's food needs almost doubled in 1986 from $204 million in 1985 to $386 million. Imports rose to still higher levels in 1987. A particularly dramatic increase was in foreign purchases of meat, which rose from $13 million in 1985 to $72 million in 1986. This willingness to resort to imports helped avoid urban food shortages, but it flew in the face of the government's stated aim of dynamising national agriculture. Furthermore, it contributed directly to the balance of payments difficulties which surfaced in 1987. Finally, it also helped sabotage incipient policies to try to change patterns of demand for food by substituting imports like wheat for home-produced grains.

The scale of imports in 1986 indicated above is also partly disguised by the extremely low international prices for some agricultural goods. There were, however, gains to be made from low world prices. ENCI, the state agency in charge of purchasing inputs, directed an interesting and novel programme by which it took advantage of unusually low world market prices to buy cheap wheat, fertiliser and edible oils abroad, to sell them to Peruvian processors and distributors at higher prices, and to use the profits to finance the Agricultural Reactivation Fund. The existence of an over-valued, frozen exchange rate made such operations especially attractive.

Largely as a result of the government's stimulation of domestic demand in 1986, Peruvian agriculture had one of its best years in decades. Though probably those most integrated into the market – the richer farmers – benefited most, the positive effects were felt also in small-scale peasant agriculture. The problem was that lack of detailed policy coordination, coupled with the lack of forward planning for agriculture and for the economy as a whole, meant that the boom proved impossible to sustain. The rural revival was as strong as the urban boom which lay behind it. When the macroeconomic downturn took place in 1988 and 1989, rural society was to suffer most.

THE PROBLEM OF THE STATE AND ADMINISTRATION

The return to a more interventionist style of economic management under Alan García once again highlighted the problem of the poor quality of public administration in Peru. What was to be done to improve the way in which public policy was elaborated and put into effect?

The experience of the Velasco regime had brought this problem into focus during the 1970s, when the rapid growth in the powers and responsibilities of the state had not been matched by the institutional development to implement reform. Some of the shortcomings of the Velasco government in putting its chosen policies into effect can be attributed to the weaknesses of the administrative machine. In particular, the development of a centralised bureaucracy was not parallelled by that of state institutions at the local level. A government which considered itself 'above' politics was not well disposed to listen to and collaborate with representative popular organisations on the ground.

Despite its critique of the bureaucratic, authoritarian state apparatus it inherited from the military regimes, the Belaúnde government did little to make government more agile. It failed to carry out its plans to engineer a substantial reduction in the size of the public sector which it tended to consider the root cause of so many of Peru's economic problems. It also did little to streamline the bureaucracy. If anything, the effect of public spending cuts and the erosion of real pay in the public sector tended to demoralise the bureaucracy, make it less efficient and more open to corruption.

However, the more neo-liberal climate under Belaúnde did encourage growing criticism of the statist model. It was at this time that the most strident attack on the nature of the Peruvian state was written. Hernando de Soto's *El Otro Sendero*[14] highlighted in a graphic fashion the way in which unhelpful bureaucracy got in the way of initiative and enterprise. The examples he used were thoroughly credible, such as the 289 man-days it took his group of researchers, posing as applicants to set up a clothing factory, to get official permission to go ahead. But what made *El Otro Sendero* polemical was that it took the argument several steps further, positing that the state was itself one of the main causes of poverty through its stultifying effects on the potential for small-scale producers in the informal sector of the economy.

Another critique of the bureaucratic state arose in a very different quarter: from the other 'Sendero', Sendero Luminoso. Sendero evolved from an extreme left-wing tradition bitterly opposed to the military reformism of Velasco (see pp. 96–101). In developing its guerrilla war, Sendero sought to give high priority to the destruction of the state at the local level, killing or driving out its main 'representatives': local governors and mayors, engineers and others working on state-sponsored development projects, judges and petty officials. For Sendero, the revolutionary struggle was one of destroying the existing state structure in all its manifestations.

Irrespective of these points of view, Alan García came to office arguing the need for a less liberal, more interventionist approach to economic management. Reiterating many of the preoccupations of the Velasco era, García and his top advisers emphasised the key role to be played by the state in stimulating national development, particularly if the benefits of that development were to be more equally distributed. The challenge facing the new government was threefold: to strengthen the state apparatus, to make it more effective in the design and implementation of public policy, and – at the local level – to make it more democratic and more responsive to people's needs.[15]

A key priority for any government which believed in reinforcing the role of the state was to ensure that that the public sector was put on a sound financial footing. This was all the more important for a government like García's which could not count on raising foreign loans to help it with current or capital spending. As it turned out, the García administration did little to reform the tax system and thereby take fiscal advantage of the benefits of heterodoxy. Higher-than-usual growth in 1986 and 1987 should have translated into higher government income with both indirect and direct taxes yielding more. Lower-than-usual inflation should also have helped boost income by reducing the losses incurred in the period of delay between taxes falling due and finally being paid.

In practice public sector income fell in 1986 and 1987 – substantially. Total income (current and capital) of the whole of the public sector (excluding financial enterprises) fell by just over 20 per cent in real terms in 1986. In 1987, it fell by just over 50 per cent. In relation to GDP, central government tax income fell from 14.5 per cent of GDP in 1985 to 12 per cent in 1986, to 9 per cent in 1987. Similarly, the current income of non-financial public sector companies halved between 1985 and 1987, falling from 28 per cent to 14.3 per cent of GDP. Altogether the current income of the public sector fell from 46 per cent of GDP in 1985, to 33.5 per cent in 1986, and to 26 per cent in 1987 (Table 2.8).

Table 2.8   Public sector income, 1980–7 (% of GDP)

	1980–4 (av)	1985	1986	1987
1. Central government tax income	13.8	14.5	12.0	9.0
Income tax	3.0	1.9	2.7	1.8
Profits tax	0.5	0.4	0.6	0.4
Import taxes	2.6	3.0	2.4	1.9
Export taxes	0.9	0.3	0.2	—
Taxes on sales and production	6.3	8.3	5.8	4.6
Other taxes	0.5	0.6	0.3	0.3
2. Current income of non-financial public sector companies	24.9	28.0	18.2	14.3
3. Current income of other state sector entitles[1]	3.6	3.4	3.9	4.0

[1] Includes other public institutions, social security contributions, local government income etc.
Source: Central Bank, *Memoria*, Lima, 1988.

There were several reasons for the fall in public sector income during the first two years of the García government.[16] First, one of the initial measures it took in 1985 was to reduce the sales tax (VAT) from 11 per cent to 6 per cent. The idea was that reactivation coupled to supposed lower evasion rates would compensate for the loss of income. This turned out not to be the case. The sales tax yield fell from 3 per cent of GDP in 1985 to 1.3 per cent in 1987. A second cause was the freezing of petrol prices. Like the cut in VAT this was an integral part of the heterodox stabilisation formula. The Belaúnde government had come to rely increasingly on this tax to offset the declining yield of direct taxation after 1980. It brought in as much as 5 per cent of GDP in 1985, having become a key source of government income but also a major source of cost inflation. As a result of the freeze, the yield fell to as low as 2.2 per cent in 1987. Thirdly, an overvalued exchange rate reduced the income on imports raised through tariffs. Fourthly, price controls fell heavily on the public sector companies which had to finance them. Finally, the government increased the number of tax exonerations it extended to the private sector in its attempts to get private companies to invest more.

The government therefore faced a difficult dilemma in introducing its heterodox policies: the stabilisation package had a high fiscal cost. The Treasury thus had to look for ways to offset the effects of lower taxes by ensuring that it gained from the upturn in economic activity. But the results were disappointing: the public sector ended up paying much of the bill itself. Meanwhile, the APRA government does not appear to have devoted much thinking to a comprehensive reform of the tax system, aimed at widening the tax base and hitting tax evasion.

The tax base in Peru, traditionally, has been very narrow. In 1987, for instance, 800 larger companies accounted for 75 per cent of Treasury tax receipts. Of these receipts nearly 60 per cent of the total came from twenty-four of Peru's largest firms, the majority of them state enterprises.[17] Meanwhile, at the Ministry of Industries there were 10 000 registered industrial firms. Comparatively, three times as many Ecuadoreans (in relation to the total population) made an income tax return in 1983 than did Peruvians; and five times as many Ecuadoreans presented a sales tax return, according to IMF figures. Similarly, nearly forty-four times as many Chileans proportionately made a sales tax return; and twelve times as many an income tax return. Clearly, the size of the black economy in Peru distinguished it from Chile, but the tax authorities in Peru have been notoriously unsuccessful in finding ways to widen the tax base, despite increased funding in recent years, more staff and the introduction of computerised technology.

Nor have the tax authorities shown great success in clamping down on evasion. The dimensions of evasion are hard to calculate and, itself a significant point, few serious attempts have been made to quantify the problem. In his study, Jorge Vega estimates that tax evasion amounted to at least 4.4 per cent of GDP in 1987, the equivalent of 40 per cent of the tax income for that year. Evasion broke down into three main sources: sales tax (equivalent to 3 per cent of GDP); profits tax (1.3 per cent); and personal income tax (0.1 per cent). In 1984, a special office within the Treasury was opened to tackle the problem of tax evasion. But the results were once again very disappointing: in 1985 only 2.9 per cent of the total tax yield was recuperated, in 1986 3.8 per cent, and in 1987 3.7 per cent.

The main problem which has encouraged evasion and 'hiding' from the tax authorities is at once administrative and judicial. As Vega points out, an average firm could expect a visit from a Treasury auditor once in every fifty-five years; an average individual once in every 138 years. The low effective penalties for tax evasion combined with the small probability of being caught out, provide every incentive not to pay. Lacking the administrative machinery to tax increased sales, income and profits, the García government ended up itself shouldering much of the fiscal burden of heterodoxy, and thus weakening the very state institutions it wanted to fortify.

As well as needing to provide state institutions with an adequate financial base, the new government needed to introduce changes to strengthen the bureaucracy institutionally, to make it more efficient. The problems inherited from the past were all well known: the slow speed of policy implementation; the lack of coordination between different parts of the bureaucracy; institutional rivalries; the problem of unaccountability and corruption especially at the higher levels of administration; lack of drive and initiative at the lower levels; poor morale; bad pay; inadequate training... [18] No one was more conscious of the limitations of the public administration than Alan García himself, who tended to see it as an obstacle to his proposals for change.

The system of government which evolved under García was both highly personalist and highly centralised. Decision-making was conducted first and foremost in the presidential palace with one man, the president, the mainspring of political initiative. At the same time, the independence of government ministries, departments and other institutions of state was curtailed with the president seeking to intervene in the daily business of policy execution. After 1985, García's ministers were half-jokingly referred to as his 'secretaries'.

From the earliest days of the new government García made no secret of his distrust for the centralised bureaucracy in Lima. He sought to move at a much faster pace than the sluggish bureaucratic machine, trying to make a political virtue of being seen to break through red tape and to get things done. The government's concept of dynamising the centralised bureaucracy was thus further to concentrate decision-making. García abandoned a system of cabinet and ministerial coordination created under Belaúnde (in which decision-making in economic policy involved senior ministry officials with their back-up teams as well as ministers) in favour of a system in which he took all major decisions in consultation with a small group of advisers, thereafter transmitting the results to the rest of the administration.

Though this possibly made it easier to reach swift decisions it had a number of drawbacks.

One obvious disadvantage was the risk to the quality of the decisions reached. Policy tended no longer to be reached on the basic of consultation with other parties as a matter of course, but on the basis of whom the president chose to consult beyond his immediate circle. Important decisions were therefore reached in such a way as to keep them as a surprise until the last moment, but which made it more difficult to evaluate their likely effects. Such was the case, for instance, of the move in July 1985 to limit debt service payments to 10 per cent of exports, and the decision two years later to nationalise the banks. While decision-making thus came to rely greatly on the president's own judgement, his fast-moving style of government tended to encourage impetuosity and improvisation rather than carefully pre-meditated policy-making. Though in theory the APRA government stood for a more planned approach, planning was often more illusory than real. The wheels of social and economic planning turned slowly, but García's demands – often prompted by political as well as economic calculations – were immediate. Arguably the government's heterodox economic policy required much more by way of careful planning than the well-tried orthodox formulae it sought to replace, since in many ways it broke new ground. But the emergency plan, as we have seen, was not a carefully worked out scheme; rather it was an *ad hoc* short-term package tailored to the circumstances. One of the greatest disadvantages facing APRA in 1985 was the lack of a well-considered blueprint on what do to.

Perhaps of even greater importance from the point of view of institutional development within the state was the fact that this approach to government tended to ignore rather than solve the problems of public administration. García showed little disposition to improve the quality of the administrative system, a task requiring patient and sustained attention. Rather, in further concentrating power and responsibility, he helped accentuate some of the problems inherent in a centralised, executive-dominated system. Not only did he create resentment within the administration through interference and a tendency to maintain his own primacy by exploiting rivalries between and within institutions, but he showed little will to confer greater responsibility on individual ministries and departments within their own area.

Meanwhile, not much was done during the first two years to tackle such pressing problems as improving pay and training. Except at the

highest levels of government, pay in the public administration
remained low both in relation to the private sector and even public
companies. Central government wages, for instance, increased only
slightly in 1986 and 1987, much less than average wage increases in the
capital (see p. 49) and remaining at well below their 1979 level. So far
as training was concerned, the National Institute for Public Administration (INAP) became primarily what the INP had come to be under
Belaúnde, a dumping ground for officials removed from positions of
responsibility elsewhere. Individual institutions had to fend for
themselves, with only those with more cash and autonomy over their
budgets, like the INP and the central bank, able to finance training.

At the same time, the problems of government at all levels were
complicated by the government's need to reward its supporters with
jobs in the administration. García appears to have been very conscious
of this problem, aware that most Apristas lacked the professional
training to qualify them for the jobs they wanted to occupy. His initial
resistance to filling the bureaucracy with Aprista appointments caused
bitterness within the party, especially his reluctance in 1985 to give
Apristas a monopoly of the top jobs in government. Even so, the
change-over of government that year resulted in a net increase in the
size of the public sector with new place-seekers outnumbering those
who took the end of the Belaúnde government as a cue to seek
employment in the private sector or to go abroad.

Though the first two years of the APRA government released a
great deal of creative energy and the apparent will to deal with some of
Peru's more deep-rooted problems, little was done to improve the
functioning of the public administration. As with tax reform, it seems
in retrospect that an opportunity was lost to take advantage of the
government's authority to confront a number of these problems.
García's distrust of the bureaucracy and his penchant for personalist
government meant that this area received scant attention. The results
were poor planning, lack of coordination and low morale.

The third major challenge for the APRA government was to
advance in its commitment to making the state more 'democratic' –
to make it more responsive and accountable at the local level to those
who it was supposed to serve.

As we have seen, one of the long-term problems in Peru's institutional development was the lack of a fluid relationship between the
state and genuinely representative organisations on the ground. The
Velasco reforms did little to develop public institutions locally. They
remained often ineffectual, underfinanced or corrupt; sometimes all

three. While the institutions of the state were weak, however, representative organisations at the local level had accumulated a degree of political power since the 1970s, especially with the return to elected municipal government as of 1980.

On coming to office it soon became clear that if the APRA government was to fulfil its reformist and redistributive political agenda, it was going to encounter a number of serious problems in relation to the public administration locally, both in urban and rural areas. One was precisely the weakness of the state apparatus at its disposal. The areas of the country to which the new government wanted to give priority in terms of accelerating development tended to be those where the state machinery was weakest. This was the case, for instance, of the southern *sierra*, where in addition the authorities that did exist were being chased out by Sendero Luminoso. The mechanism for steering resources towards their intended beneficiaries therefore had to be created, but that depended on pacification. Another problem was that those who in 1985 came to occupy key posts in the local administration were members of APRA. Very often they were urban, middle class and conservative, and not in sympathy with the organised popular movement which sought changes. The government had to implement policy while subject to strong political pressures at the local level. In general terms, then, the proposals to switch resources to where they were most needed presented substantial administrative and political difficulties. Suitable mechanisms had to be created, and this was not something likely to be achieved quickly.

During the first two years of the APRA government, the main proposal that emerged in relation to rural areas was the creation of *microregiones*. These were designed to provide channels for the distribution of development finance. The idea was to promote a decentralisation of the functions of government in specific areas, and thereby help create a more agile, less bureaucratic system of resource allocation. They were to be established initially under the aegis of the INP, with priority going to the most backward rural areas, especially those where Sendero Luminoso was most active.[19] In practice, though physically decentralised from Lima, they were dependent financially and bureaucratically on central government.[20] Also, despite the name, most *microregiones* covered large areas. As a result they tended to be no more responsive to particular local needs than the development corporations they were supposed to subsume. Furthermore, the system of *microregiones* was a 'top-down' structure, not accountable to locally elected *municipios* or provincial councils. The conception was basically a technocratic one: how to channel finance to different parts of the country rather than how to mobilise local communities to work politically in pursuit of their *own* perceived needs. However, this new system at least had the effect of prompting further consideration of different types of institutional reform locally. At the outset, it went in tandem with García's and the Planning Institute's experiment of trying to relate to the problems of peasant communities in the *sierra* through the *rimanacuys*.

Some of the traditional problems of local administration, both in rural and urban areas, were aggravated by APRA's clientelistic impulses. It proved even harder to restrain these at the local level than in central government. As the party took office, its supporters took advantage of the opportunities for self-advancement. The result was that jobs went to the party faithful rather than those best qualified to perform them. Irrespective of the reforming impulse coming from central government, the APRA-dominated local bureaucracy frequently became more of an obstacle than a promoter of change. One particularly vivid example of this was in Puno where Apristas opposed, sometimes violently, the attempts of peasant communities to restructure landholding.[21]

Problems associated with verticality and opposition to change were also common in the urban setting, where APRA also sought partisan control over administrative institutions. Here too the party frequently ran into conflict with grass-roots organisations. In the shanty-towns the rapid growth of popular organisation had brought with it politicisation and a widespread identification with the left. The degree of organisation was not uniform: some areas developed stronger and more autonomous local institutions than others. A conspicuous example of high level of organisation in Lima was Villa El Salvador, the large *pueblo joven* on the city's southern periphery, with its strong sense of the need for self-management (*autogestión*). In such areas Apristas at the local level were forced to recognise existing popular institutions, and to work through them rather than supplant them. In less organised districts, government agencies were less respectful of local organisation, especially when run by the left. The functioning of the government's temporary employment scheme (PAIT) offers a useful glimpse of how this worked in practice.[22]

The main point is that decentralisation of state activities and their 'democratisation' proved hard to put into practice, not just for technical or financial reasons, but for political reasons. The clientelistic instincts of APRA, as the next chapter shows, clashed with existing interests on the ground. Partisan conflict – especially between APRA and the left – made 'democratisation' difficult to achieve in the absence of any understanding between these political forces at a national or local level. The tenor of relations rather was one of distrust and disconfidence.

One of the APRA government's more lasting contributions to greater decentralisation was the creation of *regiones* with a greater local autonomy. These came into existence during the last years of García's term of office. During the first two years the government did little to respond to the expectations it had awoken as a result of promises made during the 1984–5 election campaign. It was only in 1987 and after, as the government looked for new policy initiatives to take up, that more serious thought was given to regionalisation.

The quest for greater administrative and political decentralisation was nothing new in Peruvian politics. Pressures for regional autonomy from Lima were common themes in nineteenth-century history, and did not diminish with Lima's consolidation as the industrial as well as the political hub of the country. The persistence of regional pressure groups, and their radicalisation in the 1960s and 1970s with the development of *frentes de defensa*, helped ensure that regionalisation was an issue taken up by the Constituent Assembly elected in 1978 to write a new constitution. The 1979 constitution gave the executive the job of preparing procedures and a timetable. Though the Belaúnde government took the step of restoring the departmental development corporations, their focus tended to be concentrated mainly on providing infrastructure rather than carrying out wider responsibilities for development at the local level. Still, a national plan for regionalisation was finally approved in 1984.

According to the constitution, the procedure for regionalisation, following the approval of the outline plan, involved the passing of a basic law (*ley de bases*) and then laws setting out the attributes of the individual regions (*leyes orgánicas*). Under García, regionalisation only became an issue of importance after the *ley de bases* was approved in 1987. In the following years the *leyes orgánicas* were worked on by the development corporations, supposedly in conjunction with elected municipal governments. The *frentes de defensa* tended not to be involved.

One of the most conflictive issues to arise was the establishment of the functions and attributes of the new regional governments, and especially the role of popular and representative groups within the assemblies, and the relationship between the assemblies and existing provincial and departmental authorities. Another difficult issue, which arose in the drafting of the *leyes orgánicas*, was the territorial delimitation of the new regions. In several parts of the country, the merging of separate departments into a single region did not necessarily lead to the formation of coherent geographical, economic or even cultural units. Also, for smaller departments whose capitals would play only a very subordinate role in the new scheme of things, the risk of loss of status and possibly employment excited small-town pride. In San Martín department in the *ceja de selva*, for instance, with a strong left-wing *frente de defensa*, there was great opposition to being merged into a new region whose capital would be the Aprista coastal stronghold of Trujillo.

Yet another source of difficulty was the establishment of a system for financing the new regions with their legislative and executive functions. One of the goals was to ensure effective financial autonomy of Lima, but without further exacerbating differences between the regions able to subsist by taxing local industries (e.g. oil and mining) and those not. It was inevitable that some regions lacking plentiful raw materials would remain dependent on the central government for the bulk of their income.

But despite these difficulties, the regionalisation programme made important advances after 1987, contrasting with virtual paralysis in other areas of policy-making. This was in good measure the result of the enthusiastic support of Alan García who saw the opportunity to deal with one of Peru's enduring structural problems, while at the same time trying to revive his government's flagging popularity by appealing to the local demand for greater autonomy from Lima. In theory, at least, the programme involved an important degree of decentralisation with a greater degree of popular participation in decision-making. Regional assemblies were to be formed by people elected directly and by representatives of organisations like local *gremios* and trade union federations. The often autocratic and unaccountable development corporations were to be merged and subjected to the political control of elected assemblies. But it remained to be seen how, following the election of new assemblies in 1989 and 1990, they would work in practice, especially in instances where the party in control locally was not in power nationally, and where the new regions were beholden to the national Treasury for the money to make them work.

3 APRA's Political Triumph

APRA's landslide election victory was to an important degree the victory of Alan García. It confirmed the supremacy he had been able to build up since he was elected party leader in 1982. For Apristas it was the moment that the party had been awaiting for sixty years; and they had García's dynamic leadership to thank for getting the party into office at last. Also, APRA's majority in Congress and the division of the opposition into two separate camps put the party and its leader into a position in which they enjoyed the political initiative. For good or for bad, the party's political fortunes became intimately bound up with the public *persona* of Alan García.

The results (see Table 3.1) confirmed the success of García's strategy to widen both the social and geographic base of the party's support. The party's share of the total vote (not counting null and void ballot papers as part of the whole) rose from 27.4 per cent in the 1980 presidential elections – a low point in APRA's electoral performance – to 33.1 per cent in the November 1983 municipal elections, to 53.1 per cent in 1985. APRA's share of the vote had thus increased dramatically. Traditionally, as we have seen, the base of APRA's social support socially came from sectors of the working and lower middle class with a strong regional concentration in the north of the country, especially in La Libertad and Lambayeque departments, where the party had its historic roots and most organised political presence.

The social composition of the APRA vote in 1985 included support from all sectors of society: from members of the élite, the middle classes, the organised working class to the inhabitants of the *pueblos jovenes* and peasant communities. The party had come to represent a truly poly-classist 'alliance'. It had also become a national party in a way that it had never been in the past. Though the percentage of votes cast for APRA was still highest in the traditionally Aprista north (La Libertad 77 per cent, Lambayeque 64 per cent), APRA still won enough support in 'non-Aprista' areas in the south like Cuzco and Puno to win a majority there. While APRA had always enjoyed some support among popular sectors in Lima, it had never been the dominant political force in the capital. In the 1980 municipal elections, for instance, it got 16 per cent of the vote. Its share increased to 27 per cent in the 1983 municipal election, won by Alfonso Barrantes and the Izquierda Unida. But in 1985, APRA got 51 per cent of the vote in greater Lima which accounted for just over 31 per cent of the country's total electoral population.[1]

Table 3.1   Election results, 1980–6 (% of valid votes)

	1980(Gen)	1980(Mun)	1983(Mun)	1985(Gen)	1986 (Mun)
Acción Popular	45.4	35.9	17.4	7.3	—[1]
PPC	9.6	10.9	13.9	11.9[2]	15.2
APRA	27.4	22.7	33.1	53.1	47.8
Izquierda Unida	13.8[3]	23.9	28.8	24.7	30.8
Others	3.8	6.6	6.8	3.0	6.2
Total	100.0	100.0	100.0	100.0	100.0
Null and void	22.3	14.3	17.8	13.9	11.1
Abstention[4]	18.2	30.2	35.5	8.9	22.0

[1] Acción Popular did not participate in the 1986 municipal elections.
[2] In 1985 the PPC participated as Convergencia Democrática, in alliance with dissident Apristas (Townsend supporters) and some independents.
[3] This is the sum of votes for individual left-wing parties and which ran separately in the 1980 presidential elections.
[4] % of registered voters.
Source: National Electoral Committee (JNE) quoted in Tuesta, *Perú Política en Cifras* (Lima: Friedrich Ebert Foundation, 1987).

This election victory was not the product of a well-oiled national party political machine, even though in 1985 APRA's organisation was more efficient than it had been in 1980. The landslide was fundamentally due to the way in which Alan García managed to swing over very large numbers of uncommitted voters by personifying the quest for a 'new beginning' in Peruvian politics. The importance of the 'floating voter' in Peruvian elections is illustrated by the substantial swings in voting behaviour since 1980, notably in the fortunes of Acción Popular. The most stable vote appears to be that of the PPC. García's success in galvanising the uncommitted voter in 1985 (primarily to AP's detriment) is also indicated by the relatively low number of null and void votes and particularly by the very low abstention rate in 1985.

García's appeal to the uncommitted voter was based partly on his dynamism, youth and on his ability to communicate with his audience. These qualities stood in stark contrast to the aloof, patriarchal style of Fernando Belaúnde, who – as cartoonists would have it – peered down condescendingly on the suffering of the real world from a cloud. García's success also owed something to having launched his presidential campaign well in advance of his main adversaries, and having painstakingly visited even the remotest villages in the country. But, perhaps most importantly, he sought to transmit an ideology which found a strong echo among a people tired of seeing the government which they had elected apparently giving more importance to foreign creditors than to Peruvians. The nationalist tone of the party's propaganda was designed to appeal to a broad constituency, going way beyond the loyal Aprista voter. Indeed, the old partisan slogans to the effect that APRA alone could save Peru were dropped in favour of slogans which sought to attract Peruvians of all colours, like 'Alan García: My commitment is to all Peruvians'. Other sectarian party symbols like the Aprista star were also dropped in favour of the image of the dove designed to appeal to this wider public. In the classic populist mould, the party was to be the reflection of society as a whole.

The supremacy achieved by García within APRA itself owed much to historical factors. First and foremost APRA was a party which has always excited strong loyalties among its militants. In part this was the legacy of Haya de la Torre whose authoritarian leadership did not brook political rivalries or internal dissidence. As we have seen, in some respects APRA evolved more along the lines of a religious movement than a modern political party. Discipline was a crucial element of Aprista political culture, with those charged by the leader to enforce discipline, the so-called *búfalos*, playing an important role in the relationship between the leadership and the mass following. Traditionally, the party provided much for the loyalist, but retribution for those who refused to toe the line.

The rapid rise of Alan García also coincided with a particularly unhappy chapter in the party's history. Haya's death from cancer in 1979 left a large political vacuum. One of the problems inherent in his absolute leadership was, of course, that of succession. His demise almost immediately brought ideological rifts out into the open which the pre-eminence of the old man had kept subordinate during his lifetime. The more progressive wing of the party, led by Armando Villanueva, found itself locked in conflict with the conservatives under Andrés Townsend. APRA's poor electoral performance in 1980 served to worsen the split and enhance the struggle for the party's political soul. In 1981 APRA split, the party machine supporting Villanueva but key members of the old guard, notably Luis Alberto Sánchez and Ramiro Prialé, siding with Townsend.

It was in this context that Alan García, who had established himself in the party as its secretary of organisation and then had made his oratorical mark in the House of Deputies, emerged as a factor of unity. Ideologically, he belonged to the more progressive wing, but he maintained close ties with the old guard, especially with Sánchez. Though Haya left no obvious heir apparent, his sympathy for the young García (Haya supported his studies in France and Spain) enhanced his legitimacy in party circles. But García's election as general secretary also owed much to his own political skills in working with divergent factions and gaining their trust. Having won the confidence of key conservatives like Sánchez, he held out the possibility of providing the party with a more modern, social-democratic image, breaking the party's close identification since the 1950s with conservative politics.

García's rise to power also owed much to Haya's legacy in a different way: the dearth of political talent within the party. Haya's inability to tolerate rivals and his control over mobility within the party made it difficult for those with new ideas or with ambitions of their own to stay within the rigid discipline of the party ranks. APRA's identification with the right also put off new entrants and prompted splits, like that of APRA Rebelde in the 1960s. The majority of Peruvian intellectuals in the 1970s found affinity in the much more dynamic politics of the Marxist left than in APRA, which seemed at the time almost moribund as a political force. García, therefore, did not have to face great competition from alternative talent within the party rivalling his own, especially once he had managed to leap-frog the generation of leaders which had failed so signally to make their mark in the 1980 elections.

But perhaps most importantly of all was García's ability, in the wake of defeat, to provide the party with the real chance of achieving electoral victory. His skill in projecting a new image to a much wider electorate was the crucial political virtue: it offered the taste of success for a party which had thirsted after office for so long, but which had always found executive power so elusive. Once he had clinched the leadership his evident qualities set him aside from others in the party. His growing popularity in the country, cultivated painstakingly in the build-up to 1985, was the guarantee of his hegemony within APRA.

The landslide election victory of 1985 confirmed that *liderazgo* within the party. It gave APRA not only a majority in both houses of Congress, but offered the militants of the party the prospect of influential and sometimes lucrative posts in both the central government and in the regions. García's supremacy within the party was further enhanced by the popularity of his government's policies, in particular its heterodox economic policy and the return to growth based on an increase in real incomes. With both García and his party riding high in the opinion polls right through to the end of 1986, there was no serious challenge to his leadership. It was only by the end of 1986 and the beginning of 1987, when the signs began to appear of the economic troubles which lay ahead, that he began to face serious problems from within APRA.

Alan García grasped the point, however, that a big vote from traditionally non-Aprista sectors of society did not mean that the party's new support base was either structured or unconditional. The electoral front which had brought him to power had to be maintained and solidified. An important theme of his first two years in office was the attempt to build on the support he had won in the polls. García, it soon became clear, was someone unusually sensitive to his standing with public opinion, particularly among the poor mass of the population.

This bid to build on his party's electoral success was – as we shall see – a process regarded with considerable apprehension among the parties of the left. The growth of the left-wing vote in Peru in the late 1970s and 1980s had taken place to APRA's detriment at a time when the party's future looked bleak. Few at the time predicted its swift resurgence. The parties of what formally became the Izquierda Unida at the end of 1980 managed to articulate strong social support, especially among the most organised sectors of the popular movement. That support base was perhaps most visible in the trade union movement which played a key role in mobilising popular opinion against the military government after 1975, but it was also strong among the urban *pueblos jovenes*, and influential as well in rural Peru, partly through the peasant federations, partly as a result of the influence of the radical church. The revival of APRA under Alan García came as a direct challenge to the left not just in terms of its prominence in national politics but in terms of the popular sympathy it elicited at the local level. Some commentators on the left, frightened by the positive public reaction to García's initial successes in the economic sphere and by APRA's attempts to build grass-roots organisations, saw him trying to turn the party into a political machine akin to the Mexican Partido Revolucionario Institucional (PRI), a party with tentacles in all sectors of society exerting through the control of the state an effective political monopoly at the local level.

The social sectors which the new government sought to mobilise were those which had emerged politically over the previous twenty years but which had the weakest organised expression: the 'marginalised' urban poor and the rural peasantry. These were the sectors which Alan García said would receive attention from the new government in terms of social policy, the base of what he called the 'social pyramid'. This analysis divided Peruvian society into two fractions: a 'modern' sector, at the top of the pyramid, the beneficiaries of Peru's skewed pattern of economic growth (which included the 'relatively privileged' working class); and the 'traditional' or informal sector at the bottom – including the urban poor and the rural peasantry – which had been largely by-passed by the pattern of growth in the past.

This classification of the working class as a relatively privileged group was, of course, significant. On the one hand, it implied that any redistributive policies would not be intended to benefit this sector, a matter which had important implications for policies on wages and subsidies. On the other, it implied that APRA would not set out to compete or contest the predominance of the left in this sector. It was a tacit recognition of the marginal importance of the Aprista-dominated Confederación de Trabajadores del Perú (CTP) compared with the strength of the Communist Party-dominated Confederación General de Trabajadores del Perú (CGTP) which had progressively come to dominate the labour scene since the early 1970s. In the early 1980s, the CGTP had gained the affiliation of most of the powerful independent federations – the miners, the teachers, government employees, electricity workers, peasant workers, etc. The CTP, once Peru's most important confederation, was composed mostly of small, conservative federations, and was tainted by its right-wing leadership, its bureaucratic structure and its conciliatory approach to employers. Though García managed eventually to engineer the replacement of Julio Cruzado, the CTP's long-running general secretary, and to boost a more progressive leadership within the CTP, he did not seek to use control of the state to promote the CTP to undermine the CGTP. Rather, respect for the left's domination of the union movement seems to reflect García's preference to build up the party's presence among more numerous and less organised social groups and not to challenge the left's bedrock of organised support. Also it was characteristic of his preference to by-pass established organisation in appealing directly to the people.

In seeking to attract the urban poor and the rural peasantry, García did, however, try to encroach on political worlds in which the left had made significant advances during the 1970s and early 1980s. The potential for collision was evident, and came particularly to the fore during the course of 1986 when APRA sought to challenge the advances made by the left in municipal politics three years earlier, especially in low-income districts in Lima. For a party which saw its role as trying to correct social imbalances, and which simultaneously sought to expand and structure its social base, it was obviously to its advantage to set in motion programmes which would channel public funds to groups it thought it could win over – even if this meant picking quarrels at the local level with the left. Policy towards the left was therefore ambiguous.

In designing programmes to meet the needs of the urban poor and to mobilise support for APRA, the government was influenced by the experience of Sinamos during the Velasco regime. The office with responsibility for this under García was Cooperación Popular. Cooperación Popular had originally been established by Belaúnde to channel aid to communities in the *sierra* and *ceja de selva* where it sought to consolidate party support for Acción Popular. Under García, Cooperación Popular was more urban in its emphasis. Some of those put in charge of Cooperación Popular had previously been associated with Sinamos but who had fallen from favour when Sinamos was disbanded by Morales Bermúdez.

The most important programme developed under García to reduce urban poverty was the PAIT (see pp. 52–3), whose main purpose was to provide temporary employment for the unemployed. PAIT, which came under Cooperación Popular, responded, at no great cost to the Treasury, to much-felt social needs. It also had an overtly partisan profile, and sought to build up Aprista influence in the *pueblos jovenes*.[2] The great majority of PAIT coordinators at the local level were APRA militants, and those who became involved in PAIT activities were encouraged to participate in party activities and in demonstrations of support for the government. The numbers involved in PAIT were increased substantially in the run-up to the November 1986 municipal elections. Not surprisingly, the activities of PAIT were criticised by the left as being a way of using public funds for party purposes. Not only did it contribute to APRA's grass roots organisation, but it helped to debilitate left-wing municipal or neighbourhood organisation. Chronically underfunded, local municipalities in the poorest areas of Lima (mostly run by the Izquierda Unida between 1983 and 1986) found the PAIT scheme intervening in areas which, nominally at least, fell within their sphere of competence. Also, since PAIT was able to offer cash payments to those it involved, it tended to undermine municipal self-help schemes and neighbourhood community development projects run on the basis of voluntary labour, many of which identified with the left.

Two other schemes, both closely identified with APRA's attempt to build up its presence in the shanty-towns, complemented the work of PAIT, though they were much smaller in scope. These were the Direct Assistance Programme (PAD) and the IDESI programme of subsidised credit to small-scale businesses in the informal sector. PAD, presided over by Alan García's wife, Pilar Nores, was aimed particularly at women's organisations, notably *clubes de madres*, where it often conflicted with the activities of pre-existing social organisations, closely identified with the left and the radical church, such as the *comedores populares* and (in Lima) the municipality's *Vaso de Leche* campaign.[3]

We have already seen how in rural areas as well, the new government set out to change the pattern of social spending in such a way that it would channel funds to the poorest. In this case attention was directed towards the peasant community, which, in numerous speeches, García identified as representing the soul of the real, historical Peru. The APRA government set out to underpin its electoral support by trying to build support among the communities, using the special agricultural promotion programmes and the newly established structure of *microregiones*. At least at the outset, the García government put considerable emphasis on the need to find solutions to the problems of extreme backwardness and poverty in the southern *sierra* in particular. The expansion of the activities of Sendero Luminoso up to 1985 served to emphasise the importance of a 'new deal' for the highland peasant communities. In a bid to target the five departments of the *trapecio andino*, the government established a number of aid programmes to direct funds to peasant communities, including the Microregional Development Fund, Direct Assistance to Communities, in addition to credit and price support schemes.

The series of encounters or *rimanacuys* organised during the course of 1986 between the presidents of peasant communities and the president of the republic were designed primarily to boost García's profile in rural areas. Arranged by one of García's closest confidants,

Javier Tantaleán, head of the INP, five *rimanacuys* took place: in Piura, Huancayo, Cuzco, Puno and Pucallpa. Rather than directly promoting APRA as such, the idea was to forge a direct link – president to president as the government's publicity liked to describe it – to provide both sides with an opportunity to listen to the other. It was perhaps significant that no *rimanacuy* took place – nor was one apparently contemplated – in the Ayacucho Emergency Zone, where from a strategic point of view perhaps the government needed to listen most attentively to what the *comuneros* had to say.

Given the 5000 representatives of peasant communities who participated in the five *rimanacuys*, it was a successful exercise, providing the government with valuable information on the complaints and sources of disatisfaction of *comuneros* over much of highland Peru. Never before had a Peruvian president been able to project himself personally to so many legitimate representatives of the peasantry with all the potential political benefits which this could bring. It was an attempt to create a direct relationship which, as in the case of the *pueblos jovenes*, sought to by-pass intermediaries. In this instance it meant by-passing the established peasant confederations like the Confederación Campesina del Peru (CCP) and the Confederación Nacional Agraria (CNA) and other organisations with strong mass support hitherto dominated by the left. García's speeches to the *rimanacuys* bear testimony to his awareness of the continuing importance of the peasant community, of the need for effective decentralisation and of the advantages of small-scale agriculture. But though in the short term they helped boost his political profile among a largely non-Aprista sector of the population, and though the president was good at winning over the sympathies of sceptical audiences, the future of the relationship was to depend crucially on how the *rimanacuys* were followed up. The last of the *rimanacuys* was held in Pucallpa, just before the November 1986 elections. As García's attention turned to other issues in 1987, the experiment in communication with peasant Peru was not to be repeated.

APRA AND THE LEFT

The formation of the Izquierda Unida in September 1980 was a milestone in the development of the Peruvian left. It represented the decision of the parties of the Marxist left, which had shown their electoral potential in the 1978 Constituent Assembly elections, to put behind them the bitter ideological wranglings and internecine feuds which had fragmented them in the 1970s. It was also the culmination of a process which had begun three years earlier in which the parties of the left, many of them committed to armed struggle, came within the ambit of the formal political system. By September 1980 only one group stubbornly rejected participation in the newly established parliamentary democracy: a hitherto almost unheard of group, Sendero Luminoso. The Izquierda Unida became a major force in Peruvian politics winning 23.9 per cent of the vote in the November 1980 municipal elections and 28.8 per cent in the subsequent municipal elections of November 1983.[4] Indeed, comparatively, during the early 1980s the Izquierda Unida became one of Latin America's leading left-wing political forces, with a strong following in the unions, neighbourhood organisations among the urban shanty-towns, and among the organised peasantry.

The relationship between the Marxist left and APRA had never been an easy one. Even at the outset in the early 1930s they had clashed, their respective leaders, Haya de la Torre and Mariátegui, representing different political strategies and ideologies and competing for political influence among organised workers. In the cold war atmosphere of the 1950s, APRA became stridently anti-Communist while the Communist Party rounded on what it saw as APRA's fascist and populist tendencies. The two political forces vied for control of the labour movement. Up until the 1960s APRA retained control of the CTP, still at that time the main union federation. But during the 1970s the left made inroads on the unions and the CGTP marginalised the CTP. In establishing a *modus vivendi* with the Velasco government, the Communist Party rapidly gained union strength at APRA's expense. During the late 1970s newer, more radical Marxist parties made most headway within the union movement. By the early 1980s, before García started campaigning for the presidency, there was considerable confidence on the left that it, not APRA, was the popular force of the future. This confidence was reinforced by the creation of the Izquierda Unida in 1980 and its success in the 1983 municipal elections in Lima and elsewhere.

In this context it was not surprising that Alan García was acutely conscious of the potential challenge from the Marxist left. Not only was the left in competition with APRA in vying for popular support, but García saw it as being well placed to articulate Peru's profound social divides and to channel possible discontent with his government. García was therefore concerned to retain the political initiative, wherever possible to keep the left in check, and to stop it – or the parties within it – from adopting ever more radical political positions. The growth of Sendero Luminoso and the possibility that it might influence the more radical parties of the Izquierda Unida to move outside the formal political system only served to increase this concern.

Divisions within the Izquierda Unida made it easier for García to exert a degree of control over the left after 1985. During the Belaúnde administration the divides within the left were partly masked by common opposition to government policy, especially IMF-supported stabilisation policies and counter-insurgency policy in Ayacucho. Also the advantages of unity of action became more obvious, especially after the 1983 municipal elections. Nevertheless, even before 1985, rivalries on the left were never far from the surface, and party coordination a cumbersome process, despite the leadership role conferred on Alfonso Barrantes, an independent, as mayoral candidate in 1983 and presidential candidate in 1985.

After 1985, however, the left immediately encountered serious divisions over how to react to the new government, especially when in its first few months it took up many of the issues on which it had itself long been campaigning. The first point on which different groups pulled in different directions arose no sooner than the results of the first round of voting were announced. García failed to reach the '50 per cent-plus-one' of the total vote needed to make a second round of voting unnecessary. Barrantes' decision to recognise García as the outright winner and thus avoid a second round caused serious discrepancies. The more radical groupings within the Izquierda Unida, notably the Partido Unificado Mariateguista (PUM), saw an opportunity in a second round to embark on a further propaganda campaign, and – perhaps most importantly – to use a new round of campaigning to differentiate the left from APRA from the outset. Barrantes prevailed, backed by the more moderate social democratic parties, notably the Partido Socialista Revolucionario (PSR) led by Enrique Bernales, the first vice-presidential candidate on the Izquierda Unida slate in 1985. Even at this stage the lines were being drawn within the Izquierda Unida into two camps: the 'moderates' who emphasised the need to preserve democracy above all other considerations, and the more radical parties which sought to use the space offered by democracy further to develop popular organisation and to make it more politicised.

With nearly 25 per cent of the vote in the 1985 presidential elections, the left became the second force within the new parliament, and was much the most important block within the opposition. It had 15 of the

60 seats in the Senate, and 48 out of the 180 seats in the House of Deputies. Its parliamentary presence reflected the weight of its three most significant parties: the pro-Moscow Communist Party (PCP), the PUM and the Unidad de Izquierda Revolucionaria (UNIR), dominated by the previously pro-China Communist Party, Patria Roja. Together these accounted for nine senators and thirty-three deputies. While UNIR and PUM were on the left of the Izquierda Unida's ideological spectrum, the Communist Party was more or less in the centre. The three senators who received most votes in the elections were (in order of their electoral support) Javier Diez Canseco (PUM), Jorge del Prado (PCP) and Rolando Breña (UNIR). Enrique Bernales came in fourth place, despite the advantage of the extra visibility he gained by being one of Barrantes' running mates on the presidential slate. These results indicated the effective muscle of the main parties in the Izquierda Unida both in terms of deciding who should be on the lists of candidates for the Congress, and in terms of their genuine electoral support.

During the first few months of the new government its dynamism and the apparent radicalism of its policies proved disconcerting for the left. García took up several issues which had previously been the patrimony of the left: unilaterally limiting debt payments; breaking with the IMF; and annulling the oil contract of Belco, the second largest foreign oil company in Peru, and expropriating its assets. The initial and unexpected success of his heterodox economic policies in bringing inflation down and boosting economic growth also made opposition more difficult. Furthermore, the APRA government seemed to be making headway in taking steps to safeguard human rights an area in which the left up until 1985 had made most of the running. A Peace Commission was established in 1985 and emphasis was increasingly put on challenging Sendero Luminoso through social reform and economic reactivation. Especially striking was García's summary dismissal of three of the highest ranking military officials when the news emerged of army involvement in a massacre of peasants at the village of Accomarca in Ayacucho in August. His audacity and initiative thus took the wind out of the left wing's sails.

García's ability to maintain influence over the left was greatly helped by the close relationship he was able to develop with Alfonso Barrantes, who, up until November 1986, retained his post as mayor of Lima. The job gave Barrantes scope for manoeuvre independent of the Izquierda Unida, since it involved negotiation with central government on a regular basis on a wide number of issues. Increasingly,

Barrantes came to act as an intermediary between the government and the left. Relations between Barrantes and García were visibly cordial. This was criticised within the Izquierda Unida, but – given the importance of Barrantes's official post – the critics within the left could not do much, especially when he was selected once again as the Izquierda Unida's candidate for mayor in the 1986 municipal elections. It helped Barrantes, however, to reinforce his image as a 'moderate' and to distance himself in the public eye from the more radical parties of the left. It also helped Barrantes to negotiate the financial support required to continue with municipal spending programmes in the capital. In turn, for García he was a valuable ally who made it easier to exercise a degree of influence over the more radical left.

Though the 'honeymoon' in García's relations with the left lasted longer than most observers in 1985 thought it would, a degree of disenchantment soon set in. Once again the problem of human rights surfaced when the findings of a commission appointed to investigate the Accomarca killings were blocked by the APRA Senate majority, and nothing was done to reprimand those responsible. It also became clear that there was more rhetoric than substance in the government's commitment to limit annual debt payments to 10 per cent of exports, and – following the Belco nationalisation – relatively favourable concessions were granted in the jungle to the much bigger and more important multinational, Occidental Petroleum.

The incident which did most to shatter the working relationship between Alan García and the left was the June 1986 massacre of 250 Senderista inmates in two of Lima's top security jails. Acting on García's orders, troops were sent in to quell a synchronised 'rebellion' by Senderista prisoners in the prisons of Lurigancho, Santa Bárbara and El Frontón, an island off the coast from Callao. García's responsibility in ordering the intervention, the brutality with which it was carried out, and the elaborate attempts subsequently to conceal those responsible, all helped to drive a wedge between the government and the left. At the very least García was seen as guilty of major political misjudgement in his handling of the issue. It gave the initiative to the more radical sectors of the Izquierda Unida, particularly the PUM, which had long been the party to give greatest priority in its political work to human rights issues. By contrast the position adopted by Barrantes and the more 'moderate' groups on the left was much less critical but more pragmatic: they deliberately avoided any antagonism towards the security forces. García's image abroad was also badly dented, especially in the social-democratic world: the 'rebellion' in the jails was timed by Sendero to take place exactly as García was playing host to a congress of the Socialist International.[5]

Another factor that caused growing conflict within the Izquierda Unida and led to a questioning of Barrantes's role was the issue of internal reorganisation of the coalition. The system which evolved since 1980 of an executive committee (*comité directivo*) composed of general secretaries (or their representatives) of all the parties, a representative of the 'independents' and Alfonso Barrantes as president, failed to reflect the different weight of the political forces involved. It under-represented the larger parties like the PUM, UNIR and the Communist Party with their superior strength in the Congress, unions and other popular organisations; and it gave correspondingly more to the smaller parties, such as the Partido Comunista Revolucionario (PCR) and the PSR, not to mention small clientelist groupings supporting individual leaders like FOCEP and Acción Popular Socialista (APS).

Attempts to reorganise and streamline Izquierda Unida ran into a number of obstacles. The most important of these was Alfonso Barrantes himself, who always opposed – though not openly or in public – the conversion of Izquierda Unida into a single political machine. If the institutionalisation of the left was to take place, then Barrantes was set to lose the role of broker between competing political forces. Smaller groups would have to give way to majority resolutions. The 'little' parties would lose out, and those without a party, like Barrantes himself, would probably lose out most. The Izquierda Unida would also probably shift in a more radical direction, something which Barrantes tenaciously opposed.

So, by the second half of 1986 the system by which García kept the left in check through his relationship with Barrantes and the Izquierda Unida 'moderates' looked like breaking down. At the same time, conscious of this, the more radical groups on the left began to flex their muscles, keen to differentiate themselves in the public eye from the government and anxious to seize on embarrassing incidents like the prison massacres which undermined García's political standing nationally and internationally.

GARCIA, EMPRESARIOS AND THE PARTIES OF THE RIGHT

The presidential election results of 1985 were a major blow to the political standing of the main parties of the right, Acción Popular and the PPC. Having faced three years of recession, high rates of inflation and falling living standards, Peru voted massively for a change from the policies espoused by Belaúnde and his ministers. The pattern of *tercios* whereby the vote was split roughly three ways between the left, right and centre was altered significantly by the swing to the left. The right-wing vote in 1985 was reduced to under 20 per cent.

The results were particularly humiliating for Belaúnde's Acción Popular. It got just 7 per cent of the vote compared with over 45 per cent in 1980. Had Belaúnde been the candidate he might have fared marginally better, given his personal standing, but he was constitutionally barred from immediate re-election. Acción Popular's candidate instead was Javier Alva Orlandini, general secretary and party boss. His lack-lustre campaign performance failed even to rally the party faithful. The only places where Acción Popular's percentage share of the vote reached double figures were in departments like Amazonas and San Martín where communities, especially in the *ceja de selva*, had benefited from Belaúnde's pet development schemes, notably the marginal highway, a road link along the eastern flank of the Andes.

The rebuff to the PPC was not so crushing as that dealt to Acción Popular. It won just under 12 per cent of the vote in 1985, compared with 10 per cent in the presidential elections five years earlier. It probably picked up disaffected Acción Popular voters in urban areas, notably in Lima where it won 19 per cent of the poll in 1985. The PPC had taken steps to distance itself from the Belaúnde government when, in 1984, it prudently ended the arrangement agreed in 1980 whereby it helped provide the government with a majority in Congress in return for rights of nomination over the Ministries of Industry and Justice.

Reflecting the discomfort caused to local industrialists by the liberalisation of import tariffs, the PPC had become increasingly critical of the economic model introduced by Manuel Ulloa and his team from 1980 onwards. Its better showing was also due in part to a stronger party organisation in Lima and to the figure of its candidate and founder, Luis Bedoya Reyes, who was still remembered by some in Lima as having been one of the city's more successful mayors during the 1960s.

As a result of the 1985 elections, the right wing's representation in parliament was reduced from 137 deputies and senators (122 for Acción Popular and 15 for the PPC) before 1985 to 34 afterwards (15 for Acción Popular and 19 for the PPC). Its capacity for manoeuvre within the Congress was reduced by the ideological distance separating the right-wing parties from the Izquierda Unida. There was little common ground between the two wings of the opposition, except on such conjunctural matters as votes of censure against the Aprista majority.

The reduction of the right's parliamentary presence to a small, politically impotent rump brought with it important consequences. On the one hand, it produced a virtual suspension of party political activity outside Congress. Acción Popular even refrained from fielding candidates in the November 1986 municipal elections, fearing that they would have brought yet another humiliating defeat. Though the PPC did participate in the municipal campaign, the poor performance of Bedoya as candidate for mayor of Lima, running alone against APRA and the left, came as a serious blow to his political ambitions.

The other important consequence was that the lack of any strong right-wing parliamentary representation made it easier for Alan García to deal direct with the economic interest groups which normally had closer ties with these two parties. One of the salient features of García's first two years in office was his ability to deal on a person-to-person basis with Peru's main private-sector groups, by-passing not only the elected representatives of the right in Congress, but also the private sector *gremios*, like the Sociedad Nacional de Industrias (SNI), the exporters' association (Adex), and the Confederación Intersectorial de las Empresas Privadas (Confiep), an umbrella private sector organisation set up in 1984.

García adapted a strategy of talking direct to the largest industrial concerns, and ignoring the smaller ones. During 1986 the owners of the largest economic groups became known as the 'twelve apostles'. These included the Romeros and Raffos (owners of the Banco de Crédito, by far the largest private bank in Peru), the Brescias, the Ferreyros, the Wieses, the Nicolinis, the Bentíns, the Lanata Piaggio group, La Fabril (Bunge and Born), the Picassos, the Olaechea-Alvarez Calderón group, and Cogorno. García seems to have consciously avoided dealing with Confiep wherever possible, aware of the partisan political interests involved, preferring instead to achieve a degree of coordination and contact with the business community on an intermittent basis through the annual conference for executives, CADE.

Unlike the left, APRA's 1985 presidential campaign never sought to vilify Peru's business class. Indeed, traditionally, APRA's political message had never been 'anti-capitalist'. It sought to harness the energies of local capitalism to a political purpose which was nationalist and reformist. Alan Garcia, as candidate, was careful not to attack local business interests. In fact he did his best to attract business to the Aprista cause. Some like the Romero–Raffo group went so far as to contribute to his election campaign. Many others, despite their reservations about APRA, saw an APRA victory as the most likely outcome, and preferred to be on the winning side. Also, despite their reservations about García's populism, many believed genuinely that an APRA government offered a viable social democratic mid-way between the economic liberalism of the Belaúnde government and the left-wing radicalism of Izquierda Unida.

García underlined his interest in establishing close collaboration with the private sector in his inaugural speech to Congress in 1985. While extolling the importance of the state in economic management, he stressed the point that the development of private enterprise should go hand-in-hand 'with the common good' and he rejected what he called 'dogmatic egalitarianism and sterile statism'. Private enterprise was to have an important role to play in domestic capital accumulation. The message was reiterated the following October at the annual CADE conference in Ica when García appealed for investment. In the wake of the 1985 CADE, mechanisms for more permanent consultation between the government and the representatives of the private sector were introduced under the auspices of the Instituto Peruano de Administración de Empresas (IPAE), the organisers of CADE. This, known as 'CADE *permanente*', did not seek to involve Confiep, or representatives of private sector *gremios*, even though on occasions meetings were held between government officials and Confiep. On top of this, from mid-1986, the government pushed ahead with what it called '*concertación selectiva*', meetings between senior officials (including García himself) and the 'twelve apostles' to coordinate investment policy. The continued marginalisation of Confiep and its impatience at being excluded from the process of policy formulation were revealed by a conference it organised in October 1986, in which it was guardedly critical of the government. As if to put Confiep in its place, Garcia managed to get many of the '12 apostles' to come in person to the 1986 CADE, which took place shortly afterwards in Huaraz, something which most of them did not usually bother to do. Once again at CADE, García argued forcefully that the continued success of his government depended crucially on private sector investment. In announcing the existence of letters of intent signed by the 'twelve apostles', he reaffirmed where the main axis lay in relations between government and the private sector.

The initial reaction of the business community to Alan García's attack on inflation was positive. After nearly eighteen months of policy drift during the last phase of the Belaúnde government, at least it seemed that initiatives were being taken and pursued with some determination. While there were doubts about the new government's real intentions in the longer term, the main short-term worry was that the price freeze announced in July 1985 would cut into profits. In practice the freeze was at best partial, and by October 1985 there were already signs that the increase in purchasing power was filtering through into a revival of domestic demand. By the end of the year Lima's financial press was beginning to declare the recession officially over, reporting a sharp upturn in demand for cars, clothing, shoes, food products and drinks.[6]

García's standing with the private sector owed much to the extraordinary pace of economic reactivation which took place in 1986, taking most of the pundits by surprise. As we have seen, the sectors which benefited most from the reactivation were manufacturing and construction. Manufacturing grew by 18.6 per cent and construction 30 per cent, their best performance for years. Though employers found themselves having to pay higher wages to their workforce, this was more than offset by expanded output, turnover and profit.

The government also showed ability to strike deals with specific industrial sectors which were to the advantage of both. One such deal was an agreement reached in March 1986 where the government assented to a relaxation of the price freeze on pharmaceutical goods on condition that Peruvian and foreign-owned drug manufacturers set aside funds to finance a special programme of low-cost medicines for popular distribution at between half and a third of their usual price.[7]

But while manufacturers supplying the domestic market benefited from government policy, this was not the case with exporters – especially exporters of minerals who did not receive the same incentives as exporters of non-traditional goods. Exporters became increasingly hostile as 1986 drew on and the inti became progressively more overvalued. By June private sector mining companies were claiming that they were being hit by large losses, and were pushing hard for a higher exchange rate for the inti against the dollar, tax cuts, lower interest rates on pre-export financing, and loans for selective bail-outs. It is a notable feature of García's approach to the private sector that he did not look for close policy coordination with, for instance, mining interests. But, at the same time, it should be stressed that the biggest traditional exporter by far was the state itself through its ownership of Centromin, Hierroperu, Mineroperu, Petroperu and Petromar (the company which took over Belco's nationalised assets). The public sector export companies carried the brunt of the cost of reactivation.

The big question that presented itself in terms of the government's relations with the private sector was whether the strategy of working with the 'twelve apostles' would actually bring the hoped for results: domestic investment in selected areas of the economy. The series of contacts established in late 1986 ended in the formation of the National Investment Council at the beginning of 1987, in which the twelve were represented. And while there was much speculation in the specialist press during early 1987 as to whether investment would get beyond the stage of 'letters of intent', there were indications that overheating of the economy would lead to new inflationary pressures if it was not forthcoming quickly. By the end of the first quarter the government itself was beginning to have doubts about what could be achieved voluntarily, and in April it introduced its compulsory bond purchase scheme, a move criticised by Confiep as simply a form of expropriation.

So, despite the *modus vivendi* established between García and the leading lights of the private sector during the first two years of economic expansion, the links were founded more on mutual self interest than on strong trust or confidence on either side. With growing concern that the government's model could not be sustained and that a crunch was approaching, it was perhaps hardly surprising that Peru's major capitalists were having second thoughts about putting their money on the line. Probably their thoughts were already turning more towards how to get their money out of Peru rather than investing more. Meanwhile, for his part, García was preparing his volte-face to attack the private sector head on by nationalising the private financial system.

TROUBLE IN SIGHT

For APRA party organisers the November 1986 municipal elections yielded some very positive results. It saw APRA candidates for the mayors of provincial and district municipalities sweep the board across the country. While APRA had won 75 provincial municipalities in 1983 to Acción Popular's 35, Izquierda Unida's 33 and the PPC's 2, in 1986 APRA got 159 municipalities to Izquierda Unida's 10 and only one for the PPC. Politically the main prize was Lima where an Aprista, Jorge Del Castillo, replaced Alfonso Barrantes as mayor, winning by a narrow margin and amid claims of fraud. But APRA also mopped up other Izquierda Unida-run cities including Huaraz, Cuzco, Huancavelica, Huancayo, Puno and Pucallpa. APRA increased its share of the vote in every department of the country in 1986 over 1983's results, in some cases dramatically. In Puno, APRA won 52.7 per cent in 1986 (8.7 per cent in 1983), winning in all but three out of twenty provinces; in Cuzco it won in all thirteen provinces with 57.5 per cent of the vote (20.9 per cent in 1983).

But seen from a different angle, the results were less of a stunning political victory. Though sixteen months after taking office the polls still confirmed the popularity of APRA and the García government, the party's share of the vote actually fell in relation to the presidential election results, even though one of Peru's main political parties, Acción Popular, did not participate. APRA got 47.8 per cent of the vote, compared to 53.1 per cent in 1985. By contrast the percentage share for the Izquierda Unida reached its highest ever, 30.8 per cent as opposed to 24.7 per cent in 1985. On the right the PPC got only a slightly higher percentage than it did in 1985,[8] despite Acción Popular's absence.

The geographical distribution of the vote showed APRA consolidating its strength in former Izquierda Unida strongholds in the south. Support for the Izquierda Unida fell in departments such as Arequipa, Huancavelica, Puno and Tacna. At the same time, the Izquierda Unida managed to increase its share of the vote in the north, on occasions substantially. In Cajamarca its vote increased from 18 per cent to 25 per cent, in La Libertad from 11 per cent to 23 per cent, in Lambayeque 20 per cent to 35 per cent, and in Tumbes on the frontier with Ecuador, from 23 per cent to 34 per cent.

In Lima, compared with 1983, APRA made big advances winning in 19 of the city's districts compared with 7 in 1983. The Izquierda Unida, by contrast, won in 20 in 1983 and only 9 in 1986. But, as was the case nationally, APRA's percentage of the total vote was rather less than it was in 1985. While the Izquierda Unida retained control in many of the most populous slum areas, it did so often with much reduced majorities. APRA candidates pushed out Izquierda Unida mayors in highly populated, poor neighbourhoods, such as Carabayllo, Lurigancho, Villa Maria del Triunfo and San Juan de Lurigancho, as well as in poor inner city areas like Rímac and La Victoria, underlining the volatility of the poor urban vote.

The climate of public opinion behind the voting patterns is the result of a complex interaction of influences both local and national which requires more detailed analysis than is possible here. A survey conducted three months after the elections in three separate areas (Carabayllo and Villa El Salvador in Lima, and in the department of Cuzco), each with big swings to APRA in relation to the 1983 elections, confirmed that voters were influenced by the way in which they had benefited from the economic reactivation. There were clear perceptions that there was more employment and that living standards had improved. Moreover, at the local level there were many who felt that the promises made by the left in 1983 had not been fulfilled, and that though there was less corruption than before, the left's record in terms of public works projects completed had not come up to expectations.[9]

APRA's special social promotion programmes – PAIT, PAD and IDESI in the cities, subsidised credit and government hand-outs in rural areas – also appear to have had an impact. The scale of PAIT in Villa El Salvador, for instance, greatly increased in the months just before the elections. It was widely seen as having an important effect in reducing public support for the Izquierda Unida and its otherwise extremely popular mayor, Miguel Azcueta. In rural areas of Cuzco development agencies reported a tactical vote for APRA: communities decided that they stood more chance of receiving funds from government sources if they voted in mayors belonging to APRA, even though in general Apristas in Cuzco had never been closely identified with the interests of peasant communities.

The 1986 municipal elections helped to widen the gap further within the Izquierda Unida, and to place further strain on its relations with the government. In the first place, both the PUM and UNIR were openly against Barrantes being reselected as the candidate for mayor of Lima. During the campaign splits and rivalries came out into the open, damaging the Izquierda Unida's public profile. Finally, when Barrantes lost by scarcely 3 per cent against Del Castillo, the more radical groups on the left were exasperated by Barrantes's refusal to take the lead in a campaign to nullify the results in view of the alleged fraud. Forced by the radicals to speak in a public protest meeting in Lima, Barrantes – for the first time in his political career – was greeted with whistles and jeers. No sooner had García's ally lost the post which gave him standing and a certain autonomy in relation to the rest of the left than he found himself the victim of growing radicalism within the ranks of Izquierda Unida.

Hostility to Barrantes on the left was made even more evident a few months later in May 1987, when at the inauguration of the 9th Congress of the Communist Party Barrantes was again booed at and heckled by a substantial number of those present. Most hostile was the youth section of the party, which had come to adopt markedly more radical positions than the traditionally moderate, pro-Moscow party leadership. It represented a significant shift within Izquierda Unida and was a particularly bitter blow for Barrantes whose position within the Izquierda Unida had usually received strong support from the Communist Party. The results of the Congress marked a swing to the left within the party, with the replacement of 'moderates' on the party's central committee by more radical voices. Alfonso Barrantes resigned as president of the Izquierda Unida shortly after this. Though his presence in the executive committee had been intermittent for some time, from this moment onwards he ceased to have any direct links with the Izquierda Unida.

This growing radicalisation within the Izquierda Unida had a number of causes. In the first place, the left saw itself as a victim of the growing number of restrictions being placed on democratic freedoms in Peru by the APRA government. As a result of the counter-insurgency campaign of the Armed Forces against Sendero Luminoso, the scope for political organisation in many parts of the country, especially in areas under direct military control, was becoming very circumscribed. Many Izquierda Unida supporters and militants had been the victims of arbitrary killings or imprisonment for supposedly 'terrorist' offences.

A second reason was that the growth of Sendero Luminoso and the Movimiento Revolucionario Túpac Amaru (MRTA) reduced the political space available to the Izquierda Unida, especially in rural areas. While many of the parties of the left maintained a Marxist–Leninist ideological stance and an adhesion, at least in principle, to the validity of armed struggle, the apparent success of Sendero in vindicating a strategy of violence acted as a pole of attraction for the more radical sectors, especially among the young. At the same time, in areas like Ayacucho where organisations and politicians who supported the Izquierda Unida found themselves caught in the cross-fire between Sendero Luminoso and the military, armed self-defence increasingly became the only option to forced migration.

A third cause of radicalisation was the loss of a number of municipalities in the 1986 local elections. While municipal concerns occupied the energies of many on the left after 1983, anchoring them into the formal political system (though often with few rewards), the loss of a stake in the system had the effect of diminishing loyalties, especially among political forces which were only semi-loyal to the system in the first place.[10]

Finally, as we have seen, the political dividends of heterodoxy were beginning to diminish by the first half of 1987. Real incomes were no longer rising at the same rate as before, and the economic future looked increasingly bleak. It was in these circumstances that the CGTP, on 19 May, launched its first one-day general strike since the APRA government came to office, reflecting the shift to the left within the Communist Party. Immediately prior to the one-day strike, however, members of the police force went on strike. Not only with the CGTP stoppage did the police strike have obvious security implications, but it raised the whole issue of indiscipline within the police force and fears among the the security forces of creeping unionisation. It also excited historical comparisons: a strike by police in Lima preceded the military coup which toppled General Velasco in 1975. Senior armed forces commanders are reported to have been 'disgusted' by the way the government handled the dispute, negotiating directly with the strike leaders.[11] The Finance Ministry was not pleased either since the wage award was set to cost up to US$75 million a year, just as the sharply deteriorating fiscal climate was becoming clear for all to see.

The government thus faced the threat of growing union militancy. The boom of 1986 had led to a relative increase in union power after years in which falling real incomes and high unemployment had eroded the real muscle of the unions. With the strong recovery of purchasing power and the lack of a pool of skilled workers, unions began to sense that they could push harder in their negotiations over pay. With full order books, firms discovered a new-found interest in keeping their workforce happy, and were often prepared to settle for wage increases which were well ahead of the rate of inflation. Some were also worried by the inroads reportedly being made by Sendero Luminoso among the unionised workforce in Lima's factories (see p. 191).

By mid-1987, García was also facing considerable problems within his own party where his overarching authority was beginning to be called into question. The most important complaint among party militants from 1985 onwards was that Alan García had deliberately robbed them of the fruits of office. García preferred to bring in independents or former Velasquistas into key roles. He also sought to tap the skills of the left, a source of more intellectual and professional talent than his own party. And, with García's radical-sounding tone there were many on the left, especially within its more social democratic currents, who found no difficulty in working for him. A major problem, then, was to find ways of satisfying the frustrations within APRA.

García's high-handed methods of doing things were a source of irritation within APRA. His autocratic style of leadership, in particular his dealings with his party in Congress, led to outbursts of anger. One of the first to criticise García in public was Jorge Torres Vallejo, the vociferous and independent-minded Aprista mayor of Trujillo, who was later expelled from the party. More importantly in terms of party unity were the manoeuvrings of Luis Alva Castro, prime minister and finance minister since 1985. As early as 1986, Alva Castro was preparing the terrain within the party for his candidacy in the 1990 elections, priming himself up as a serious rival to Alan García. The most obvious obstacle to Alva Castro's ambitions was the possibility that García might be tempted to run for a second consecutive term, although to do so would mean introducing an amendment to the constitution, for which he would need two-thirds of support in a Congressional vote.

By the beginning of 1987 relations between the two men were coming under increasing strain, provoking split loyalties and the formation of groups within the party. The split became particularly evident when Alva Castro openly defied García by standing against García's chosen candidate, Rómulo León, in a race for the presidency of the House of Deputies. Alva Castro swung the majority of APRA deputies behind him. His resignation as prime minister and finance minister in June 1987 caused further open discord, with García responding that 'good' Apristas did not resign or shrink from their responsibilities. With the heterodox model heading for trouble, Alva Castro, it seemed, was abandoning the sinking ship, taking the credit for its successes but not wishing to have his reputation tarnished by subsequent failures.

By the middle of 1987 García's political pre-eminence seemed based on much shakier foundations than a year earlier. Not only did he face the problem of schism within his own party ranks with Alva Castro attempting to rival his authority, but the methods used to keep the left in check appeared to be breaking down. García appears to have been extremely conscious also that his own personal popularity in the opinion polls was on the wane, and that this personal popularity was his most precious asset. Though the November 1986 municipal elections had confirmed APRA's electoral strength nationally, it was clear that its political presence was still largely disorganised and could disappear as quickly as it had been created. The main threat to the APRA administration at this stage appeared to be the possibility of the left mobilising against the government as the economic situation deteriorated, thereby regaining and capitalising upon the electoral support won in 1985 and in 1986 by APRA. No one predicted that the main challenge would come from the resurgent right, not the left. But then no one predicted that García, in a bid to regain the political initiative, was about to announce such a dramatic move as his decision to nationalise the private financial industry.

4 Sendero Luminoso and the Guerrilla Challenge

SENDERO LUMINOSO AND ITS SIGNIFICANCE

By the time Alan Garcia took office in 1985, Sendero Luminoso's war against Peru's political establishment – 'the old reactionary Peruvian state' as Sendero would call it – was already five years old. Indeed, Sendero had existed as a political grouping since 1970. Its first armed strike, symbolic in retrospect, but largely unnoticed at the time, had been to burn the ballot boxes at Chuschi, a small township in the province of Cangallo in Ayacucho, on the night prior to the presidential election on 18 May 1980. It thus turned its back on electoral politics, the way forward chosen by most of Peru's Marxist parties at the end of the twelve-year-old military dictatorship, asserting that armed struggle was the only way forward. Five years on Sendero remained unvanquished. A group whose methods and style initially generated more ridicule than preoccupation had come to exercise profound political influence.

Sendero's influence by 1985 spread far beyond the Ayacucho region, its birthplace. During the early 1980s, partly as a consequence of the counter-insurgency strategy adopted by the Belaúnde government, the radius of Sendero's attacks came to cover a wide swathe of the Peruvian *sierra*. If we include the other armed groups which Sendero had effectively subsumed by 1985,[1] its political and military influence stretched from Puno in the south as far north as La Libertad and Cajamarca. But its political influence was greater than the area over which it held sway, the number of acts of sabotage it perpetrated or the numbers killed in armed attacks. Alongside the effects of the debt crisis, Sendero probably did more than anything else to undermine the standing and authority of Peru's first elected government since the 1960s. In part this was because Sendero's persistence made a nonsense of the government's constantly reiterated claims to have matters under control. There was a substantial part of rural Peru where it no longer exercised control. It was obvious by 1985 that, despite the large-scale deployment of troops and police in Ayacucho and elsewhere, Sendero's activities continued to grow.

94

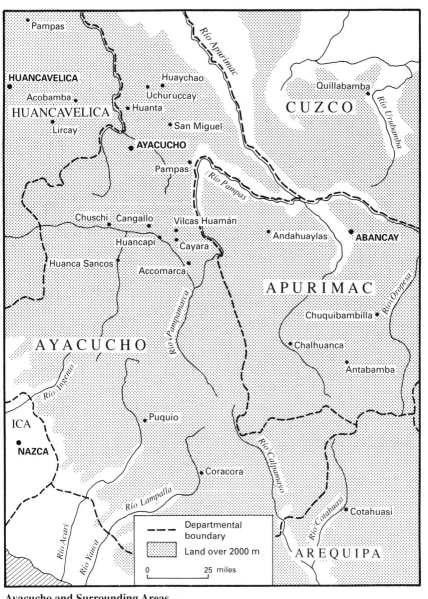

Ayacucho and Surrounding Areas

Perhaps even more importantly, the war against Sendero forced the Belaúnde government to cede ever increasing amounts of political responsibility to the military, when one of its main claims to legitimacy and popular support was that it was an elected, civilian government. The clearest example of ceding political control was the declaration of the Ayacucho Emergency Zone in late 1982 and the conferring of political as well as military responsibility over the three departments of Ayacucho, Apurímac and Huancavelica to the armed forces. The moral standing of the Belaúnde government was further undermined by the problem of human rights violations committed by the military in its campaign to crush Sendero. The government found itself obliged to support the military, irrespective of the massacres of innocent people which took place. Criticised by Peruvian and international human rights organisations alike, Belaúnde turned a blind eye to the charges they made, claiming in one of his press conferences that he just threw Ammnesty International reports into the dustbin. The opposition parties, especially the Izquierda Unida, but also to a lesser extent APRA, took up human rights as a key isue to discredit Belaúnde and his government.

Sendero's insurgency also helped fuel animosities between the civilian government and the military establishment. Senior military officers were concerned about how far Belaúnde was prepared to go in giving them the unequivocal backing they demanded. Though Belaúnde had no wish to upset the military and was scrupulous in respecting military autonomy in such areas as promotions and budgets, the growth of violence (especially the death toll) in Ayacucho also created tensions. It became clear that military repression was not working, and as on each occasion new atrocities were revealed it became more difficult politically for the president to continue giving the military *carte blanche*.[2] This was a dilemma which was also to face Alan García after 1985.

THE ORIGINS AND DEVELOPMENT OF SENDERO

By 1985, Sendero Luminoso was by no means just an Ayacuchan phenomenon. As well as spreading over a wide area of the Peruvian *sierra* it was already building a presence in other parts of the country, notably in the coca-producing valleys along the *ceja de selva* and in the capital itself. Despite this advance, Ayacucho still remained the heartland of Sendero. Why was Ayacucho such fertile ground for the development of this extreme left-wing, highly dogmatic and very violent political grouping? The degree to which Sendero's growth responded to the specificity of circumstances in Ayacucho helps explain some of the constraints that faced Sendero in starting up operations in other parts of the country.

Ayacucho, and with it Huancavelica to the west and Apurímac to the south-east – the so-called *mancha india* – combines several features which makes it propitious for the development of guerrilla warfare. It is a mountainous terrain, remote and isolated with very poor land communications. It is a terrain in which it is difficult to locate guerrilla bands, still less to attack and destroy them. The highest and most remote areas also provide refuge in moments of retreat. As a consequence of its remoteness, this is the part of the *sierra* where the presence of the Peruvian state and its representatives has traditionally been weakest. Typically, for instance, the presence of police and other local authorities is concentrated in a few larger communities or small towns, where even there they are vulnerable to attack. By almost all the conventional indicators, Ayacucho and surrounding areas are also the poorest part of Peru. Indeed income levels on average in the three departments are among the lowest in Latin America. Child mortality rates are extremely high, life expectancy low and illiteracy widespread.[3] It is an area which has long been marginalised from the mainstream of economic development, even in comparison with other parts of the Peruvian *sierra*. As a consequence there has traditionally been a strong regionalist resentment against the economic domination of Lima and the coastal cities, which has proved relatively easy over the years to articulate. It is also a region characterised by a strong ethnic differentiation, in which a native-born guerrilla organisation can profit from racial tensions and win the confidence of the local population in defending them (having first provoked a military response) from what appears as an army of occupation.

There were, however, disadvantages too. It was not an area of any great strategic importance to the national economy, being one mostly of subsistence agriculture and small-scale mining. So as to strike at targets of real economic importance, Sendero had to initiate operations elsewhere, notably in Lima and in the central *sierra* to the north. Nor were these departments ones where significant wealth could easily be tapped to finance guerrilla warfare, except along the *ceja de selva* where cash-crop agriculture including coca was more common. While Sendero was confined mainly to Ayacucho, the scale of military activities was limited by the guns and ammunition it could rob from the police and army, and dynamite from local mining operations. It remained an *artesanal* kind of guerrilla army.

Sendero's origins are to be found in the 1960s in the University of San Cristóbal de Huamanga in the city of Ayacucho. The university was, however, not typical of most of Peru's provincial universities in several important respects. Re-established in 1959, it had a strong vocational orientation directed towards practical disciplines like agronomy, engineering, veterinary science, nursing and education, with obvious relevance for regional development needs. Its curriculum indeed highlighted the removal of 'obstacles' to development, and there were strong ties between the campus and rural projects. Its intake included not just the sons and daughters of Ayacucho's wealthier and more privileged families but involved a wide social spectrum, with an unusually large number of students from humble, often rural back-grounds. Another peculiarity of the university was its prestige and standing in the economic, political and cultural life of Ayacucho. Education was the main source of employment in the city. At its height there were some 10 000 students in a town of 70 000 inhabitants. Education was as important to the local economy as mining was in Cerro de Pasco, or sugar cane to the towns of La Libertad or Lambayeque.

While the economic backwardness of Ayacucho and the lack of a significant industrial or commercial base enhanced the role of the university, the absence of a strong economic élite also helped make it a fertile ground for the development of radical politics. From the early 1960s the Communist Party was able to build a significant presence, skilfully exploiting economic discontent and raising regionalist issues. It was the motive force behind the creation of the Frente de Defensa del Pueblo. The Frente started out as a pressure group in resistance to central government attempts during the first Belaúnde government to cut funding to the university. It turned into a broad-based regional pressure group with wide social support, the forerunner of regionalist pressure groups that developed elsewhere in the 1970s and 1980s.[4]

Though Sendero's presence in urban politics in the 1970s was clandestine, the legitimacy it enjoyed in Ayacucho owed much to the radical tradition and the strength of regional feeling developed in the 1960s. It sought to build a presence in the university, especially among trainee teachers whom it mobilised in opposition to the Velasco government's educational reforms. Ayacucho was an area where the expectations raised by the Velasco reforms were never met in practice. The rhetoric of land reform and assistance to the peasantry, for instance, rang hollow in a region largely unaffected by changes in land tenure, especially when, as in 1969, protest was met by severe repression. Sendero rejected outright what it called the 'fascism' of the military government. It clashed with other parties on the left, notably the pro-Moscow Communist Party which supported military reform- ism. Maoism, generally, in the 1970s came to be the political expression of sectors with a sense of social, political and occupational frustration during the military government, of which school teachers were a prime example.[5]

Both the ideology and structure of Sendero Luminoso are also rooted in its origins and development prior to 1980. Sendero came into being as a result of successive splits within the Peruvian communist movement: first within the Communist Party itself at the time of the Sino-Soviet division in 1964, and then subsequently within the pro-Chinese Patria Roja and its more extreme offshoot Bandera Roja in the highly charged ideological debates within the left of the late 1960s. It was in 1968 that, returning from China, the head of Bandera's military commission, Abimael Guzmán, Sendero's foun- der, arrived in Peru to find himself expelled from the Bandera mainstream. Only a small group, mostly from Ayacucho where Guzmán was a philosophy teacher in the university, stayed with him. The origins of Sendero Luminoso were thus in a small group of radicals, isolated from the political mainstream.

This isolation from mass politics, coupled to the intellectual back- ground from which Abimael Guzmán and his friends came, meant that Sendero became a small, tightly knit organisation, welded together by strong ideological cohesion. Guzmán spent at least eighteen months in 1970 and 1971, after the final split with Bandera Roja, intensively studying Marxist writings, particularly those of Mao and Mariátegui, to perfect points of ideology and revolutionary strategy. He developed the notion of bureaucratic capitalism as a critique of the Velasco government, a sort of pseudo-capitalism masking a 'semi-feudal' social structure. Such was the importance of ideology to Sendero that it became virtually a religion, a set of unquestionable and immutable doctrinal precepts. To the outside world, its apparently dogmatic ideology – especially its preoccupation with the Chinese model – made Sendero seem far removed from the real problems facing rural villagers in highland Peru. In fact, however, the dedication to ideological purity was to become one of Sendero's most important sources of strength. It implied absolute loyalty, unity of purpose and submission to the will of the party. Indeed, one of Sendero's most remarkable features, paralleled to some extent in the history of APRA, was the degree of commitment of its members to the cause.

Particularly as it moved into its military phase from 1980 onwards, Sendero came to be organised on a tight cell structure with a highly vertical chain of command. Indeed, its organisation operated in the function of its very militaristic outlook, and the militarisation of the party was seen as being one of its more important contributions to Marxist revolutionary practice. Decision-making, at least on strategically important questions, rested in the hands of the Central Committee. Yet it is unlikely that this consisted of more than a handful of people. The inner core of the party in fact passed into clandestinity when military operations began with the attack on Chuschi in 1980.

At the centre of Sendero, ultimately the source of all authority, was the figure of Abimael Guzmán, 'President Gonzalo', the 'fourth sword' of the world revolution after Marx, Lenin and Mao. No one knows for sure whether Guzmán is alive or dead. He has not been seen in public since 1980.[6] But whether he is or not, he has remained the dominant figure in Sendero. His disappearance has probably enhanced certain superhuman qualities in the popular imagination. He has become almost more of a legendary figure than a real person.

Because of its clandestinity we are afforded few glimpses of how Sendero works in practice. The activities of Senderistas in prison, however, offers an insight which confirms the ferocious discipline and authoritarianism exercised within its ranks. This was clearly the case in the two Lima prisons, Lurigancho and El Frontón, which received the majority of captured Senderistas until the June 1986 prison massacres. With the prisoners held in blocks, but not in solitary confinement, Sendero effectively administered its own sections of the prison, excluding the prison guards and imposing an iron discipline over their inmates. Instead of breaking their morale, prison life helped to reinforce revolutionary convictions. In fact, as was the case with APRA in the 1940s and 1950s, the prisons provided a sort of ideological university, overcoming the dispersal which necessarily arose from tight, cellular, clandestine forms of organisation.

For a party which puts a premium on the 'correct' application of scientific Marxism, the revolutionary strategy as elaborated by 'President Gonzalo' played a central role in determining its actions. Sendero Luminoso's strategy broadly followed basic Maoist prescriptions which were fiercely defended by the pro-Chinese Communist Party following the Sino-Soviet split. However, the weight given to the peasantry in spearheading the process of revolution also had its roots in Mariátegui, whom Senderistas admire not only as the founder of the Peruvian Communist Party (of whose tradition they see themselves as the true disciples) but for his contribution in relating Marxist thinking to Peruvian circumstances. It is worth remembering that the name Sendero Luminoso is derived from the phrase 'Por el Sendero Luminoso de José Carlos Mariátegui', the name of the student group in Ayacucho university in which Guzmán and others held sway in the late 1960s. The notion of the prolonged popular war originating in rural areas, surrounding the cities and finally choking them, however, is derived from the Chinese experience. But whereas it took Mao twenty-seven years to achieve, Sendero believes that the revolution will come more quickly in Peru.

While proclaiming the achievements of the Maoist revolutionary tradition and lauding the Gang of Four in its propaganda, Sendero developed its own thinking on strategy. It divided its experience between 1980 and the end of 1986 into three different periods, each with its separate plan. The first was an initial phase which lasted from May up to the end of 1980. This was the *Plan de Inicio de la Lucha Armada*, involving the 'militarisation of the party through (military) actions', primarily in rural areas. The second was from 1981 onwards to the end of 1982, known as *Plan de Desplegar la Guerra de Guerrillas.* Then in 1983 the Central Committee sanctioned the *Gran Plan de Conquistar Bases* which involved reorganisation of the party, the creation of the Popular Guerrilla Army (EGP), the formation of organisations to win support in both rural and urban areas, and finally the implementation of the military plan. From 1987 onwards, Sendero moved into a fourth stage with the *Gran Plan de Desarrollar Bases*, which sought to develop an alternative power to the 'reactionary' state and from there progressively to conquer power throughout the country. In its strategic design the emphasis was on the encirclement of Lima.

Naturally, in practice Sendero's strategic development does not correspond to such a unilinear plan. Still, though faltering and uneven, Sendero's development through these different phases is unmistakable.

THE BATTLE FOR HEARTS AND MINDS

Although Sendero's initial growth was chiefly among students and teachers from the university in Ayacucho, from 1977 onwards it set out to build a presence in rural areas. Though in 1980 it was still not essentially a peasant-based organisation, its advance in rural areas was rapid between 1980 and 1982. Government sources say that by the time the army was drafted in at the beginning of 1983, Sendero controlled 85 per cent of the northern and central provinces of the department. Apart from the general characteristics of the region, two factors help explain this surge.

First, there was no strong rural landed class capable of obstructing Sendero's advance. Though the pattern of landholding had not been greatly affected by the agrarian reform of the 1970s, many of the old *hacendados* had left the region. Those who remained were not big landowners, nor were they economically powerful. The expansion of Sendero did not therefore encounter any vigorous opposition from a strong landowning class. Rural conflict was rather to be found between rural communities, or even within them.

Secondly, also partly a result of the lack of agrarian reform, pre-existing peasant organisation was weak. This meant that Sendero did not run into opposition from existing interest groups; or when it did these were not strong enough to resist its inroads. In other parts of the *sierra* the agrarian reform and the activities of government agencies like Sinamos had had a crucial bearing on peasant organisation, even if indirectly, by forcing those by-passed by land reform to redress their grievances. While peasant unions were weak in Ayacucho, there was also no radical church hierarchy in this part of the country promoting and protecting grass-roots economic and social organisation. The church in the department was extremely conservative in orientation. The contrast between Ayacucho and Puno, for example, where Sendero's advance was to be blocked by the strength of local peasant organisation and a radical church, is very striking.

Sendero therefore encountered little to oppose it as it moved through rural Ayacucho and neighbouring departments in 1981 and 1982. It moved in a terrain suited to guerrilla warfare, and was helped by social and economic circumstances and the lack of organised opposition. But its success was also due to its understanding of how to exploit the sources of social conflict. Not only did it impose itself by instilling fear among the *comuneros*, but also because it took steps to support them against their main perceived adversaries. These were not so much landowners (though Sendero did initially attack a few *haciendas*), but more frequently petty bureaucrats, abusive local authorities, commercial middlemen and cattle rustlers. By killing such people or driving them out, Sendero began to win grudging support. It brought a degree of security and built on the peasant's distrust of outsiders. It also appeared as a moralising force: not only did it inveigh against the corrupt and the exploitative, it took on those who behaved badly within the communities. It dealt harshly, for instance, with drunkards and adulterers, both common enough in highland communities. Sendero's 'revolutionary justice', though harsh, corresponded to perceived needs among the peasant population. Violent though its methods were, they were not without a logic.

However, it also made mistakes which undermined such support and played into the hands of the authorities. One such major error turned out to be the insistence that peasants should stop producing for the market, confining themselves to producing just for their own needs. In its insistence that Peruvian rural society was 'semi-feudal', it is possible that Sendero underestimated the real commercial links that bind the rural economy, even in the most remote areas, with the market economy. Though integrated on disadvantageous terms into the wider economy, community income – even in apparently remote corners of Ayacucho – was dependent on the market. Such actions as insisting on communal work to the exclusion of private production, closing down local fairs and markets, and interrupting the transport of goods to and from urban centres did not help promote Sendero's popularity among peasant communities. There were already signs that by the time the army began to move into rural Ayacucho at the beginning of 1983, some communities were already resisting Sendero's inroads. For instance, the news that highland communities near Huanta were fighting back against Sendero was the reason for the killing of eight journalists at Uchuruccay in early 1983, an incident which caused a big political scandal.

Another major difficulty for Sendero was its ability to honour commitments to defend peasant communities in the face of offensive action from the armed forces. This was particularly the case during the counter-offensive of 1983 and 1984. Sendero, whose political control of the communities was not based on permanent presence in them, quickly lost the support it had gained when, in its absence, the full weight of military repression fell on the *comuneros*. Indeed, as we shall see, counter-terror became one of the main forms by which the authorities recuperated territory 'lost' to Sendero. Sendero was thus forced back on to the defensive, and to act with much greater caution than it had employed in 1981 and 1982. It did not disappear, however, and typically used the cover of darkness to visit communities and to maintain pressure on them.

Counter-insurgency strategy went through various stages during the Belaúnde government as the authorities unsuccessfully wrestled with the problem of how best to deal with Sendero Luminoso.[7]

The first stage, between 1980 and 1982, had been to treat the problem essentially as if it was a matter of common delinquency, using exclusively the resources of the police forces to combat it. Though the *sinchis* – a division of the Guardia Civil with training in counter-insurgency methods – spearheaded operations in Ayacucho, the police exhibited none of the skills required to win over sympathy among the local population, still less to nip the Senderista insurgency in the bud either militarily or politically. The police authorities showed themselves corrupt, poorly trained, and prone to undisciplined, arbitrary and abusive behaviour. The military authorities, even those actually based in Ayacucho, did not get involved.

The second period began in December 1982 when the government finally decided that control of counter-insurgency should pass from the police (under the Interior Ministry) to the jurisdiction of the Armed Forces Joint Command. The cabinet at the same time ratified the decision of the National Defence Council creating the Ayacucho Emergency Zone, thereby suspending a number of constitutional rights. General Clemente Noel y Moral, the first civil–military commander of the zone, was vested with considerable autonomy in the field of counter-insurgency. Under his aegis the emphasis was placed on dealing with the problem militarily: using military force as the principal means to eliminate the enemy. Though the 'enemy' in this case was Sendero, it is clear from military writings produced at the time that the 'enemy' was perceived as being that of 'communism' of which Sendero was but one manifestation.[8] The Peruvian military, as elsewhere in Latin America, has long been influenced by the doctrine of national security and the existence of the 'enemy within'. The logic of internal war is, of course, that there is a cost in terms of human life, but – especially at the local level in Ayacucho – the military proved remarkably unwilling to distinguish between 'communists' and the rest of the population; and particularly between different types of 'communist', between Sendero on the one hand and the supporters of the legal left, the Izquierda Unida, on the other.

But increasing public concern about human rights violations in the Emergency Zone from Uchuruccay in February 1983 onwards, coupled with growing scepticism about the results being achieved, led to pressure to adopt other methods. The emphasis in counter-insurgency thinking passed to trying to adopt social and economic

strategies to counteract the backwardness which was seen to nurt
rural violence.

The beginning of a third phase was marked by the twin appointments of General Julian Juliá as commander-in-chief of the Army and General Adrian Huamán as the civil–military commander in Ayacucho. Both these appointments at the beginning of 1984 reflected the shift in emphasis away from a purely military to a more political and developmental approach to the problem. The 'new strategy' was discussed extensively in the military journals of the time. General Huamán, whose own *serrano* social background and ability to speak Quechua facilitated a more communicative style, spent time developing links with peasant communities. The idea was to win back political support among the communities through such direct assistance as food donations and promises of community development.

At the same time, military operations continued and human rights violation increased. Total casualties rose from 2800 in 1983 to 4300 in 1984. Huamán extended two policies begun under Noel y Moral. One was the creation of peasant militias under close military control. Referred to as *rondas campesinas*, these bore little resemblance to earlier *rondas* established independently by peasant communities in Cajamarca to defend themselves from attacks by outsiders such as cattle rustlers. The other policy was to remove population physically from the highest altitudes, where Sendero had freer rein, down into the valleys into specially constructed camps – 'strategic hamlets' similar to those used in Guatemala and before that by the United States in Vietnam.

At the local level the Huamán strategy involved the army assuming more than just a military role. Huamán insisted on having control over development programmes, reducing the autonomy of the local development corporation, and on himself determining the allocation of resources from central government. In short, he helped build a sort of 'military state within a civilian state', a policy which especially if applied more widely raised serious questions about the nature of Peruvian democracy. Huamán's self-confident style also rankled with Belaúnde, especially when he began to use the media to criticise the government for its failure to provide sufficient funding. Belaúnde finally dismissed him in August 1984.

Belaúnde was concerned that the more 'political' approach to the problem threatened to involve ceding too much power to the military. He also saw his government's prestige being sullied both nationally and internationally by the frequency and scale of human rights

r Huamán's dismissal was one of inter-
, waiting to see what initiative a new govern-

viding samples of contrasting counter-insurgency
Belaúnde period highlighted some of the problems that
ating a guerrilla like Sendero Luminoso.

and foremost, Sendero proved practically impossible to
rate and infiltrate. This was in great measure due to Sendero's
tight clandestine organisation, but it was made more difficult by the
lack of confidence of local peasant communities in the military
authorities. Lacking local roots and predisposed to arbitrariness, the
military appeared as if it were an army of occupation. At the same
time, Sendero Luminoso was difficult to distinguish from the population in which it moved: in the classic Maoist phrase, Sendero militants
were 'like fishes in the water'.

Secondly, as we have seen, in spite of its dogmatic Maoist language,
Sendero was able to build political support around social and ethnic
marginalisation, reinforced by the effects of military presence. In many
areas it managed to destroy pre-existing support for the left in rural
areas, thereby eliminating alternatives.

Thirdly, a coherent and unified approach to counter-insurgency was
dogged by institutional rivalries between the three branches of the
armed forces, and between the three independent divisions of the
police force, the Guardia Civil, the Guardia Republicana, and the
Investigative Police (PIP). These made it more difficult to establish a
single, coherent counter-insurgency strategy. Reinforced by mutual
distrust at the uppermost levels of command, these divisions also
meant that there was no proper sharing of intelligence or material
resources. For reasons which are not entirely clear, control of the
Huanta district of Ayacucho, for instance, was vested in the navy,
which operated as a fiefdom with considerable independence of the
army in Ayacucho. Though the airforce kept out of counter-insurgency
almost entirely, airforce planes and helicopters were not made readily
available to the army.

Finally, Sendero Luminoso's military capacity was persistently
underestimated, with the result that inadequate logistical support
was made available opportunely. This was not just the case of
expensive and relatively sophisticated equipment like helicopters, but
also true of more basic equipment like road transport facilities and
even field radios.

THE 'OTHER' GUERRILLA

The Belaúnde administration also saw the birth of another guerrilla organisation, distinct from Sendero in terms of its origins, its ideology and its strategic designs. The Movimento Revolucionario Túpac Amaru (MRTA) was the resurgence in Peru of a more time-honoured type of guerrilla warfare which had its origins in the Cuba-inspired *foquista* insurgencies of the 1960s. And not only were the two guerrilla groups from different stables. As we shall see, in as much as they sought to appeal to the same social groups, they were to come into direct conflict with one another. The MRTA, however, sought to occupy a political space between the Izquierda Unida and Sendero in the long-term perspective of becoming the armed 'wing' of the Peruvian left.[9]

The MRTA made its debut in mid-1984, four years after Sendero's attack on Chuschi. Its style was notably different from Sendero's. First, it was urban rather than rural. At the outset its targets were typically symbols of imperialism such as the US Embassy, Citibank branches or American fast food outlets like Kentucky Fried Chicken. At least to start with, they also avoided killings, though they were involved in a number of kidnappings. And, in stark contrast with Sendero's hermetic style, the MRTA revelled in 'armed propaganda' taking care to take the credit for their actions and seeking maximum publicity for themselves and their political demands. In international terms their nearest equivalent was the Colombian M-19, with whom they were to develop links, and whose taste for the sensational they emulated. Also, like the M-19 – and quite unlike Sendero – their ideology was strongly nationalist, the enemy being more Peru's exploiters abroad, particularly the United States.

The institutional origins of the MRTA are to be found in the fusion of two small left-wing splinter groups in the early 1980s: a section of the so-called Partido Socialista Revolucionario – Marxista Leninista (PSR-ML) and a section of the Movimiento de Izquierda Revolucionaria, known as El Militante (MIR-EM). Both of these groups were excluded from the Izquierda Unida when it was created because larger sections of the same parties had joined it. The formation of the Izquierda Unida in 1980 brought in most, but not all, of the dozens of small leftist groups within the pale of parliamentary politics. The PSR-ML was itself a splinter group from the predominantly Velasquista PSR, while the MIR descended indirectly from APRA Rebelde in the 1960s. The larger of the factions of the MIR, along with others from the PSR-ML and Vanguardia Revolucionaria (VR) joined to form the PUM which, while supporting armed struggle in principle, did not feel the moment to be opportune to withdraw from parliamentary politics. Underlying the agreement to launch the MRTA was the conviction that democratic government would not last long in Peru, and that in the event of a coup the 'legal' left within the Izquierda Unida would be forced into clandestinity and to taking up arms against a military government. This, of course, was also part of the thinking of Sendero, whose objective became precisely one of sharpening the contradictions to such a point that a military coup would be the outcome. But in the case of the MRTA, there would be much more ideological common ground with the rest of the left than in that of Sendero Luminoso.

APRA's landslide victory in 1985 and the overwhelming popularity of Alan García made such a line of thinking rather less plausible. The MRTA's position was made even more difficult when it seemed that García was going a long way towards meeting just the sort of demands which the MRTA had been making: breaking with the IMF, instituting a debt moratorium, raising real wages and ending 'dirty war' methods of counter-insurgency in Ayacucho and elsewhere. The MRTA's response was to call a truce while evaluating the ways in which the government went about putting its promises into practice. It was a truce which was to last eighteen months, until January 1987, during which the MRTA sought to consolidate its nuclei of support mainly in the student world in Lima and among the rice and maize farmers of San Martín department, where the MIR had long had one of its main bastions. The truce ended when the MRTA launched its first rural guerrilla operations in the north of San Martín in the district of Juanjui.

GARCIA: A NEW APPROACH TO COUNTER-INSURGENCY?

When Alan García assumed office the reaction among members of the armed forces was, on balance, positive. The old military antipathy for APRA was a thing of the past, being effectively buried with the reforms of General Velasco and the subsequent collaboration between Apristas and the military during the transition to constitutional rule. The institutionalist positions within the armed forces still predominated. These interpreted the military's functions as being confined to self-defined areas of security. They did not seek more direct participation in politics which were still seen as being potentially divisive and dangerous to the military's corporate identity. García's wide electoral support provided a degree of political stability based on consensus. Furthermore, García's forthright style and his capacity to take the initiative both went down well in military circles, as did his nationalist, reforming ideology. The big question mark in the relationship was how he would seek to conduct counter-insugency strategy against Sendero Luminoso.

Initially, García laid stress on two aspects of policy: there would be more emphasis on the developmental rather than the purely military approach; and counter-insurgency would have to be conducted observing internationally recognised norms regarding human rights. García took steps to assert himself in his constitutional role as commander-in-chief of the armed forces. One of his first acts as president was to fly the flag of the commander-in-chief atop the presidential palace alongside the national flag. He did not wish to fall into the same trap as Belaúnde in being seen to abdicate responsibility to the military in counter-insurgency and other matters. On the contrary, he publicly sought to assert that authority.

The first two or three months brought with them surprises in this just as in other aspects of policy. Shortly after being sworn in, García announced a reorganisation within the police force, involving the dismissal of senior police officers suspected of corrupt activities. This was done swiftly without prior consultation or negotiation with the forces concerned. Then, in response to the Accomarca killings and the evidence of a cover-up afterwards, García took the dramatic and unprecedented action of dismissing the president of the Armed Forces Joint Command, the commander of the powerful second military region based in Lima (also responsible for the centre of the country), and the civil–military Commander of the Ayacucho Emergency Zone. At no point in Peru's recent history, certainly not since the transition back to civilian rule in 1980, had a president behaved in such a high-handed way with the military hierarchy.

The difference of tone in asserting civilian control was also clear in the emphasis placed upon development as part of a counter-insurgency strategy. Support for agricultural activities, as we have seen, was to be channelled through the new *trapecio andino* programme to all the highland departments of the south, but especially to those of the Emergency Zone. A Peace Commission, initially including leftist as well as Aprista parliamentarians, was to look into methods of providing lasting peace.

The reaction of the military to these developments was mixed. On the one hand, officials were impressed by García's popularity. At the same time they were not prepared to countenance any changes within the military system imposed from outside. Though the dismissal of General Enrico Praeli, the president of the Joint Command, was a striking gesture, it did not affect the institutional powers of the armed forces; it did not change the basic rules of the game.[10]

The '*desarrollista*' sentiment found an echo, however, as it had done under Huamán.[11] As of September 1985 the military started to hold back on military operations and more attention was given to military public works programmes. In part this was a reaction to criticism over human rights violations; in part it was also an effort to define a specific period in which to show whether or not the government would mobilise the resources of the state and direct them to solving problems arising from social and economic backwardness. The minister of war, General Jorge Flores Torres, who was more of the Huamán school of thought and who appeared to have enjoyed a good working relationship with Alan García, spoke of the need for economic development, education and 'psychological' actions to neutralise Sendero.

However, by the beginning of 1987, the '*desarrollista*' phase had run its course, and a vacuum in counter-insurgency strategy had begun to open up. By that time it was clear that in practice the new resources being pumped into the Emergency Zone were minimal and that even fewer projects were being started, still less completed. The system of the *trapecio andino* and the *microregiones* it embodied existed only on paper, and the Development Corporation in Ayacucho continued to be starved of funds.[12] Most of the projects initiated were in fact carried out by the army, and as such tended to have a military rather than a developmental logic. Even so, repairs to vital lines of communications – especially bridges blown up by Sendero – were ignored. Though the activities of Sendero were designed to frustrate any kind of government development strategy – killing or threatening to kill engineers and agronomists – the main reason for the absence of any progress was the lack of substantial economic support from the central government.

In this context, the killing of the 250 Senderista prisoners in the Lima jails was once again an event of particular importance. Though it is clear that Alan García gave the orders for this action, he was quick to distance himself from the political consequences.[13] He demanded those responsible to be sanctioned. 'Either they go, or I do,' was his succinct reaction.

For the military the event was important because it punctured the image of Alan García as the defender of human rights, particularly internationally. Sendero's uprising in the jails caused García maximum political embarrassment, timed as it was to coincide with the meeting of the Socialist International. As a result of these incidents, García caused considerable resentment in the military by his refusal to take full responsibility for his actions. But the incident and the aftermath demonstrated once again the operational autonomy of the armed forces in counter-insurgency.

By early 1987 there were signs of a rethink in military strategy on counter-insurgency. Not only was it clear by that time that the developmental approach had failed to make headway, but Sendero was also increasing its own military offensive. This offensive involved the upgrading of its policy of assassinations so as to target figures of national importance. At the same time, the scale of Sendero's advance into new areas, especially the central *sierra*, had became evident from a wave of mayors resigning their posts in these departments, faced with death threats from Sendero. In March 1987, the military decided to deploy substantial reinforcements in the Emergency Zone and elsewhere in a bid to stop Sendero's advance.

Another major issue which soured García's relations with the military at this point was his insistence on the creation of a single Defence Ministry, merging the functions of the three military ministers in charge of each of the three services into a single cabinet post. Alan García's decision in March 1987 to submit a draft law creating a single ministry raised animosity in sectors of the armed forces. The announcement produced a flurry of public criticisms by senior retired military officers. The resentment was most acute in the navy and the airforce, the two services whose political power was most threatened. Throughout the period García tended to enjoy better relations with the army than the other two services which traditionally adopted more conservative positions. The strength of feeling aroused was indicated by the decision of the commander of the airforce, General Luis Abraham Cavallerino, to push for the resignation of the war minister, General Jorge Flores Torres. When García, in his capacity of supreme commander of the armed forces, announced Cavallerino's dismissal, Cavallerino ordered Mirage jets to buzz the presidential palace. It was the first overt sign of *golpismo*.[14]

Other than the fact that García did not consult widely with the military before announcing his legislative proposal, the main reason for apprehension in the military was the fear that, beyond just asserting civilian control by possibly appointing a civilian as the new minister, the government sought to *apristizar* the military. There were rumours that the new minister might even be Armando Villanueva, an Aprista of the old style. The Defence Ministry issue therefore rekindled old anti-Aprista animosities, and prompted the question of whether or not the government was seeking to alter the relationship between the civilian authorities and the military, as established in 1980. But, having raised the issue, García was once again forced back on to the defensive because of the stir it caused in the military establishment. Though the three military ministries were combined in one, García was obliged to appoint the new commander-in-chief of the Army, General Enrique López Albújar, as the new minister.[15] If the intention was to strengthen civilian control over the military, then the move backfired. Under López Albújar, who remained defence minister until May 1989, the new ministry was little more than a renamed War Ministry.

García's first two years in office, therefore, saw the attempt of the new government to assert the position of the presidency in terms of its ultimate control over the military establishment. The dismissal of the heads of the police, his sacking of the president of the Joint Command, and his personal initiative in pushing through the Defence Ministry legislation were all indications of this. But while there may have been misgivings among the military, García's personal popularity was a decisive factor in keeping the upper hand. By early 1987, however, there were signs that autonomy in counter-insurgency – the key everyday preoccupation of the military – was passing back into the hands of the armed forces. The attempt to promote a *desarrollista* alternative in Ayacucho had come to nothing. García therefore faced the same danger as his predecessor of having to pay the political cost of a war in which the death toll of innocent victims grew ever higher. Meanwhile, in terms of his direct relationship with the military establishment, he had raised animosities through his handling of the Defence Ministry issue, even though his final acceptance of the head of the army as the new minister was seen as a climbdown. The president's authority in military circles, as in others, was waning.

THE EXPANSION OF SENDERO'S RADIUS

For Sendero Luminoso the electoral victory of Alan García and the subsequent change of government made little difference. Despite the size of his victory and the clear swing to the left in 1985, Sendero treated the new government as if it were the same as the old. Probably the main difference in Sendero's thinking was that García's popularity made it that much more urgent to unmask the pretence of democratic institutions. President 'Gonzalo' is alleged to have said in the fourth plenary of the Central Committee held in April or May 1986 that 'we have to hit the new reactionary government of APRA head on, pitching ourselves against the armed forces. This is what we have defined, this is what we are doing.'[16] The battle against the new government therefore formed part of a strategy defined well in advance. Sendero's aim throughout 1985 and 1986 was basically to build up organised popular support (*bases de apoyo*) around armed actions, and to expand the ambit of the popular war to other areas of the Peruvian *sierra* beyond the main initial theatre of operations in Ayacucho.

Partly as a result of the counter-insurgency offensive in Ayacucho forcing Sendero to fan out into other areas, partly as a result of conscious policy, the geographical extent of Sendero's military and political influence spread notably between 1984 and the end of 1986. By early 1987 it was concentrating much of its energy on the highland areas of the centre-north (notably the *sierra* of La Libertad, Ancash, Pasco and Huánuco); developing armed actions in the south (especially in the north of Puno); and building up what was to become a very solid presence in the coca-growing Alto Huallaga region of San Martín and northern Huánuco. Armed attacks in Lima itself also had become more frequent.

Though the extent and range of Senderista attacks had military strategists concerned about the security forces becoming overextended, they should not lead us to exaggerate Sendero's real strength. The so-called 'liberated zones', where Sendero had established itself by forcing the authorities to retreat, were largely to be found in the highest and most remote areas. The development of '*bases de apoyo*', particularly in the more strategically valuable parts of the country, was often no easy matter. Two areas exemplify this: Puno in the south, and Pasco in the central highlands.

Puno is a department of considerable significance in any strategy to develop widespread guerrilla warfare in Peru. Not only is it a region with strong social tensions over the distribution of land (exacerbated by the agrarian reform) and with a long political tradition of rebellion, but it is also important in view of the access it provides to neighbouring Bolivia, potentially useful as a source external supply and a safe haven in case of retreat.[17]

By late 1986 Sendero's attacks in northern Puno – particularly in the provinces of Azángaro and Melgar – had become increasingly frequent. The first Senderista attack in Puno had been as early as 1982 in the Ayaviri district of Melgar, but until 1985 attacks had been sporadic. The location of Sendero's attacks in 1985 and 1986 was significant. Azángaro and Melgar are the Quechua-speaking areas of a predominantly Aymara-speaking department. Sendero seems to have found it considerably more difficult to appeal to the Aymaran population especially in the south of the department around Lake Titicaca. Melgar and Anzángaro, on the other hand, were not only Quechua speaking but also areas where the *altiplano* meets the mountains. Sendero not only found it easier to impose itself but also had access to safe refuge.

The evidence up to late 1986 and early 1987 shows that Sendero had managed to create nuclei of support in these areas. Through selective assassinations and death threats it had managed to displace often unpopular local officials. The police had been forced to retreat from rural areas to the more important townships. However, Sendero had difficulty in winning over a peasantry with its own strong traditions of local organisation. The peasant unions were also fortified by their ties to a strong radical church and by their links to CCP, itself closely identified with the PUM and the Izquierda Unida. Conscious of these obstacles, Sendero seems at times to have worked in a rather different way than in Ayacucho, seeking in some instances to win over local leaders with some standing in their communities, rather than simply trying to eliminate them.[18]

The department of Pasco was another area where, by 1985–6, Sendero was stepping up its campaign of violence. There, the first attack had been back in 1980, soon after the Chuschi incident in Ayacucho, when local Senderista sympathisers blew up the offices of Acción Popular. By 1984, however, Sendero had built up considerable influence in the highest, least accessible and poorest peasant communities. It used exactly the same methods: killing or driving out local authorities like governors and local mayors, and imposing its own 'revolutionary' authorities. When Sendero began to appear with greater regularity in lower-lying areas and got closer to the main urban area, the mining centre of Cerro de Pasco, the government decreed three provinces (two in Pasco and one in next-door Huánuco) as Emergency Zones.

The presence of Sendero in Pasco revealed one of the difficulties implicit in pursuing a strategy in which the peasantry was to be the main motor of the revolution, but where ideologically the most advanced and best organised groups in society were wage-earning miners, not subsistence peasants.[19] Senderistas who tried to win over the mine-workers of Cerro de Pasco made little or no headway. One of the main reasons for this was that their ideological barrage had little impact on workers whose main grievance was low wages or poor working conditions, and who long ago had put their faith in trade union activity as the best way to improve working conditions. Sendero, in contrast, showed little interest in collective bargaining.

A third key area of advance for Sendero at this time was in the coca-producing Alto Huallaga. Coca has been grown from time immemorial in Peru for domestic consumption, often to reduce the effects of hard work at high altitudes. Traditionally, the main area of cultivation was the jungle valleys of Cuzco and in particular those of Lares and La Convención. The colonisation of the jungle valleys further north between the 1940s and the end of the 1960s also brought with it the practice of coca agriculture. The boom in production for export – for the manufacture of cocaine – started in the 1970s, and was concentrated primarily in the Huallaga river valley. With the surge in demand for cocaine in the United States, coca agriculture and narcobusiness grew rapidly, organised to a large extent vertically by the Colombian mafias. It had the effect of transforming the economy of the Alto Huallaga region, and notably that of Tingo María, the main urban centre.

Under pressure from the US government, and alarmed at the sudden escalation of the cocaine trade, the military government of General Morales Bermúdez declared coca agriculture illegal, except for a small fraction of production (mainly in the traditional areas of Cuzco) destined for the domestic market, to be sold exclusively to a state monopoly, the Empresa Nacional de la Coca (Enaco). It was from this time onwards that serious attempts got under-way to reduce coca acreages through a programme of eradication and substitution. Three agencies were set up, all funded by the US government: Corah (Proyecto de Reduccion del Cultivo de la Coca en el Alto Huallaga) to coordinate eradication and control programmes; PEAH (Proyecto Especial Alto Huallaga) to promote substitution of coca and to promote alternative agricultural development; and Umopar (Unidad Movil de Patrullaje Rural), a special detachment of the Guardia Civil to deal with enforcement.

Throughout the second Belaúnde government the activities of these three organisations suffered from inadequate funding and equipment, as well as from hostility from local coca growers to their activities.

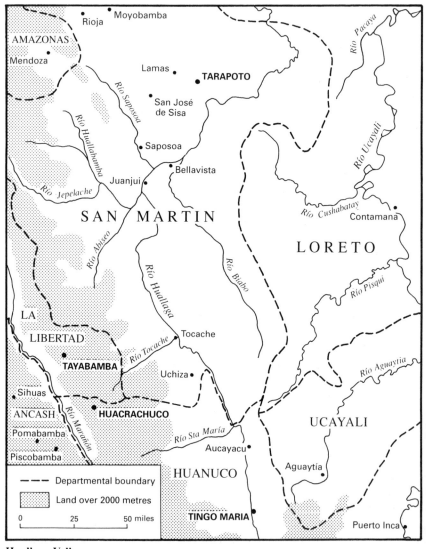

Huallaga Valley

The three were ill-prepared to deal with such a fast expanding business, and the paltry results of eradication/substitution contrasted with the expansion in area of land planted with coca. Though estimates as to the extent of coca planting vary according to the source, Peruvian police figures point to the total area increasing from around 10 000 hectares in 1980 to 195 000 in 1986. Meanwhile, only 2651 hectares were eradicated in 1983, 3134 hectares in 1984 and 4828 hectares in 1985.

By 1985 the main area of production had shifted northwards from around Tingo María to more remote locations further down the Huallaga river, centred around the towns of Uchiza and Tocache. At the same time, attracted by the relatively high wages for those growing coca or transforming the leaves into paste, thousands of migrants were moving into the Alto Huallaga, mostly from more impoverished regions in the *sierra* to the south. Coca had become a major source of employment nationally, and in Alto Huallaga *the* source of employment.

Though there is some evidence of Senderista activity in Alto Huallaga as early as 1980 (and that of Puka Llajta in and around Tarapoto), there was no concerted attempt to build support until 1984. Sendero's advance in 1985 and 1986, however, was fast and furious. The key to that advance was Sendero's ability to put itself at the head of the mass of small-scale coca producers and to defend their interests from their two main adversaries. On the one hand, they were constantly in conflict with the drug traders, the Colombian *narcotraficantes* and their Peruvian associates, mainly over prices. Typically these would buy coca leaves at the lowest possible price, taking advantage of producers' ignorance of the market, and using the threat of violence to silence those who complained. On the other hand, it was the producers rather than the traffickers who were hit by their crop being declared illegal and by the attempts of government agencies to eradicate it. Working through the area community by community, Sendero was able to build up strong grass-roots support with remarkable speed, chiefly by responding to the coca growers' sense of defencelessness and providing them with effective protection against the mafias and the eradicators.[20]

The situation in Alto Huallaga was, of course, very different from the reality of Ayacucho on which Sendero's strategy and military prowess had hitherto been based. The Alto Huallaga is Peru's 'wild west'. It is an area of colonisation and inward migration based on tropical agriculture, an area transformed economically by the bonanza in coca production, and one far removed from any vestiges of the 'semi-feudalism' of the *sierra*. Despite its dogmatic-sounding ideology, Sendero showed in the Alto Huallaga a notable pragmatism in responding to the needs and concerns of those it chose to work with. Though it would tend to enter a village, assemble the people and give its usual ideological harangue, it took care to tailor the message to those to whom it was intended. Not only did it offer the coca grower protection from the *narcotraficantes* and the likes of Corah and Umopar, but more generally it offered to organise the sort of services such as justice and even infrastructural improvements which governments in Lima had conspicuously failed to provide. Sendero did not, for instance, repeat the demands it made of peasants in Ayacucho that they should not market their produce. Instead, it argued that if US 'imperialists' wanted to poison themselves by consuming cocaine, then it should give them a helping hand. Sendero did, however, inveigh against Peruvians themselves taking drugs.

Most observers believe that the Alto Huallaga did not enter into Sendero's original strategic design, but that it was 'discovered' almost by accident. The 'discovery', though, was to offer substantial military advantages. It allowed Sendero to open up a new front in an area where the institutions of the central government were notoriously weak and where the local population proved unusually receptive to what Sendero had to offer them. In widening the scope of the guerrilla war, it encouraged greater dispersion of the armed forces and the police. Moreover, the Alto Huallaga was itself an important source of food for Lima, especially for rice and maize, though coca agriculture had by 1986 and 1987 led to sharply reduced acreages of other food crops. It therefore fitted into the strategy of cutting Lima off from its main sources of food. Finally, and most importantly, Sendero found in the Alto Huallaga the supplies of cash and armaments it needed to increase its military sophistication. By taxing the *narcotraficantes*, Sendero found itself able to raise substantial sums of money with ease, and was able to use it to acquire weaponry in a part of the country where arms were easy to come by. From 1986 onwards, Sendero started to ambush police and army patrols with greater regularity and more success. The numbers of members of the military killed began to rise as a result. It also began to have the confidence to launch attacks on police and military installations, the most notable of which was the destruction of the Uchiza police compound in 1986. But it was the attack on Tocache in March 1987 – it took the police two months to retake the town – which marked the final confirmation that in Alto Huallaga, at least, there was indeed '*tierra liberada*'.

Part II

The Downturn, 1987–90

5   The Economy from Boom to Bust and Beyond

THE ATTEMPTED BANK NATIONALISATION

President García's fateful decision in July 1987 to nationalise the private banking industry was in many ways, both politically and economically, a watershed in his government's fortunes. It stands out, separating the period of fast growth of the first two years from the subsequent economic downturn in 1988 and 1989, a period dubbed 'hyperinflation with hyper-recession'. It also represents a key point in the personal political fortunes of Alan García. Having made himself the mainspring of political life in the country since 1985, he committed the most conspicuous political blunder. It was a mistake from which it proved impossible to recover his political standing.

Like most apparent turning points, it cannot be disassociated from the context in which it took place. Though it accelerated the deterioration in relations between the government and key groups in the private sector, it was not in itself the main cause of the economic difficulties that befell Peru in 1988 and 1989. Some sort of economic crisis would almost certainly have developed if the nationalisation had not been attempted. Nor was it the only factor in explaining the erosion of the government's initial popularity. The pattern of Alan García's popularity curve (see Figure 6.1 on p. 159) shows that though he and his government had already lost some of their political gloss by the middle of 1987, the most abrupt fall took place the following year, between May and October 1988 as the full weight of economic shock measures took their toll.

There were already signs well before July 1987 of the approaching economic difficulties. It was clear, for instance, that balance of payments difficulties were looming. The main points of disagreement among commentators were over how soon the crisis would come and how severe it would be. Some aspects of heterodoxy were already being modified: price controls were being eased; the inti was being devalued once again; and measures were being introduced to stop the fall in foreign reserves by rationing foreign exchange.

Doubts were also being expressed in the financial press and elsewhere about the wisdom of the government's strategy of depending on the main private sector economic groups to provide the investment finance to sustain the economic model. The government answered by producing lists of projects, especially in agroindustry, for which the private sector had pledged investment money. Most of these projects were small scale, however.

Mutual suspicions between government and business about the real motives of the other remained strong. The government was wary about the real intentions of the private sector and sensitive to the problem of capital flight. The private sector also distrusted APRA's intentions, thinking that the García government was a wolf in sheep's clothing, whose talk of '*concertación*' was in fact a subterfuge for more explicitly socialist goals. This mutual distrust had already surfaced in the row in April 1987 when the government tried to force businesses to buy profits-related treasury bonds. It was a clash which anticipated the much more serious political wrangle over bank nationalisation.

Still, García's announcement in his annual speach to Congress on 28 July 1987 of his intention to nationalise the privately owned banking system, including finance companies (*financieras*) and insurance companies, came as a bolt from the blue. It was not a move which the bankers appear to have anticipated,[1] still less the political parties or their representatives in Congress. It took the whole country by surprise.

Who knew how much of the president's plans, how long in advance is still unclear. According to a source quoted by the Peru Report, the move got the go-ahead from the president fifteen days before it was announced, and García's main advisers – César Ferrari, Daniel Carbonetto, Gustavo Saberbein, Carlos Franco, Javier Tantaleán and Remigio Morales Bermúdez – were all in on the scheme in advance. The prime minister Guillermo Larco Cox, who replaced Luis Alva Castro in June, also was apparently informed, although only a few days beforehand. According to the same source, however, the possibility of nationalisation was discussed as early as March when the economic team became disillusioned by the response of the main private sector groups, the 'twelve apostles', to García's investment challenge made at the November 1986 CADE meeting in Huaraz.[2]

In his book *El Futuro Diferente*, published in 1982, in which García dedicated himself to describing his party's ideology past and present, he had been critical of what he referred to as 'financial circuits'.[3] By this he meant the close economic relationship between banks and economic interest groups in Peru. The phrase came back to the fore again in his July 1987 speech to Congress when he lambasted these financial circuits as being 'the main pillar of economic power and inequality', arguing that their ability to capture and direct credit was 'the mechanism for the distribution of social surplus'. The reasons which García put forward for his decision included his view that only if banking was conducted by the state would historic social and geographical inequalities be overcome. What was needed in Peru, García maintained, was for credit to be 'democratised'. Only then would 'credit be made available and liquidity provided to all economic agents, like the small and medium-sized firm, cooperatives (*empresas asociativas*), informal producers and traders, peasant communities etc'. These he saw as being 'systematically discriminated against by the private financial system'.

However, increasingly isolated on both the left and right, and challenged within his own party, García's main motives for nationalisation were primarily political. He wanted to regain the political initiative and to mobilise public opinion behind a cause which, like the stand on debt in 1985, would revive his and APRA's flagging political fortunes. Even so, the economic motives should not be brushed aside. García appears to have believed that the private banking system – notably the Banco de Crédito – through its offices in New York and the Bahamas – was providing a duct for capital flight, and that the increase in the flows of capital flight in the first half of 1987 was *prima facie* evidence of the private sector's insincerity in 'betting on Peru', to use his phrase from the 1986 CADE meeting. While García began to doubt that his dealings with the 'twelve apostles' were having the effects he desired, he began to be concerned, according to one of his officials, about the way in which the dominant groups in private banking and insurance were using their influence over the exchange houses (*casas de cambio*) to manipulate the exchange rate. He was particularly concerned by the possible links between 'the purchase of coca-dollars, liquidity in the currency market and capital flight'.[4] These were accusations which the bankers naturally denied, even though it was well known that since the early 1980s prominent commercial banks had played an active role in the intermediation of coca-dollars.[5]

Whatever the main reasons for García's nationalisation move, the whole operation was not one carefully worked out in advance. No clear or specific plan seems to have existed as to what the government would seek to do with the financial institutions it acquired. Nor was there a surplus of talent available to run those institutions once they were in state hands.

Considerable confusion arose because of the lack of clarity as to which kind of financial institutions would be affected. It was not evident, for instance, whether it involved foreign owned banks with commercial banking outlets in Lima, or the privately owned regional banks. Nor was it clear whether the government really intended to nationalise insurance companies, with their large shareholding in hundreds of other private companies. On this point, speaking after the event, Daniel Carbonetto, the president's chief economic adviser, said that the main point of including the insurance companies was simply to provide a negotiating instrument. 'The core of the law,' he said 'was to expropriate the Banco de Crédito, the Banco Wiese, the big banks. The rest was secondary. Clearly, if your goal is to end up with these banks in the hands of the state, strategically you begin by claiming much more in order to leave room to negotiate. The insurance companies are a negotiating piece...'[6]

García's major political miscalculation was to think that nationalising the banks would prove to be a popular cause, and that public opinion would rally behind him, as if it represented the same sort of major social conquest as Velasco's agrarian reform. García also failed to foresee the right-wing opposition's capacity to mobilise against the move. The response to the president's own attempts to mobilise support in poor districts of Lima for nationalisation was never more than lukewarm. Though, of course, Peru's top bankers had never been popular heroes in the country's political folklore, neither were they the villains of the piece. As Juan Francisco Raffo, the Crédito's manager remarked shortly after the campaign against nationalisation got going, 'even bankers are popular now, at least for the time being'.[7]

A further big mistake was to believe that APRA alone would carry the measure through. When it came to voting in Congress, Aprista senators played a conspicuous role in trying to water down the measure. Meanwhile, no prior arrangement had been reached with the Izquierda Unida and its representatives in Congress. They tended to regard García's initiative with suspicion, believing his main motive to be to outflank the left. In nationalising the banks, Alan García abandoned one system of alliances without preparing a new system of alliances to replace it.

The nationalisation issue became the primary focus of political attention for the six months which followed García's speech to

Congress. It was to become a long drawn out battle, starting in the Congress and moving on to the courts, in which the president's original proposal was gradually whittled down, rendered ineffectual and ultimately abandoned. August and September were dominated by the bill's progress through parliament. In the months following the promulgation of the new law on 9 October, the government sought to implement it, while the bank owners tried to get it declared unconstitutional. The authority of the government was effectively challenged. One prominent banker even taunted the government's resolve to intervene physically by sleeping in his office. The Banco de Crédito managed to dodge the law by handing over the majority ownership of the bank to its workers, thereby diluting the original shareholding while still maintaining indirect control. It was only a year after the law was originally passed that the issue was finally laid to rest: in October 1988, Guillermo Wiese was reinstated as chairman of the Banco Wiese. The wheel had come full circle and the *status quo ante*, with the exception of the Banco de Crédito's more diversified shareholding, had been restored.

The effect on the banking system itself was a temporary withdrawal of deposits from the main private commercial banks, in favour of the three state-owned 'associated' banks, the Popular, the Internacional and the Continental. There was a nervous run on the Banco de Crédito and the Banco Wiese in particular. Some of the money withdrawn from the private banks seems to have been channelled into consumer spending, a factor which may have helped to perpetuate the demand boom through to the end of 1987 and the beginning of 1988.[8] However, as the panic reaction waned the Banco de Crédito regained its market share, and only the Wiese continued to lose its share until its own situation returned to normal the following year. Despite the upset of the nationalisation bid, the Peruvian banking system remained surprisingly buoyant, hit more by low volumes of business and negative interest rates than institutional uncertainties.[9]

Perhaps more economically disruptive in the longer term was the way in which the nationalisation issue side-tracked government energies and attention at a crucial moment for policy making. With both Luis Alva Castro's resignation as finance minister and the appointment of a new central bank president in mid-1987, it was *the* moment for serious reflection on the changes that needed to be introduced to avoid the coming crisis. But for at least three whole months the energies of the Finance Ministry and the central bank, in common with many other government departments, were absorbed by the banks issue. Similarly, the energies of the Congress were also taken up, through to October 1987 at least, with the required legislation. Other legislative business – some of it very important – a new hydrocarbons law for instance – was side-tracked.

The most important economic effect was the negative repercussions on the government's relationship with the private sector. García ended up with the worst of both worlds: having punctured any confidence built up during 1986 with the economic revival and the attempt to court business interests, he then failed to impose his objective of creating a financial system in which the state could direct capital flows in an attempt to establish a more equitable pattern of development. From July 1987 onwards the Peruvian business community realised that any trust it had vested in García and his government had been misplaced. It came to believe that the bank nationalisation was just the first step in a chain of confiscatory moves whose inescapable logic was the ever further expansion of state ownership at the expense of private property and private enterprise.[10] Furthermore, the economic prospects by this time were becoming so bleak that business could no longer offset its anger over bank nationalisation with the possibility of buoyant sales and high profits. The economic basis for harmony was therefore also missing.

The sour mood of the private business community was clear at the November 1988 meeting of CADE in Iquitos to which – unusually – no senior members of the government were even invited. The private sector *gremios* like Confiep, marginalised by García during the first two years, saw their opportunity to attack the government. They played a central role in the resurgence of the right wing as a political movement at this time, with the eventual formation of the Frente Democrático (Fredemo) (see pp. 170–8).

By the end of 1987 many senior Apristas and others at the top levels of government were painfully aware of the blunder incurred by the attempt to nationalise the banks. Their concentration turned towards how to engineer a not too politically costly retreat, and to repair the damage done to relations with private business. As early as October, Gustavo Saberbein, Alva Castro's replacement as finance minister, was talking of the need to introduce measures to restore private sector confidence by accelerating the privatisation of public sector companies. Carbonetto even spoke of selling off 'twenty or thirty companies' by the end of the year to get rid of what he called the 'Nicaraguanisation fear'. But confidence was not easily to be rebuilt, even after the government had abandoned the whole nationalisation scheme.

The attention of most businessmen turned to how to survive the coming collapse in local demand as the economy went from boom into 'hyper-recession'. And politically their thoughts turned to how to get a more business-oriented government elected in 1990.

THE RETREAT FROM HETERODOXY

Not only were the prospects for the future by the end of 1987 gloomy, but economic performance began to reflect these forebodings.

The official monthly inflation rate began to creep up. The monthly average inflation rate in 1986 had been 4.2 per cent. The average for the first quarter of 1987 was 5.8 per cent, falling slightly to 5.7 per cent in the second. In the third quarter it rose again to 7.1 per cent hitting 7.7 per cent in the last quarter (see Figure 5.1 on p. 137). Annualised rates illustrate this acceleration more forcefully. At the beginning of 1987 inflation was running at an annual rate of 65.1 per cent. By July the rate had risen to 82.2 per cent; by October to 98 per cent; and by December to 114.5 per cent.

INE statistics for output in the economy as a whole – eliminating seasonal variations mainly affecting agriculture – show the boom of 1986 petering out during the course of 1987. The index which stood at 103 in March 1986 (1979 = 100) reached an average of 120 in the first quarter of 1977, and there it stayed: 120 in the second quarter, 122 in the third, and 123 in the last. The demand-led boom had thus begun to level out, albeit of at a fairly high level. The official 1987 growth figure of 7.8 per cent, based on an average for the year compared with an average for 1986, is therefore misleading, reflecting growth in the last part of 1986 rather than in 1987.

More worrying for the government were the indicators for the external sector of the economy. Over 1987 as a whole there was a trade deficit of $521 million, the biggest trade deficit since 1981. It compared with a surplus of $1172 million in 1985 and a deficit of only $65 million in 1986. This was not due to poor export performance – exports increased in value from $2.5 billion to $2.7 billion with higher world prices for copper and crude oil – but to the surge in imports. Imports rose from $2.6 billion in 1986 to $3.2 billion in 1987, the highest rate since the import influx at the time of Belaúnde's trade liberalisation in 1981–2. While the import bill stabilised at about its average quarterly level of 1986 in the first two quarters of 1987 ($763 million in the first quarter and $646 million in the second), it rose in the third quarter to $860 million and in the fourth to $913 million.

It was therefore the strength of demand for imports – possibly in part a mask for capital flight through overinvoicing – which reduced Peru's stock of foreign reserves during 1987. The figures for both central bank reserves and those of the banking system as a whole for 1986 and 1987 (net and gross) are set out in Table 5.1. The sharp fall in the third and fourth quarters of 1987 is evident by whichever standard is used, with net international reserves of the banking system actually turning negative in January 1988.

As we saw earlier, the erosion of foreign reserves made it more difficult for the central bank to stabilise the exchange rate. By the end of 1987 a big gap had developed between the official exchange rate (33 intis to the dollar) and the street rate (92 intis to the dollar). Fluctuations in the street rate for the dollar became a key indicator of the state of economic confidence, in a way that was not the case in 1985 and 1986. As the fall in reserves made it more difficult for the central bank to intervene to protect the inti, the demand for the reserves that remained became even more intense, further pushing up the price of the dollar in intis.

Table 5.1   International reserves, 1986–8 (millions of US$)

1986	Banking system		Central bank	
	Gross	Net	Gross	Net
March	2692	1446	2457	1541
June	2432	1178	2185	1278
September	2334	1177	2065	1239
December	2108	866	1861	958
1987				
March	2059	738	1800	820
June	1940	707	1725	790
September	1741	527	1456	533
December	1471	81	1130	43
1988				
March	1208	− 177	888	-194
June	1189	− 249	945	-180

Source: Central Bank. Figures quoted in the National Statistics Institute (INE) *Informe Económico*, Lima, 1989

At the same time as high demand prompted high imports and the outflow of foreign reserves, the government – as we noted earlier – did nothing to shore up the fiscal accounts of the public sector. Tax revenue to the central government declined from 12 per cent of GDP in 1986 to 9 per cent in 1987, partly as a result of tax cuts and exonerations conceded in 1985 and 1986, and partly because the acceleration in the rate of inflation once again undermined the value of tax receipts. Government spending fell marginally from 13 per cent of GDP in 1986 to 12 per cent in 1987. Meanwhile, with many large public sector companies making more substantial losses in 1987 than in 1986 – the largest loss-makers were those most responsible for subsidies (notably ENCI, ECASA and Electroperu) – the public sector deficit rose from just over 5 per cent of GDP in 1986 to nearly 7 per cent in 1987.

It was with growing consciousness of the significance of these imbalances and what they portended for the future – an external and domestic economic crisis – that by the last quarter of 1987 the government's attention turned to rebuilding relations with the main multilateral financial institutions: the World Bank, the IMF and the IDB. This change in the official stance towards the multilateral lenders was also partly stimulated by awareness of the government's political and economic isolation in the wake of the bank nationalisation move.

In September 1987, a discreet two-man IMF delegation visited Lima, following an approach made to the IMF a month earlier by the Peruvian government. At this time the prime minister, Guillermo Larco Cox, talked of plans to resume debt payments to the World Bank, and the need to make the 10 per cent limit on debt servicing more flexible. In a new debt repayment plan released by the Economy and Finance Ministry, new priorities were published for debt repayment which gave multilateral organisations higher priority than before.

Tentative approaches to the multilateral lenders thus coincided with a shift in official policy thinking. In October, Daniel Carbonetto admitted that 'we now agree that there should not be an exchange rate lag, nor an anti-export bias in our model'. A devaluation of the inti was accepted as a necessity, ending the commitment to maintaining a frozen exchange rate. An overhaul of public finances was also agreed upon as a priority to reduce the size of the deficit. Two of the fundamental canons of Peruvian heterodoxy were thereby beginning to be challenged.

In November 1987, more contacts were made with international financial bodies. The first formal talks since December 1984 took place with the IMF, and – perhaps trying not to upset what could have been the beginning of a lasting rapprochement – the staff report presented to the IMF board was couched in conciliatory language, avoiding overt criticism of the APRA government's economic policy. An appeal by the government for a meeting with the steering committee of international banks, however, provoked a less diplomatic response. Citibank, which headed the committee, replied presenting a bill for $427 000 for expenses incurred in previous fruitless negotiations and costs of telexes sent to the 279 banks represented by the steering committee.

The government's big hope was that re-establishing links would lead to new lending and help meet the country's financial needs in 1988 and 1989. To this end Javier Tantaleán, head of the INP, and Gustavo Saberbein, the finance minister, were dispatched to Washington. The idea was to try to raise $1 billion from the IDB for balance of payments support and funding for priority development projects. On top of this $2 billion was to be sought from the World Bank on the basis of the government's economic plan for the period through to the change of government in July 1990. Alan García seems to have come round to the idea that his goal of a 4–5 per cent growth rate in 1988 was only feasible with the renewal of official lending, and he also appears to have believed that the World Bank would be conciliatory towards Peru in order to bring it back within the pale of the international financial system.[11] When a World Bank mission visited Peru in December 1987 it reminded the government of the Bank's recommendations which included establishment of a single 'competitive' exchange rate, reduction of the fiscal deficit and the establishment of real interest rates. Its team's findings and recommendations were to form the basis of a Bank report on Peru published in December 1988.[12]

The retreat from heterodoxy began in earnest with a 24 per cent average devaluation in October 1987. It was marked by a series of economic packages starting in December 1987, and thereafter in March, July and September 1988. The September package, more drastic than any of its predecessors, was followed by a further tough package of measures in November 1988. However, none of these packages of adjustments led to the achievement of the external, economic lifeline needed to help stabilise the economy.

Decision-making at this time revealed lack of coordination and a loss of direction. While prominent members of the economic team reluctantly came round to accepting a return to orthodoxy if that was what was needed to get fresh dollars, García balked at the political price involved. The result was a set of half-measures and compromises. In December 1987, just as an adjustment plan was being devised under the auspices of the World Bank, measures were introduced to devalue the inti and reduce the number of exchange rates, but which ignored World Bank recommendations for fiscal and monetary reform.

In March 1988, García's top advisers, notably Saberbein, Coronado (the central bank president), Tantaleán, Carbonetto and Morales Bermúdez, thought they had persuaded García to go for a full-blown orthodox shock to be followed by a six-month 'heterodox' price freeze. The heterodox advisers accepted the need to deal with fiscal imbalance and the need to get rid of subsidised exchange rates for certain types of imports. Their plan sought to reduce the fiscal deficit to 'zero' through sharp increases in taxation, the elimination of tax exonerations, the unification of exchange rates, a 70 per cent increase in the retail price of petrol, higher tariffs for goods and services produced by state companies, and the elimination of subsidised credit to farmers in the *sierra*.

But, even though public opinion had been primed for these measures, García's last-minute intervention led to the package announced on 9 March being substantially different from that agreed by the cabinet (and subsequently leaked to the press) only a few days earlier. Worried by the political impact of measures which would have sent March inflation upwards towards 40 per cent for the month, García opted to scale down the price adjustments, increase the amount of wage compensation, and to do the adjustment in two stages with a 120-day price freeze in between. A member of the government's economic team is quoted as having said 'it only takes a couple of hours to work out and alter a couple of coefficients. Computers are marvellous'.[13]

Further adjustments in June and July – corollaries to the March package – did little to inspire confidence and convince the public that short-term (let alone longer-term) problems were being addressed. In June, the price freeze was lifted and some adjustments were made, notably a 58 per cent increase in petrol prices. The average exchange rate was devalued once more and the number of exchange rates reduced from nine in May to four in July. In July, regulated prices were increased, as were public sector tariffs like the prices of water, electricity and telephones, as well as bus fares. To offset the social cost the government authorised a 70 per cent increase in the minimum wage, 50 per cent for government employees and 55 per cent for workers in the private sector.

A key problem in what became known as 'gradualism' was that it was impossible to attack the twin deficits – fiscal and trade – on a piecemeal basis. The effects of price increases simply fed through into the following month's inflation rate, wiping out any real-terms increase that had initially been made, and preparing the ground for another package which would have the same effect. A rise in the retail price of petrol in December would have nil effect by March as the higher inflation it helped generate wiped out the effects. Similarly, the impact of a devaluation in restoring a competitive exchange rate was quickly neutralised by the inflation it helped produce. Attempts to raise domestic interest rates suffered the same fate.

Moreover, the mechanisms of effectively freezing prices between packages no longer had much effect. The monthly inflation figures for the first part of 1988 are indicative. Having achieved an average monthly rate of 7.7 per cent in the last quarter of 1987, the effect of the December package was to send the monthly rate up to 9.6 per cent in December and 12.8 per cent in January 1988. Then in March, as a result of that month's adjustments, the inflation rate rose to 22.6 per cent. In the 'freeze' which followed, the rate fell to 17.9 per cent in April, 8.5 per cent in May and 8.8 per cent in June. By June the annualised inflation rate was up to 230 per cent, the highest in Peru's recent history. Then, with further petrol price adjustments in June and devaluation in July, the monthly rate took off again – hitting 30.9 per cent a month in July and falling slightly in August to 21.7 per cent, before September's price bombshell – a monthly inflation rate of 114 per cent.

A second major problem which came to light was that stabilisation became more difficult as the government lost effective control over the exchange rate, especially as the relevant exchange rate for more and more transactions became the parallel or street rate. One factor which exacerbated this was the increasing demand for dollars as a hedge against inflation and for speculation.[14] Another was the fall in reserves which made it harder for the authorities to intervene in the foreign exchange market. But despite faster devaluation from late 1987 onwards and the reduction in the number of exchange rates, the government was unable to close the gap between the official exchange rate and the street rate (Table 5.2). Every time there was a devaluation the street rate devalued even more.

Table 5.2   1988 exchange rates: inti/US dollar (end of period)

	A	B	C	B as % of C	A as % of C
	Official (MUC)	Financial	Parallel		
1987					
December	33.00	62.82	92.00	68.3	35.9
1988					
January	33.00	63.08	89.50	71.3	36.9
February	33.00	71.69	103.00	69.6	32.0
March	33.00	75.00	105.00	71.4	31.4
April	33.00	75.00	150.50	49.8	21.9
May	33.00	75.00	176.50	42.4	18.6
June	33.00	75.00	177.50	42.2	18.6
July	33.00	125.00	204.00	61.3	16.2
August	33.00	125.00	283.50	44.1	11.7
September	250.00	250.00	425.00	58.8	58.8
October	250.00	250.00	505.00	49.5	49.5
November	250.00	500.00	690.00	72.4	36.2
December	500.00	500.00	1700.00	29.4	29.4

Source: Central Bank *Memoria 1988*, Lima 1988.

By the middle of 1988 the government could no longer claim to have an anti-inflation policy. The implicit assumption came to be that only a massive price shock would detain inflation by closing the fiscal gap and improving the external balances dramatically. But once again, the realisation of such a leap in the dark was detained by García's fear of the political consequences, as well as the uncertainly as to whether it would in fact succeed.

Even so, an adjustment of a typically orthodox type was taking place: demand in the economy was being cut as purchasing power fell. Despite the government's inclusion of wage adjustments as part of these overall packages, real wages fell as inflation consumed the nominal increase conceded. And as demand fell, so too did the demand for imports. Whereas in the last quarter of 1987 there was a trade deficit of $126 million, by the second quarter of 1988 the accounts were just back in the black with a surplus of $27 million. In the third quarter there was a surplus of $89 million. Balance of payments problems were being dealt with in time-honoured, recessionary fashion.

SHOCK TREATMENT

By August 1988 the deficiencies of 'gradualism' were clear for all to see: inflation was getting faster not slower. The price adjustments implemented were having less and less effect as the inflation to which they helped give rise nullified the impact. At the same time, though, the erosion of reserves was not being effectively staunched: by the end of September net international reserves of the banking system reached a new low of -$318 million. Even President García, whose personal last-minute intervention had supported 'gradualism' in March, came round to the view that drastic measures had to be taken, and that politically it made more sense to take them sooner rather than later.

Two key considerations appear to have brought him round to this view. The first was that as of June 1988 his popularity among the urban poor, as expressed by the opinion polls, began to slump badly under the impact of accelerating inflation and falling real wages. The second was that even though it had become clear that APRA's chances of winning the 1990 elections were already much diminished, it was better for the brunt of the recession to fall in 1988, giving rise to the possibility of a modest recovery in 1989. García therefore came round to accepting that an all-out 'war' on inflation was the best course of action in the circumstances. In doing so, however, he appears to have accepted the argument that a drastic one-off shock to reduce the fiscal deficit to zero would halt inflation in its tracks. But then, there were few alternatives on offer.

The indication of a change in official attitude was clear from the resignation of the most conspicuous author of 'gradualism', the finance minister César Robles, who had replaced Gustavo Saberbein, on 1 September. In the cabinet reshuffle which ensued he was substituted by Abel Salinas. Salinas in his various capacities since 1985 as minister of the interior and then of mines and energy, had emerged as one of the more able and independent-minded members of the cabinet. He was given the unenviable task of almost immediately announcing the shock package on 6 September.

At its inception the plan was known as '*Plan Cero*'. Its objective was 'zero inflation, zero speculation, zero shortages, zero fiscal deficit, zero exchange rate deficit and zero Central Bank credit to the public sector'. In most respects it was extremely orthodox, involving a massive devaluation, fiscal adjustments and monetary squeeze. The main heterodox element was that the package would be followed by a 120-day freeze on wages, prices and the exchange rate. The idea was that following a huge one-off inflationary 'hiccup' in September, inflation would be down to 'zero' by November.

The main ingredients of the package were the creation of a unified exchange rate at 250 intis to the dollar (close to the street rate which reached 283 the end of August), a 75 per cent devaluation on the average previous rate; a big adjustment on prices and tariffs of state enterprises varying from 90 per cent to 300 per cent; a series of new taxes including a temporary 4 per cent tax on exports; a doubling of previous domestic interest rates; and a commitment from the central bank not to finance any resultant fiscal deficit. So as to mitigate the effects there was an increase in the minimum wage, a one-off bonus to all workers and a wage rise to workers in the public sector. The subsequent freeze of prices was not to be imposed until ten days later, giving all producers ample time to protect themselves by increasing their prices in advance of the announced four-month freeze. Finally, the exchange rate was also to remain frozen until the end of the year.

The inflationary impact of the September package was enormous. As many imported items such as pharmaceutical products sextupled in price, as petrol prices rose fourfold and producers used the ten days to increase their prices to cover themselves from the anticipated effects of the price freeze, the overall consumer index rose 114 per cent. This was more than three times the March rate, itself an historical record. The price rise immediately wiped out the effect of the pre-wage freeze increase. And within weeks the system of price controls (except for forty-two staples) had been abolished. This abandonment of the freeze on prices ended any residual heterodox nuances. Even Daniel Carbonetto, the member of the heterodox team to last longest, took this as his cue to resign.

One of the unwritten assumptions underlying the package was that it would convince multilateral lenders, particularly the World Bank, of Peru's final retreat from heterodoxy and its willingness in future to play by the internationally accepted rules of the game. The decision was taken, however, not to look for World Bank endorsement before the plan was launched, but rather to seek it afterwards. This had the advantage of making it seem that the shock had not been imposed on an unwilling government by the international financial community. Also, it had the advantage of seeming more plausible to the World Bank. Since March, when the Bank-approved package had been neutralised at the last moment, distrust of García had increased at the Bank's headquarters in Washington. To approach the Bank with the package already decreed, it was thought, was a better way of ensuring a positive reaction.

This was, however, a big gamble. Economy and Finance Ministry officials believed that the renewal of lending from such sources would help produce a 4 per cent growth rate in 1989. But it was most unlikely that large-scale financial flows via project funding would get off the ground quickly, partly because of the lack of viable projects in a state ready to receive funding. Also, by this time, Peru's arrears to the IMF and World Bank were such ($600 million to the Fund and $400 million to the Bank) that arranging the bridging finance to clear the arrears first would be no easy matter. Even 'friendly' countries would think twice before lending such sums. Last but not least, there was no guarantee that the World Bank would react positively to the package, especially as it included such elements as an increase in wages, a price freeze, and the exchange rate freeze. But it was in the belief that the substantive disagreements between Peru and the Bank had been overcome that Abel Salinas left Lima at the end of September for the annual meeting of the IMF and World Bank in Berlin. Though he was treated politely, Salinas returned without the hoped for promises of new money.

The 114 per cent surge in prices in September, followed up by a further 40 per cent of inflation in October gave formerly academic discussion about hyperinflation considerable practical relevance (Figure 5.1). The September shock treatment did not halt inflation. In October, prices rose by 40 per cent and in November by 24 per cent. Once again the effects of the package tended to be undone by the inflation that followed. For instance, the positive fiscal effects were not as dramatic as had been hoped, and by late October it was becoming increasingly difficult to hold the line about not printing money to finance the fiscal gap. At the same time, the central bank had lost effective control over the parallel dollar exchange rate. Though the official rate had been set (and frozen) at 250 intis, the parallel dollar then jumped to 500 intis by the end of October, creating an even larger gap than before.

Though the monthly import bill fell – especially for consumer goods and industrial inputs – so too (though not as dramatically) did exports, hit by the effects of a lengthy strike in the mining industry. Usable foreign reserves by this stage were close to zero. The World Bank, which returned with a mission in late October, made dire warnings on the imminence of uncontrollable hyperinflation if the fiscal deficit was not reduced. Other observers, on the other hand, put the emphasis

137

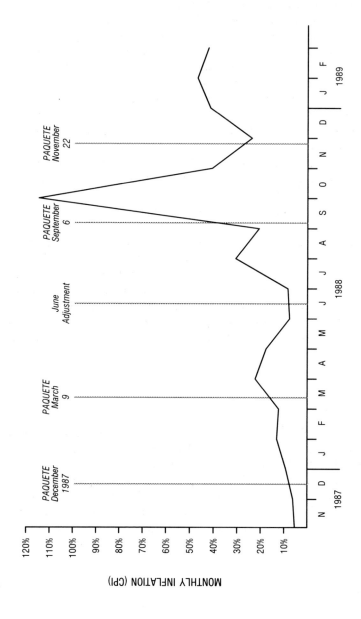

Source for monthly inflation rates: National Statistics Institute. *Informe Económico*, Lima, 1989.

Figure 5.1 Monthly inflation and adjustment measures, 1987–8

more on the government's inability to control the exchange rate as the likely detonator of hyperinflation. The pressure was on the government to do something by early November.

The 22 November package was more García's than Salinas'. Salinas had submitted yet another hard package to the president, but as in March and to a lesser extent in September, what was announced differed from the original Economy and Finance Ministry draft in terms of the scale of adjustments involved. The overall shape of the package, however, was not unlike its predecessors. The inti was devalued from 250 to 500 to the dollar; prices for basic foods rose between 40 and 270 per cent as subsidies were reduced; and the price of petrol rose 140 per cent to 600 intis a gallon; and domestic interest rates went up. At the same time, the minimum wage was pushed up from 15 000 intis a month to 24 000 in a bid to allay the effects of the package on the poorest.

No sooner was the package announced than Salinas resigned. In his letter of resignation he made a hard-hitting attack on García, recalling how his programme had been prepared only to be discarded as the president chose the measures which he wanted to be announced. In his place García appointed a former president of the Congressional budget commission, Carlos Rivas Dávila, a close collaborator within APRA and the fourth finance minister within the space of a year. Under Rivas Dávila the quest was to begin again to seek rapprochement with the IMF and the World Bank. But it was to prove equally fruitless as in the past.

THE SOCIAL COST OF ADJUSTMENT

Peruvians have got used to inflationary and recessionary economic 'packages' over the years. As we have already seen, the economic history of recent times has been one of short-lived economic booms with resultant increases in incomes overall, interspersed by ever longer periods of recession in which incomes fall further, and those who suffer most are those least able to defend themselves. But whereas the hitherto unprecedented economic contraction of 1983 had been, at least in part, a result of acts of God, the 1988–9 downspin was wholly man made.

As before, the method by which recession in the economy was induced was through the acceleration of inflation, which meant that income levels throughout the economy tended to lag behind the rise in prices. Inflation in 1988 reached the figure of 1722 per cent for the year, a record only to be broken by 1989 when it hit 2776 per cent. As the wage figures in Table 5.3 show with striking clarity, real incomes fell as increases lagged further and further behind accelerating inflation. It was in many ways a repeat performance of what happened in 1977–8 and in 1983–4, though the fall was more dramatic, especially taking place as it did against the background of the high expectations generated by the boom of 1986–7.

In 1988, economic activity contracted by nearly 9 per cent, and in 1989 by 12 per cent, together a much bigger downturn than in 1983. As a result of this, average real income per head of the population slumped by 22 per cent between 1987 and 1989, when it stood at the same level as it had at the beginning of the 1960s. With the exceptions of those whose income was already in dollars at one end of the spectrum, and those who were effectively self-sufficient and non-participant in the wider economy at the other, all Peruvians were hit by this new bout of what has been aptly termed 'hyper-stagflation'. The boom in demand had previously pushed GDP up to its highest level in March 1988 – 127 on the index used by INE (1979 = 100). It thereafter fell precipitously, averaging 118 in the second quarter, 109 in the third and 91 in the fourth.

In charting the economic downtown the decisive point was the September *paquetazo*, with its all-time record monthly inflation. Not only did the package generate large increases in the retail prices of basic foods such as bread, flour, pasta, eggs and chicken, but it increased the cost of transport by quadrupling the price of petrol. Unifying the exchange rate led to a sudden spectacular increase in 'essential' items like medicines. Pharmaceutical inputs had previously been imported at the most preferential rate of exchange of 33 intis to the dollar. Changes in the exchange rate caused prices to rise by more than six times. The purpose of Abel Salinas's *paquetazo* had been to reduce domestic demand; and it did precisely that.

Though watered down, the November 'complementary' *paquetazo* also contributed to the recession. According to the figures for Peru's national accounts, domestic consumption in 1988 as a whole was 8 per cent lower than in 1987, while in 1989 as the effects of 1988 filtered through, private consumption fell a further 16 per cent.

During 1987 and early 1988 the problem facing most consumers had been the lack of goods to buy as shortages developed and queueing began; by late 1988 and on into 1989, the problem in the country's main markets was not so much one of supply (though some shortages continued) but that most consumers lacked the money to buy, and in many cases to meet even the most basic needs. In the wake of the September *paquetazo* market-sellers told of beef and chicken going bad while housewives queued up for bones and pig fat; no one bought whole fish, they complained, only the heads and tails.[15]

The available statistical information gives us some idea of the fall in purchasing power in the cities, and in particular in Lima from where the figures are mainly drawn. Though the minimum wage fell slower than other wages because of periodic increases aimed at reducing the impact of adjustment on the poor, even these were half their September 1988 value by February 1989. The wages of other income earners in the urban economy tended to fall faster, as Table 5.3 shows.

Table 5.3   Wage levels, 1987–9 (1979 = 100)

	Minimum wage	Central government wages	Private sector wages White collar	Blue collar
1987 (average)	75.2	69.4	108.8	90.8
1988				
January	71.3	83.5		
February	63.7	74.6	104.9	85.7
March	83.1	89.4		
April	70.5	72.0	95.2	78.6
May	65.0	66.3		
June	59.7	61.0	97.0	76.5
July	78.0	72.2		
August	64.1	59.4	90.3	73.5
September	74.9	43.6		
October	53.2	31.0	58.3	46.9.
November	68.4	36.8		
December	48.3	28.2	60.1	45.9
1989				
January	42.2	26.2		
February	37.2	21.4	51.7	49.0

Source: National Statistics Institute, (INE) *Compendio Estadístico 1989–90* Lima, 1990 and *Informe Económico*, Lima, 1989.

The collapse of real wages among employers of the central government is particularly striking. In February 1989, government workers were earning less than a quarter of what they received in March 1988. So it was, that by February of 1989 the minimum wage was 35 per cent lower than it had been in July 1985 when APRA came to office; and wages in government departments more than 60 per cent lower. By mid-1989, according to the Labour Ministry's annual household survey, which covers both informal as well as formal employment, the overall contraction in real incomes was 64 per cent.[16]

Contraction in employment levels in the formal sector was not as immediate or as drastic as the fall in wages, since to some extent the fall in the real wages offset the fall in firms' turnover. Also, to start with at least, companies resolved to reduce the length of shifts and gave workers compulsory holidays (with or without wages) as opposed to formally sacking them. For employers, the PROEM system of providing temporary workers without job stability also made it easier than before to adjust to the downturn in the economic cycle. By mid-1988, and in particular after September, the number of PROEM contracts began to decrease, as these workers were the first to go. According to Labour Ministry figures gleaned from Lima's larger factories, the employment index as a whole fell from 104.5 at the end of 1987 (1979 = 100) to 96.1 at the beginning of 1989 (Table 5.4). The worst hit area of employment was in manufacturing industry (down from 101.3 to 88.2 over the same period) while employment in service industries increased marginally. The fall in employment levels, however, became more rapid by the last quarter of 1988 and the first quarter of 1989, when more and more factories found themselves reducing output and laying off workers.

A more dramatic picture emerges when employment in the formal and informal sectors are compared through to the middle of 1989. According to the Labour Ministy's household survey, the deterioration in the employment situation was very evident, with under 20 per cent of the capital's workforce being classified as 'adequately' employed. The contrast with 1986 and 1987 is striking (Table 5.5, on page 143).

Because the Labour Ministry defines subemployment in terms of an income level, this dramatic change may in part be an effect of falling wage levels within the formal sector of the labour market. However, it is also attributable to the swelling of the size of the informal sector and probably to the fall in income levels within it. The effects of an increasing supply of labour (considerably higher in Lima than the city's overall population increase) coupled to the effects of recession on employment levels in the formal sector, almost certainly led to a substantial increase in the numbers in the informal sector. Between

Table 5.4   Lima employment index (1979 = 100)

	General index	Manufacturing	Commerce	Services
1987				
(average)	101.5	97.7	95.9	110.7
(end)	104.5	101.3	102.3	111.3
1988				
January	101.8	97.7	97.7	111.1
February	101.7	97.9	96.7	110.9
March	102.1	98.3	97.6	111.0
April	102.1	98.1	97.5	111.4
May	101.6	97.0	97.7	111.4
June	101.2	96.4	97.3	111.5
July	101.3	96.4	96.5	111.9
August	101.1	96.0	95.1	112.5
September	101.5	96.7	95.2	115.4
October	99.7	93.7	94.8	112.5
November	97.6	90.3	94.8	112.5
December	97.4	89.2	98.1	112.3
1989				
January	96.1	88.2	93.6	112.3
February		87.4	91.6	112.4
March		86.0	91.1	112.0
April		85.1	90.6	112.0
May		84.5	90.4	112.0
June		83.8	88.9	111.8

Source: Labour Ministry. See National Statistics Institute (INE) *Informe Económico* Lima, 1989

1987 and 1989 the number of 'independent' workers in Lima grew on average by 11 per cent a year. Moreover, the shifts in occupational structure detected in the household survey reveal a growing proportion of the labour force in retailing and service sectors (nearly 70 per cent of the total in 1989), sectors typically associated with the informal sector.

In rural Peru, the effects of the economic downswing are less easy to chart statistically, given the lack of reliable and consistent information. Even so, the recession was probably just as severe, if not more so.

As we have seen, the wage-led demand boom of 1986 did not go hand in hand with an immediate upswing in agricultural production.

Table 5.5   Employment and unemployment in greater Lima (percentages)*

	1986	1987	1989*	1990
Unemployment	5.3	4.8	7.9	8.0
Subemployment	42.6	34.9	73.5	81.0
Adequate employment	52.1	60.3	18.6	11.0

Note: The Labour Ministry defines 'subemployment' as including those working 35 hours a week or more who receive less than the 1967 minimum wage multiplied by the CPI to the relevant date (1986: 1387 intis, 1987: 2460 intis, 1989: 541 561 intis).

* There was no survey conducted in 1988.
Source: Labour Ministry: *Encuesta de Hogares*, 18, 19, 20.

As a result prices rose, and for the first time in many years the terms of trade began to favour the rural producer rather than the urban consumer. During 1987, prompted by the continuing high demand and facilitated by the availability of cheap credit, there was an increase in supply. Farmers sowed 40 per cent more land with rice, 11 per cent with wheat, and 12 per cent with potatoes. As a result production grew by 6.5 per cent. Though this was slightly less than growth for the economy as a whole, it was exceptional by historical standards for agriculture.

However, when in 1988 the rest of the economy went into recession and the demand for consumer goods including food fell, the agricultural sector continued to grow. The result was that in 1988 the prices paid to farmers for their products fell sharply. Whereas the impact of the recession on industry was felt through production rather than prices, in agriculture it was the other way round.

One way to measure prices is to see how agricultural prices compared with other items in the consumer price index. Taking the official figure for 1988, inflation overall came to 1722 per cent. The inflation figure for agricultural goods was lower at 1451 per cent. When this figure is broken down, however, the disparities become clearer. The rise in consumer prices for crops as a whole was lower still at 1090 per cent, and for livestock products 1182 per cent. Meanwhile, inflation for agroindustrial products (included in agriculture rather than industry for statistical purposes) was as high as 2000 per cent.

The wholesale price index is probably a better guide to what producers actually received. Excluding imports, the overall wholesale inflation rate in 1988 was 1855 per cent according to INE. Agricultural goods (including crops, livestock and agroindustrial products) increased at only half the national average at 935 per cent, while manufactured goods, for instance, rose by 2525 per cent. By any yardstick then, agricultural prices in 1988 underwent a major slump, eroding the main source of income for most people living in rural areas, and reversing the income gains made by rural producers in the first two years of the García government.

However, farmers were not just hit by falling real prices. As the terms of trade swung against them, the cost of agricultural inputs – let alone other consumer items bought in local markets – increased rapidly. Fertilisers, for instance, which even fairly poor producers could afford to buy in 1986, became prohibitively expensive. Even when subsidised by the state, imported inputs also became impossibly expensive for most producers.

The situation facing farmers was made worse by the inability of state institutions to maintain earlier programmes which had helped regenerate agricultural production.

First, by 1988 there was a sharp fall in the amount of cheap, subsidised credit available to farmers. The value of Banco Agrario loans in 1988 was only a third of what it had been in 1987, falling from 1.76 per cent of GDP to 0.57 per cent. Comparing the last four months of 1988 – the crucial growing season when farmers most need credit – with the same period of 1987, the value of loans was less than 28 per cent of what it had been a year earlier. The real value of Banco Agrario credit peaked at the end of 1986 and in the first quarter of 1987. And, with the collapse in markets and prices, farmers found themselves increasingly unable to repay the loans contracted earlier, therefore further undermining the bank's financial standing, and reducing its capacity to lend in future.

Secondly, as the government's revenue problems became increasingly acute, the agencies in charge of purchasing agricultural production, ENCI and ECASA, found themselves short of cash and unable to make prompt payments. This became one of the most potent sources of agricultural discontent by 1988 and 1989 when delays in making payment to producers got longer and longer. In response to political pressures the government resorted simply to printing the money to pay angry producers.

Thirdly, in some areas at least, failure to maintain roads – particularly in the rainy season – was a further barrier to marketing. This was a particularly serious problem in *ceja de selva* areas like Huánuco and San Martín.

The effects of all these difficulties was that by the 1988–9 agricultural year which began in August 1988, agricultural production levels began to fall, especially in terms of the main food crops oriented at the urban market. Plantings were sharply down: 14 per cent in the case of maize, 18 per cent in the case of potatoes, 15 per cent in that of beans. Agricultural production for the first quarter of 1989 was 8 per cent lower than for the same quarter of 1988; in the second quarter 5 per cent lower. The effect of falling urban demand was equally clear for the less seasonal forms of agriculture, which were of particular importance in the patterns of urban food consumption. Production of chicken, for instance, was 45 per cent lower in January–February 1989 than a year earlier, eggs nearly 22 per cent lower.

The result of falling production was shortages in urban markets. The government, just when it could least afford to do so – and just when doing so was further to frustrate rural recovery – resorted to importing food products like rice. In normal times Peru was self-sufficient in rice, but in the conditions of 1989 it was importing from North Korea. During 1989 the government came to rely heavily on shipments of imported grains to maintain the supply of basic food in Lima and elsewhere, just when it most lacked the dollars to pay for them. Meanwhile, Peruvian producers found themselves forced by low prices for food crops to sow alternatives commanding better prices. Rice producers in the northern coastal valleys started planting cotton instead. In the jungle, farmers increasingly bowed to market logic and planted coca.

The problem of poverty, even in its more extreme forms, is – as we have seen – not a new phenomenon in Peru. Large numbers in both urban and especially rural areas have long suffered effects like malnutrition. However, the outset of the 1989–90 economic contraction had a notable impact in aggravating such problems, as well as reducing the capacity of the state to mitigate the social cost of adjustment.

The scale of the problem of extreme poverty was the subject of a study by Javier Abugattás, formerly vice-minister of the economy until the end of 1988 and an authority on basic needs in Peru.[17] According to Abugattás, the cost of providing emergency food supplies to bring diet levels up to a very basic minimum would have been around $1.6 billion a year. The minimum income needed to buy a basic basket of goods was $48 a month per person according to the study, and more than half the population of Peru received less than this. The minimum required to buy a basic intake of calories to avoid malnutrition was

$31 per person per month. A total of 6.6 million Peruvians are thought to have earned less than this in 1989. The $1.6 billion figure is worked out on the basis of supplementing the diets of this number of people. The regional breakdown of how the money would have to be distributed reflects the persistence of extreme poverty in rural areas, especially in the *sierra*. Of the total, $922 million would have to go to rural Peru (notably to the poorest departments in the southern *sierra*). However, it also reflects the incidence of poverty in urban areas, and especially in the capital.

Lack of detailed information makes it difficult to assess with any accuracy the full impact of the 1989–90 downturn on basic living conditions. At the time of writing little detailed and systematic research had been conducted; and that which existed tended to shed more light on the plight of the urban rather than the rural poor. One of the few serious studies done was carried out jointly by Prisma and the Cayetano Heredia University. This focused on demographic and nutritional change in thirty-two *pueblos jovenes*, mostly of recent origin, in San Juan de Miraflores in Lima's southern suburbs.[18] It confirms with depressing clarity how the drop in income over this period contributed to malnutrition among young children.

Since infant mortality rates are a particularly telling indicator of levels of poverty, its conclusions are worth quoting in some detail. They show that there was a notable fall in the average monthly weight-for-height ratio in the population under 3 after September 1988. This ratio is particularly sensitive to the incidence of acute malnutrition. In common with findings from countries with experience of famine, the San Juan research shows that boys tended to suffer more than girls from malnutrition, and that 1 to 2 year olds were worse affected than those under 1. Two findings were of particular importance. The first was that nutritional status underwent 'an abrupt fall' after September 1988; the second, that there was a significant seasonal variation not observed before in Lima. Putting these two points together, Prisma notes: 'if we observe each seasonal low point we see that those points decline with each successive year.' The Prisma–Cayetano Heredia team organised two special economic surveys in the area, first in March 1988 and then in June 1989. When compared they show that in these fifteen months family income per week fell by 56 per cent in real terms from 1050 intis to the equivalent of 460 intis. This meant that among half the population of the areas included in the survey, families were unable to cover the most basic calorie requirements. The report also points to an increase in all child mortality rates – infants, perinatal, 1 to 4 year olds and under-5s – though the relatively small numbers involved made it difficult to make statistical extrapolations.

The problem with the Prisma report is that its findings may not be typical of poor neighbourhoods as a whole in Lima or other cities. However, though the degree of acute malnutrition in this very poor neighbourhood may be exceptional, it seems unlikely that the *rate* of deterioration in living standards was exceptional. Its overall findings regarding the impact of the economic adjustments of late 1988 are corroborated by the experience of other non-governmental agencies working in different poor neighbourhoods of the capital.[19]

The experience of 1988–90 also underlined, despite its supposed commitment to the poor, the failure of the APRA government to respond to the crisis by providing timely social support for those most affected. The government's Social Compensation Programme, introduced in April 1989, six months after the September 1988 shock, had little direct impact because of bureaucratic inefficiency and the lack of available funds. Most of the work carried out continued to be done by non-governmental organisations working with grass-roots organisations and often with external finance. The church and the municipality of Lima (through its *Vaso de Leche* programme) also played an active role. The failure of the government to respond in an effective way to the social crisis was a powerful stimulus to those parties contesting the 1990 elections (notably Fredemo and the Izquierda Unida) to put considerable emphasis on the design of more effective social compensation programmes.

REACTIVATION?

In May 1989, with just under a year to go to the 1990 presidential elections, Alan García reaffirmed his determination to keep personal control over economic policy. His appointment of César Vásquez Bazán, a young APRA economist, inexperienced in government, as finance minister, flew in the face of strong pressure from the business community. Businessman wanted someone in the job who would inspire confidence. Vásquez Bazán, coming from the radical wing of the party, was not such a figure. He had previously drawn attention to himself for his outspoken criticism of García for failing to produce the social and economic transformation which the party had historically stood for. Despite his inexperience, Vásquez Bazán was to last in the job longer than his four predecessors, staying there right through to the change of government in July 1990.

Vásquez Bazán's main task as finance minister was to engineer a degree of economic reactivation in the build-up to the elections, and to stop inflation spinning off into an uncontrollable hyperinflationary spiral. Alan García's grudging acceptance of the recessionary policies enacted in 1988 had been conditioned by the calculation that the timing would provide the opportunity for recovery in advance of 1990. Back in mid-1988, García and Daniel Carbonetto had planned the build-up of reserves to around $1 billion as a *quid pro quo* for a pre-election reactivation. The contraction in domestic demand would reduce imports and help generate a trade surplus. The build-up in reserves achieved thereby would provide scope for a return to economic growth. García, it seems, was not willing to see his presidency ending up with APRA suffering the sort of electoral débâcle inflicted on Acción Popular in 1985, or, more recently, on Raúl Alfonsín's Radical Party, in Argentina, in May 1989.

'Reactivation' was therefore the main priority as Vásquez Bazán took over at the Economy and Finance Ministry. Indeed, by that time there were already some signs that the worst of the post-September 1988 recession was over. Production levels stopped falling in sectors such as manufacturing and construction. They even began to pick up, although from a very low base. The foreign reserves situation also began to improve. At the end of April 1989 net foreign reserves in the banking system turned positive for the first time since December 1987. This reflected a better trade performance as imports fell and exports (assisted once again by higher oil and mineral prices) rose. The quarterly total for imports fell from $764 million in the third quarter of 1988 to $573 million in the fourth and $400 million in the first quarter of 1989. At the same time, total exports rose from $634 million in the last quarter of 1988, to $850 million in the first quarter of 1989, to $932 million in the second. Despite labour disruption in the mines, high commodity prices for minerals meant that 1989 was the best year for traditional exports since the price boom of 1980. This stroke of good fortune gave the government added room for manoeuvre in orchestrating its reactivation strategy.

The other key goal of policy was to keep the lid on inflation. In the first four months of 1989 hyperinflationary expectations had been increased by monthly inflation rates of well over 40 per cent. By the end of April the accumulated rate for the first four months was already close to 350 per cent, 4500 per cent over the previous twelve months. For electoral purposes, if nothing else, it was essential for the government to reduce the inflation rate substantially. APRA had no wish to suffer the fate of the UDP coalition in Bolivia, for instance, swept out of office on a right-wing revival in 1985, amid inflation rates in excess of 12 000 per cent a year.

The main elements of economic policy-making as they evolved during the remainder of 1989 were reminiscent of some of the heterodox formulae employed in 1985 and 1986. First, the government determined to provide a stimulus (albeit a moderate one) by prompting an increase in real wages. Salaries and wages in the private sector of the economy increased in the six months from April to October, though central government wages remained static. Wages, however, did not regain their pre-September 1988 level. Secondly, the government sought to control inflation by keeping officially controllable prices low. The cost of milk to the consumer, for example, was 25 per cent lower in December 1989 than the previous May; wheat 35 per cent; electricity supply in the *pueblos jóvenes* 48 per cent; and petrol 36 per cent. At the same time, the official exchange rate was devalued more slowly than the rate of inflation. This was particularly the case from October to the end of the year: devaluation of 8.4 per cent a month compared with inflation of 27.6 per cent. Indeed, after October the government opted for a faster rate of economic expansion, with less than six months to go to the elections, by using up the dollars accumulated at the central bank during the earlier part of the year. Thirdly, monetary and fiscal policy were also geared to controlling inflation. In contrast to 1985 and 1986 interest rates were kept relatively high and a squeeze maintained over liquidity. The fiscal deficit in 1989 came down to 4.3 per cent of GDP, in part reflecting falling government spending especially on wages.

However, the results of price policies were disappointing. Though under Vásquez Bazán the monthly rhythm of inflation was reduced from the 40–50 per cent range of the first few months of 1989, it still remained stubbornly high. After falling to 23 per cent in June, it started to creep up again, hitting 27 per cent by September. New policy measures adopted in October, including the slow-down in devaluation, brought it down to 23 per cent. But then it started to climb once again to 26 per cent in November and 34 per cent in December. Despite a slight drop in the New Year, the rate was up to 33 per cent on the eve of the elections. The annual rate was still above 2000 per cent.

The promised reactivation was not very strong. Though in the latter part of 1989 there was a recovery of sorts, it was not nearly as generalised or as potent as that of 1985/6. Real wages did not rise rapidly. They did not recover their pre-September 1988 purchasing power, let alone that of 1986 or 1987. White-collar wages which stood at 107 in August 1987 (on an index taking the average for 1988 as 100) were down to 47 in April 1989 and back up to 51 by December; blue-collar wages which stood at 108 in August 1987 fell to 47 in April and only recovered to 50 by December. In terms of employment there was no evidence of a boom. Taking a different index (1979 = 100) industrial employment fell from 94 in October 1988 to 83 in July 1989, recovering only to 86 by the end of the year. We have already seen how an unprecedented proportion of the labour force was officially categorised 'sub-employed' by 1989.

In the propaganda battle in the build-up to the 1990 elections, the government was able to announce how GDP was 12 per cent higher in January 1990 than it had been a year before. The comparison, however, was somewhat misleading since the recovery was from an extremely low base. When compared with the situation before September 1988 the degree of reactivation looks much less dramatic. Also after a fairly strong recuperation in July and September 1989, seasonally adjusted GDP stagnated in October 1989 and thereafter. In particular, the amount of liquidity in the economy remained extremely low as Table 5.6 show.

Table 5.6   Growth, inflation and reserves, 1988–9

	GDP index (1979 = 100)	Manufact-uring index (1979 = 100)	Liquidity index (1979 = 100)	Reserves net-banking system US$mn	Trade surplus US$mn	Quarterly inflation rates (%)	
1988							
March	127.1	154.4	105.1	−177	-99	1Q	54.6
June	114.1	140.4	93.6	−149	36	2Q	39.2
September	110.2	114.7	48.8	−258	-54	3Q	241.1
December	94.1	88.7	35.1	−317	61	4Q	148.2
1989							
March	96.0	82.7	28.5	−51	371	1Q	198.1
June	96.1	82.0	28.5	346	439	2Q	135.2
September	100.8	95.0	31.5	649	515	3Q	97.8
December	108.3	105.4	30.1	611	192	4Q	107.5

Source: Central Bank.

The above table shows how reactivation was concentrated in the last few months of 1989, when the government was prepared to sacrifice reserves to achieve growth. The cost of the reactivation was high in terms of the use of foreign exchange. Having peaked in November 1989 at $745 million, net international reserves of the banking system fell precipitously thereafter: $472 million at the end of January 1990, $272 million at the end of February and $190 million at the end of March on the eve of the elections. The fall was partly attributable to lower exports, but mainly to a surge in imports caused by the cheap dollar and the rush of businessmen to stock up while dollars lasted in advance of a new government taking office. Even in the last quarter of 1989 imports increased to $641 million compared with $416 million in the third, their highest since the second quarter of 1988.

The speed at which foreign reserves were used up suggested that any reactivation would not last much beyond the 1990 elections. Indeed the trade balance had once again turned negative by January and February. With foreign reserves exhausted, monthly inflation accelerating once again, and with the government deliberately suppressing controlled prices like petrol, it was handing on a poisoned chalice to its successor.

6 The Political Response to the Crisis

THE POPULAR REACTION

Just as it was the García government's hope in 1985 that economic reactivation would help atenuate social conflict by enabling some much-needed income redistribution to take place, so too it was its fear that the sort of recessionary economic shock treatment forced upon it in 1988 would create a new level of social polarisation and violence which it would be hard pressed to contain. The notion of *desborde*, described back in 1984 by one of García's mentors, the anthropologist José Matos Mar[1] looked like becoming a reality in an all too dramatic way, as living standards collapsed and hopes of a better future were dashed. It was this political calculation which lay behind García's repeated last-minute interventions to cushion the social impact of the succession of economic *paquetes* announced during the course of 1988. Though such palliatives as increases in the minimum wage might detract from the economic 'coherence' of a set of measures in technical terms, the risk was that the social response might bring with it much higher costs. In a country with a relatively strong Marxist left, an uncompromising and increasingly ubiquitous guerrilla movement, high indices of social violence and a state machine ill-equipped to maintain control, such fears were not altogether misplaced.

The immediate reaction to the September *paquetazo*, the biggest single jolt to people's living standards, was not one of instant disorder and violence. In some ways the response was surprisingly muted: it was one of astonishment and incredulity rather than spontaneous anger. Though incidents of looting were reported in some markets in Lima, there was no widespread rioting or a collapse of public order. The government, of course, was quick to pre-empt demonstrations: it broke up a march organised by the CGTP before it had barely begun. Though the reaction tended to be stronger in provincial cities like Cuzco, Puno, Arequipa and Huancayo, where the economic shock treatment helped breathe new life into regional defence movements, it was not such as to live up to the government's forebodings.

152

This relatively muted response was confirmed by the limited success of a one-day national protest strike by the CGTP a month later on 13 October. Another one-day stoppage took place on 1 December in protest at the November *paquete* but with even less effect. This sort of protest strike had become the standard response of the CGTP to the announcement of unpopular policy measures, involving not only the unionised workforce but also wider sections of the population. The failure of the October and December one-day general strikes stand in contrast to previous, more successful mobilisations against government policies: the one-day strikes of May 1987, January 1988 and of May 1988. Though the government put this down to the sense of 'civic responsibility' of the population, two other explanations are more plausible. One is that the speed at which employment and family incomes were being eroded by the end of 1988 made most workers reluctant to sacrifice a day's wages and other bonuses. Some writers have gone so far as to stress the negative correlation between the degree of recession and the fall in income on the one hand, and the willingness of workers to support radical responses on the other.[2] Fear of loss of employment was particularly marked, with workers often prepared to take a cut in income rather than risk their jobs. Usually PROEM workers, who enjoyed no rights to job stability, were the first to go; unionised workers the last. The second explanation is fear. The government's methods of dealing with marches, demonstrations and such measures as the occupation of factories had become increasingly violent and arbitrary, often using the supposed presence of Sendero Luminoso as a pretext. In 1988 more than at any other time Sendero Luminoso tried to build up its presence amongst urban organised labour (see p. 190). In those industrial areas where Sendero had been active in trying to take advantage of discontent among the workers, union leaders linked to the orthodox left had tended to become increasingly defensive, faced by the threat of violence from both Sendero and the authorities. On either score, then, the risks of mobilisation were higher than before, while the confidence in the efficacy of such responses to achieve real benefits was probably lower.

The pattern of strike activity – beyond that of just one-day protest action – does not suggest, however, that workers were entirely acquiescent. The number of man-hours lost as a consequence of strikes in 1988 was more than four times that of the previous year. According to Labour Ministry figures 39.3 million man-hours were lost in 1988 as opposed to 9.1 million in 1987, with the vast majority of strikes concentrated in the second half of the year. Two points serve to qualify this picture, though. One is that the total number of hours lost in 1987 was abnormally low in relation to other years (see Table 6.1); the other is that the figures reveal the profound effect of two very large and protracted disputes – the two national strikes by mineworkers which closed down almost the whole mining industry first in July and August and then subsequently in October and November. Mining accounts for 20.5 million man-hours lost in 1988, compared with 6.7 million in manufacturing industry.

Table 6.1   Strike activity, 1984–9

Year	No. of strikes	No. of workers involved (thousands)	Man-hours lost (millions)		
			Total	Industry	Mining
1984	509	703	13.8	1.8	4.4
1985	579	238	12.2	2.8	2.5
1986	642	249	16.9	7.2	5.6
1987	720	310	9.1	3.2	3.1
1988	814	693	38.2	6.7	20.9
1989	667	224	15.2	3.2	3.4

Source: Labour Ministry, published by the National Statistics Institute (INE) in its *Compendio Estadístico* 1989–90, Lima, 1990.

The main focus of the miners' strikes was not primarily wages, though of course the falling value of wages and other benefits made the struggle more embittered. The strikes arose from the attempt of the Mineworkers' Federation (FNTMMSP) to negotiate on an industry-wide basis and to include the extension of a series of uniform benefits to all workers, irrespective of whom they worked for, or in which mine. Though initially accepted by the government (the single biggest employer), the dispute was drawn out as a result of determined opposition from private-sector mining companies and because of a series of contradictory judicial verdicts which caused the government to go back on arrangements to which it had previously agreed.

Beside the miners' strikes, the most important cause of industrial unrest was the attempt by unions to achieve a degree of wage indexation for workers, and the attempt by the government to impose limits on indexation. Traditionally, most annual wage settlements in Peru involve a wage rate being negotiated with agreed increments being added at the end of the sixth and ninth month. But with the speed-up of inflation during the course of 1988, such formulae increasingly failed to protect workers' living standards. Wage bargaining was made more bitter by inconsistencies in government policy. For instance, in August 1988 the government issued a decree which established a degree of wage indexation. Following the September package, desperate to break what seemed like a hyperinflationary cycle, it brought in an upper limit to wage increases given under the previous indexation arrangement. Then, confronted by a wave of strikes, including one involving the powerful bankworkers' union (FEB), and following judicial writs by the CGTP, it eventually backed down.[3] Still, the most common cause of strikes as 1988 ended and 1989 began were attempts by unions to establish as much indexation as possible into work contracts, and the failure of employers (often the state itself) to honour the terms of existing contracts by paying inflation-linked and other bonus arrangements, or even basic wages, in full and on time. One of the sectors most frequently on strike was that of government workers themselves, whose union confederation (CITE) the government persistently refused to recognise and whose wages, as we have seen, were among those to fall most behind since 1985.

The pattern of the popular response in rural areas to government policies and the economic downturn is, like the impact of recession, harder to document. Also sometimes it is difficult to distinguish between actions undertaken voluntarily and those undertaken because of coercion from Sendero Luminoso. However, it is clear that protest by rural producers was common, and possibly more strident and violent than among industrial workers. An interesting piece of research based on secondary sources suggests this (Table 6.2).[4] It seeks to quantify acts of protest reported in the newspapers and to differentiate them according to the degree of violence involved. Written protests (*denuncias*) come at one end of the scale, and strikes, road blocks and occupations at the other. It tries to create what it terms a 'basket' of responses, quarter by quarter, taking the first quarter of 1985 as a base of 100. Comparing man-hours lost through strikes in the formal sector of the economy – 9 times as numerous in the last quarter of 1988 compared with 1985 – it establishes that acts of protest in the rural sphere were 15 times more common, and more violent types of protest 39 times more common.

Table 6.2   The 'protest' index, 1985–9 (1985- 1Q = 100)

Year/ quarter		All types of rural protest	More violent forms of Rural protest:*	Man hours lost through strikes
1985	1Q	100	100	100
	2Q	213	450	110
	3Q	38	—	173
	4Q	88	—	46
1986	1Q	63	—	228
	2Q	438	750	98
	3Q	181	417	258
	4Q	13	—	85
1987	1Q	525	567	114
	2Q	494	817	147
	3Q	663	450	109
	4Q	775	750	66
1988	1Q	763	1716	99
	2Q	625	1408	216
	3Q	745	2623	588
	4Q	1560	3925	927
1989	1Q	4475	12900	N.A.

* Includes demonstrations, occupations of buildings and land, road blocks and strikes.
Source: J. Velazco, *Crisis y Movilización Popular* (Lima: Catholic University 1989).

In the weeks following the September *paquetazo* there were daily reports in the Lima press of impromptu roadblocks interrupting the transit of vehicles; strikes and stoppages; mobilisations organised often by departmental *frentes de defensa*; and the frequent occupations of the local offices of such government agencies as ENCI and ECASA. These last were generally on account of the government's failure to pay producers on time for their crops, the extremely high prices being charged for such inputs as fertiliser, or failure to provide timely credit. In November 1988, there was a fifteen-day strike in Ayacucho by agricultural producers; a protracted stoppage in the sugar cooperatives along the coast; and mobilisations among farmers in the jungle departments in support of better prices. At the beginning of 1989, likewise, there were protests among coffee workers and milk produ- cers, a three-week strike by rice workers in Ucayali on account of non- payment by ECASA (which culminated in eight being killed and thirty wounded as police opened fire on a march in Pucallpa), a three-week strike by farmers in Cuzco (which seriously interrupted potato supplies), and various protests organised by the peasant federation there.

Thus, though the immediate effect of government policies was not such as to spark an uncontrollable social upheaval, the social responses to the economic downturn were marked both in the urban–industrial context and (probably more so) in the rural–agricultural one. Two interrelated aspects emerge from this picture. First, the response was not so much of an offensive or particularly violent type. Rather, the resort to action seems more to have been a product of lack of viable alternatives in a situation in which the state or employers failed to honour previous agreements: wage-indexing arrangements in the case of unionised workers and price agreements or the withdrawal of credit and subsidies in the case of farmers. Secondly, protests tended to be sporadic and uncoordinated. Neither the CGTP nor the political parties of the left chose to seize the opportunity to mobilise social protest against the APRA government. Union and party leaders were conscious of the fragility of the political situation and the danger of a coup. But failure to take the initiative against the government reduced the political standing of the left and provided the right with the chance to profit from the government's unpopularity. Left-wing protest tended to be better orchestrated in the provinces outside Lima where the *frentes de defensa* operated with greater unity of purpose, but even there their room for manoeuvre was limited.

APRA'S DWINDLING PROFILE

To be jeered at by the party faithful was undoubtedly something to which Alan García was not accustomed. But this was the humiliation he had to suffer at APRA's 16th Congress, held in December 1988. It was an unmistakable sign of how the collapse in the president's popularity ratings in the country, following the September and November *paquetazos*, had undermined his standing within his party. In a climate of economic chaos and growing popular discontent, it was perhaps not surprising that many in APRA – who had previously lauded García for the 1985 victory and his initial successes in government – blamed him personally for the way in which things had gone wrong. It must have seemed to many Apristas that APRA had waited sixty years to get into government, only to dissipate the opportunity.

Both as candidate before 1985 and president afterwards, García recognised that his standing in the party was derived from his popularity in the country as a whole. Though the speed of his rise to power reflected an absence of alternative political talent, he was not without rivals within the party. Whilst he maintained his impressive popularity ratings, few in the party could or would defy him. But, once that popularity begin to diminish, once he was forced back on to the defensive, then rivalries would emerge more clearly, challenging his leadership and bringing with it the risk that the old ideological tensions, which had emerged so clearly on the death of Haya de la Torre, would once again destroy party consensus.

The speed at which García's popularity fell during the second half of 1988 is striking. Even though opinion polls in Peru are by no means a perfect barometer of public opinion, they do provide a useful guide, particularly when their findings are charted over time. One of the more reputable polling agencies is Datum, whose findings are set out in Figure 6.1 in relation to the simple question of whether those asked thought Alan García was doing a good job as president. The polls were mostly limited to Lima, and the popularity curve which we see below based on these polls excludes those who did not know or refused to give an answer. While his popularity rating had dwindled during 1986, 1987 and 1988, it was between June 1988 and the end of the year that his popularity fell most dramatically. The economic crisis, it seemed, had had a much more profound effect than the bank nationalisation débâcle.

As well as being booed and heckled, Alan García was also dealt other humiliations at the 16th Congress. He lost the post of president of the party (which had been created especially for him at the previous congress in July 1985), lost control of the party's political committee, and – perhaps more galling still – saw his main rival within the party, Luis Alva Castro, voted in as general secretary, all but ensuring that Alva Castro would be the party's candidate at the 1990 elections, and possibly the dominant force thereafter.

The split in the party leadership went back to well before 1985, with Alva Castro rising to prominence as the only person of García's generation with his own strong standing and organised following

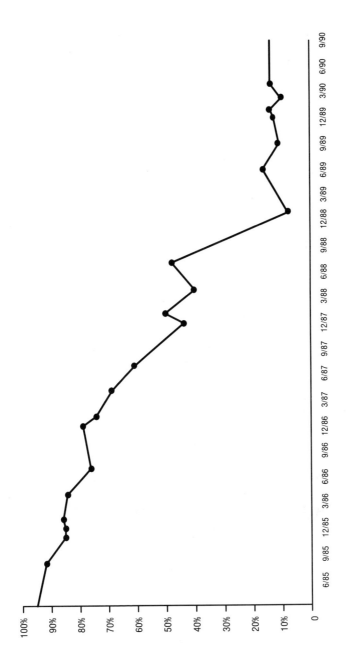

Source: Datum, on the basis of monthly opinion polls.

Figure 6.1   Alan García's popularity curve

within the party. Though lacking García's charisma and political style, he matched García in political ambition. His status in the party was recognised in 1985 when he was made second vice-president of the republic, and – more importantly – prime minister and minister of economy and finance. His powerbase within the party was centred on Trujillo, APRA's heartland, for which he was also a deputy. From 1985 to mid-1987 he was able to use the power of the patronage at his command to construct a well-defined group of collaborators, the so-called '*mocheros*', both in government in Lima, as well as in the provinces.

Alva Castro's resignation from the cabinet in June 1987 and his subsequent successful bid to become president of the House of Deputies made the break between García and Alva Castro explicit. Not only did García publicly criticise Alva Castro's decision to resign, but his active promotion of Rómulo León to stand against him produced an embarrassing setback which even then showed the limits of García's authority over the parliamentary party. Alva Castro beat León by two to one.

The dilemma for Alva Castro was how to channel latent discontent within the party about García's leadership, without overstepping the mark by appearing to seek an open split, and thereby risking the charge of treachery. The difficulty was eased by the fact that Alva Castro did not represent an ideological challenge in the sense that the schism between the reformist '*armandistas*' and the conservative '*andresistas*' in 1979–81 had been both an ideological battle as well as a struggle for power. In one respect Alva Castro's position was quite clear: he wished to succeed Alan García as president of Peru in 1990, and to that end a crucial part of his strategy was to clinch the job of general secretary of the party. Ironically, it was possibly this lack of a clear ideological position in relation to the government which made him seem a less attractive figure to those in the party rank and file most disillusioned by the performance of the García government, in failing to engineer the 'social revolution' to which the party had been historically committed.

The rivalry between García and Alva Castro – at least up until the middle of 1988 – was given more poignancy by the constant rumours that the president himself planned to be the candidate in 1990 and to run for a second consecutive term in office, and that he planned to get a constitutional amendment passed to allow him to do so. However, given the hostility of the opposition in Congress (both on the left and the right) on this point, as well as that of a number of prominent

Apristas, it was always doubtful whether he would ever have got near achieving the two-thirds majority required to change the constitution. By the middle of 1988, the most common speculation was that García himself would try to thwart Alva Castro's ambitions by standing against him for the general secretary's job, the post he had held up until 1985. But the possibility of a narrow win – or even losing – was too big a risk. In the end, García seems to have reconciled himself to Alva Castro becoming the party's general secretary, since, by the time of the September *paquetazo*, APRA's chances of winning the 1990 elections were fading fast. For García it made most sense to let Alva Castro take the responsibility for electoral defeat, and then re-establish his own leadership in time for 1995.

In a longer-term perspective, the much publicised battle of political wits between García and Alva Castro, the subject of seemingly endless comment in the local media was less serious than the growth of discontent and disillusionment among important sectors of the party rank and file. As we have seen, APRA traditionally was a party of divergent social and political interests welded together through the experience of repression and around almost blind loyalty to its founder and leader. Alan García sought to replicate aspects of Haya's leadership, masking the divergences between conservatives and reformers, the old and the young, the party at the centre in Lima and the party in the provinces. García's failure to meet the great expectations vested in him as Haya's 'heir' in 1985, combined with Alva Castro's attempts to build a separate identity within the party, brought tensions closer to the surface.

As a result of Alan García's preference to dissociate himself from the party by surrounding himself by non-party advisers, discontent began to grow within the party, especially those who saw themselves being excluded from the centre of decision-making. In addition, a sense of frustration and animosity grew up out of the lack of interest shown by APRA's main leaders in developing the party's capacity at the local level. A common complaint was that while the leadership justified putting non-Apristas in key posts with the argument that there was a lack of talent within party ranks, little was done to develop such potential talent as existed. Of all the members of the party's National Executive Committee, only the leftward-leaning Carlos Roca (systematically passed over by García for high office) spent time visiting local party groups, and taking interest in their views and activities.[5] Most party leaders, by contrast, seemed more interested in jockeying for position in pursuit of their own personal ambitions.

Throughout 1987 and 1988 a diffuse but increasingly organised and vocal opposition movement started to develop within the party, highly critical of the leadership and demanding a greater degree of respect for local democracy within the party. In the case of the student and youth wings of the party, this frequently took a stridently radical form – a matter of disquiet and sometimes embarrassment among the party hierarchy.[6]

As often as not, one of the main complaints in the provinces was the apparent insensitivity of politicians in Lima to conflicts within the party at the local level, frequently over the way in which corrupt local bosses took over the party machine, using it for their own personal ends. Such voices demanded *moralización* and *democratización*. In particular they demanded that the party nationally ensure that democratic norms were respected at the local level and that local committees were allowed regular re-election to take place. Another common complaint was that local committees had little or no say in the choice of local administrative officials, especially for key posts like prefects, subprefects and the presidents of departmental development corporations. The prefect, for instance, wielded power by virtue of his responsibility for law and order. The development corporations were the route by which most central funds were distributed at the local level, and were thus a major source of patronage. Such officials almost always were appointed from Lima, frequently on the basis of rewarding local party leaders. Often they behaved in a high-handed way giving short shrift to their opponents either within the party itself or outside it. One particular case in which the party machinery was taken over by the local prefect was that of Cuzco. There, a virulent anti-communist *andresista*, Julio Jara Ladrón de Guevara, got himself chosen as prefect and then set about encouraging the development of paramilitary units to fight his enemies. In practice, these were targeted at the left with little distinction being made between Senderistas and militants of the Izquierda Unida. Traditionally, APRA counted for little in Cuzco, as in much of the rest of the south, and such activities created malaise among more progressive members of the party. Many Apristas came to bemoan the fact, perhaps paradoxically, that Haya's authority over the party had not been replaced by a leadership powerful enough to ensure that justice prevailed at the local level.[7] In several instances conflicts led to parallel committees being set up in rival offices in the same locality. Such was the case in Nasca, Camaná, Ayacucho and in the department of Madre de Dios.

At the same, time the process of radicalisation among Peruvian youth, exemplified by Sendero Luminoso, also had its counterpart within APRA. Both Aprista students and the party's youth movement (JAP) came to assume very radical positions. The roots of this radicalisation go back to the 1960s and the emergence of APRA Rebelde. This subsequently became the nucleus of the MIR and involved in guerrilla warfare. More recently, the factors which gave rise to Sendero Luminoso also had an impact on the party. In 1983, for instance, the Confederation of Aprista Students (CUA) held a congress which they chose to name in honour of Edith Lagos, a young Senderista killed by the military, in 1982, in Ayacucho. By 1987 the radicalisation of the youth sections had become widespread. In February 1987, the party leadership had to resort to de-authorising a student party convention in which members of the National Executive Committee were whistled at and heckled, and their suggestions voted down. Also in 1987 militants occupied the party's offices in Trujillo, Huancayo and Cuzco. At the 1987 Aprista Youth congress a sizeable proportion of the delegates wanted to call the congress after Luis de la Puente Uceda, the 1960s guerrilla leader and founder of APRA Rebelde. The youth sections aimed their fire at what they saw as a self-seeking party leadership which was failing to bring about the revolutionary changes promised by Haya de la Torre in his younger days, frustrations which also found an echo among other members of the party rank and file.[8]

The fact that the party leadership, García in particular, took these developments seriously is indicated by an extraordinary address he gave in secret to delegates at the Aprista Youth congress, in Ayacucho, in May 1988. A tape-recording was made of these proceedings which was subsequently transcribed and leaked to the Lima press.[9] In it he praised what he called the '*mística*' and commitment of members of Sendero Luminoso, prepared to lay down their lives for their cause: 'These are people who merit our respect and my personal admiration since they are, like it or not, militants.' He went on to compare it with the 'inertia' and '*comodismo*' within APRA and the 'cowardliness' of the party's congressmen for their vacillation on the bank nationalisation issue. The publication of this text, of course, provided García's critics with welcome ammunition, especially those on the right who contrasted it with his other public statements on the need to repress Sendero more forcefully. It seemed a perfect demonstration of the president's hypocrisy and double standards. But it also served to show the lengths to which García had to go to try to preserve unity in a party in which the cult of leadership had traditionally placed clear limits on what was ideologically acceptable. With the political polarisation of the late 1980s the party came to incorporate die-hard anti-communists at one extreme and quasi-Senderistas at the other.

Yet, though confronted by challenges both from other APRA leaders and from radicalised youth, Alan García also enjoyed important advantages in dealing with his party. Not only did he remain a commanding personality in his own right with charisma and the ability to influence people, but he was the leader of a political movement in which loyalty to the leadership still carried with it a strong political premium, and in which leadership traditionally was vested with almost sacred qualities. García was the leader of a tightly organised movement with, in certain parts of the country at least, a well-structured and devoted popular following. While Haya de la Torre was alive, the mainspring of political action among Apristas was not so much political rationality but faith. The writings of Imelda Vega-Centeno show how important the religious element had been in the development of the party, with the 'jefe' an almost prophet-like figure leading his people to the promised land, and with Haya himself deliberately using religious symbolism to mobilise his political following. The death of Haya, of course, along with the profound social changes of the last thirty years, no doubt served to undermine the political culture which underlay *caudillismo*. But Alan García, with his often studied attempts to repeat the political mannerisms of Haya's rhetoric, did not believe that *caudillismo* had run its course in Peru, particularly in his own party with its reservoir of unquestioning loyalty.

Doubtless the negative impact of economic crisis of 1988 and 1989 took some of the gloss off the 'mystique' of leadership within the party, whittling away at one of APRA's main sources of strength. But even in adversity the party was to retain a motivated and organised mass following, a bedrock of believers, which made it certain that it would continue to be one of Peru's major political parties.

THE LEFT DIVIDED

The First Congress of the Izquierda Unida at Huampaní, in January 1989, was at once the crystallisation of a new level of organisational unity within the left, and the catalyst of a rupture with disastrous political consequences. The hopes raised by the congress were soon dissipated.

As the 3500 or so delegates congregated in this holiday centre just outside Lima, it was with considerable optimism that a new Izquierda Unida was being born, an organisation considerably greater than the sum of its parts, and capable of overcoming the inter-party feuding which had dogged its institutional development since 1980. Moreover, with the fall in APRA's popularity, the left seemed well placed to come out on top in the 1990 presidential elections.

The 1st Congress was the culmination of a lengthy process, beginning in November 1987, in which supporters of the Izquierda Unida, irrespective of party affiliations, registered themselves as members, district by district, province by province throughout the country. To the surprise of even those organising the registration (*carnetización*) exercise, more than 130 000 took the trouble to come forward and claim membership. Though the size of APRA's registered membership is a closely guarded secret, it seems likely that these figures showed the Izquierda Unida to have become Peru's biggest organised political movement. Most of the 3500 delegates to Huampaní had been elected by individual district committees which had all come into existence during the course of 1988. Three-quarters were chosen by local committees, only a quarter nominated by the political parties as such. Indeed the process of forming these committees had contributed greatly to the Izquierda Unida's dynamic at the local level. Conspicuously, there were around three times as many delegates at Huampaní than there had been at the APRA congress a month earlier.

At the same time, the congress at Huampaní led to the apparently irreversible split within the left, the result of years of growing polarisation, which was to lead to rival candidacies in the municipal elections of 1989 and in the presidential and congressional elections of 1990.

On one side of the divide was Convergencia Socialista, an amalgam of the smaller, more moderate parties of the left – notably the PSR of Enrique Bernales – which grouped themselves around the figure of Alfonso Barrantes; on the other was the more radical wing of which the main two parties were the PUM and UNIR. In between, trying to preserve the balance and to maintain unity within the Izquierda Unida, was the Communist Party (PCP). In most of the individual commissions, convened to hammer out a line on such matters as doctrine, organisation, programme and statutes, the two blocs – each labelling the other either '*reformistas*' and '*vanguardistas-militaristas*' – confronted one another with the powerful voice of the Communist Party going one way at one moment, the other the next. When it came to the plenary session, the most conflictive item of all was on the formation of the national executive committee. When the Communists at this point threw their weight behind the radicals, the delegates from Convergencia Socialista, a small minority numerically, walked out. In the feuds that followed each group based their appeal on the legitimacy, or the lack of it, of the committee elected at Huampaní.

As we have seen, the divisions within the Izquierda Unida and the lack of a method of resolving them were nothing new. However, the ideological rift became ever more pronounced as a result of the radicalisation that took place within its ranks from the middle of 1987 onwards. An important landmark in that shift leftwards was the 9th Congress of the Communist Party in May 1987. At the Congress Barrantes was lambasted for his conciliatory line towards APRA in his capacity as president of Izquierda Unida, and for acting with excessive independence of the organised political parties. The 9th Congress also witnessed a clear shift towards a more radical position, a challenge to the party's very orthodox leadership and the replacement of an important number of members of the central committee.[10] Coming on the heels of the CGTP's relatively successful 19 May one-day strike against the government's economic policies (spurred on by the PUM, UNIR and the PCP), it appeared that the *entente* between the government and the left, orchestrated by Barrantes until his resignation as president of Izquierda Unida, was a thing of the past.

The parties of Izquierda Unida were, like everyone else, taken by surprise by García's decision to nationalise the banks. Their response, was to try to go one step further so as not to be outflanked. When García, for instance, argued in favour of the democratisation of credit, the Izquierda Unida found itself obliged to demand 'the democratisation of the economy and society'.[11] The left also demanded that the state should take over the shareholdings the banks held in large industrial companies; that the majority in the banks' boards of directors should consist of representatives from cooperatives, small firms, agricultural producers, workers or representatives of professional *gremios*; and that the previous bank owners should be subject to fines and other financial penalties so as to ensure that the state did not end up paying the compensation for expropriation.

But as the measure began its long drawn-out procedure through Congress, its main defenders were to be found more on the Izquierda Unida than on the APRA benches. Indeed, the reluctance of Apristas in Congress to support the measure gave the left greater leverage than they were accustomed to have in parliament. In the televised Senate debate, the left sought to link their support for the bill to concessions on human rights, in particular the demand (which García refused to accept) that all jailed Izquierda Unida militants be amnestied. But the left did little to mobilise its supporters behind a measure which was not theirs, while Alan García found himself obliged to organise rallies in the *pueblos jóvenes* so as not be outdone by the resurgent right and its new spokesman, the novelist Mario Vargas Llosa. The issue of nationalisation, indeed, put left-wing leaders in a difficult position. They ended up supporting it, but with reservations and (especially the radicals) deeply suspicious about García's original intentions. As public opinion, galvanised by the tactics of the right, turned against what had never been a particularly pressing issue at the popular level, the Izquierda Unida found itself defending a lost cause.

The move away from the consensus-type, conciliatory politics of Alfonso Barrantes towards a more aggressive position against the APRA government became even more explicit with the National Popular Assembly (ANP), in November 1987. This was a three-day event in Villa El Salvador in Lima's southern suburbs. It congregated some 2300 representatives from all types of popular organisations, as well as those from the political parties of the left. The ANP brought together 825 representatives from trade unions, 455 from peasant federations, 310 from urban neighbouring organisations, and 258 from the regionalist *frentes de defensa*. The rest, 501, included intellectuals, professionals, students and party leaders. It was a meeting of leaders from the whole gamut of popular organisations which had grown so in number and in political weight over the previous twenty years. One notable absentee, however, was Alfonso Barrantes.

Politically, the ANP was dominated by the more radical left. The biggest single party presence was that of the PUM, followed by the Communist Party, and in third place – significantly – the Unidad Democrática Popular (UDP). The UDP was a semi-legal party, not part of the Izquierda Unida, and active as the political wing of the MRTA guerrilla movement. The UDP presence at the ANP was greater than, for instance, that of Patria Roja. The tone of the resolutions of the ANP were correspondingly radical. One called for 'development of mass struggles'; another declared that 'popular self-defence as the main element in arming the people'.[12] An opinion poll conducted during the ANP bears witness to these radical sentiments. As much as a quarter of those asked said that the Izquierda Unida should concentrate its efforts in preparing for armed struggle. Though 83 per cent agreed with the notion of participating in elections, only 16 per cent thought that Barrantes should be the candidate.[13]

Despite the wishes of some who took part in the ANP to convert it into an expression of 'direct democracy of the masses' and a new forum for popular democracy, there was little to suggest that the ANP could or would turn into a permanent institution. Its claims to do so, however, created some concern within the CGTP and the Communist Party, which saw it as a potential threat to the CGTP's primacy in the labour movement. In one of the plenary sessions there was a very lively debate over which organizations – the CGTP or the ANP – should organise the general strike which had been agreed upon. In the end, in the face of determined resistance from the Communist Party an agreement was reached, with both organizations doing so, but with the CGTP fixing the date.[14] Also, largely as a result of pressure from the CGTP, the final draft resolution of the ANP carefully avoided endorsing armed struggle. Longer term, it seems that the potential challenge to the CGTP's influence in the labour movement was an important factor in accelerating the process by which a number of independent labour federations were absorbed into the CGTP in the year that followed,[15] even at the cost of diluting the degree of Communist Party control over the CGTP.

The swing to the left within the Izquierda Unida and the growing importance of electoral calculations with a view to 1990 made ideological divides increasingly difficult to disguise. On the surface, there was the contentious issue of whether or not Alfonso Barrantes would be the candidate for the Izquierda Unida in 1990. For parties like the PSR, closely allied with Barrantes, there was no question about it; but for a growing number on the left – notably for the PUM – there was no hiding their antipathy for Barrantes. The issue was, of course, coloured by the argument that if the Izquierda Unida wanted to maximise its electoral support, Barrantes was the candidate likely to get most votes. The corollary of this argument was that if Barrantes stood as candidate, it would improve the chances of other left-wingers being elected to Congress. But, having alienated the Communist Party, as well as the two other major parties of the left, the PUM and UNIR, Barrantes lacked the organisational capacity to mount a strong campaign of his own.

But the vexed issue of the candidacy was more a symptom of deeper divisions within the left over the whole purpose of the Izquierda Unida, irrespective of its strategy and tactics. In the short term, those divisions emerged in terms of the political space the left wished to occupy; and concretely how it was to relate to APRA on the one hand, and to Sendero on the other. Was the mission of the Izquierda Unida, as the radicals argued, to attack the APRA government and to 'unmask' its reformist pretensions? Or was it, as the more moderate groups argued in a meeting of leaders in October 1987, to 'form a broad front against imperialism and the right'? On the issue of Sendero, the supporters of Barrantes – with 1990 in mind – anxious to build confidence in business and military circles, did not hesitate to argue in favour of a hard line against the guerrillas. But for others on the left this was tantamount to a declaration of war on important albeit misguided sectors of the popular movement. The PUM, for instance, with close contact with peasant organisations through the CCP, criticised Sendero but insisted that the discrepancies had to be fought out politically not militarily.

Therefore, the 'schizophrenia' on the left was the impulse, on the one hand, to build alliances towards the right in a bid to bolster the existing forms of parliamentary democracy and to win the 1990 elections by moving towards the centre; and on the other, the impulse to create and defend popular power by occupying a political space to the left, which, increasingly, was being contested by Sendero Lumino-so, the MRTA and their respective political allies.

The division revealed profound differences in interpreting the political mood of the popular movement at a time when the principal forces which seemed to be making the running were at the political extremes: the neo-liberal right of Fredemo and Mario Vargas Llosa, and Sendero. It also showed up very divergent views as to what could be hoped to be achieved, in the light of past experience, through parliamentary politics. With Sendero's armed insurgency affecting most of the country, the issue of armed struggle and its applicability was a matter of more than just theoretical importance. Attacked by the more moderate groups for its '*militarismo*', parties like the PUM refused to reject the need for armed struggle, evolving its own notion of *auto-defensa*, drawing on the experience in Cajamarca with auto-nomous community-based militias or *rondas campesinas*.

It is, however, worthwhile noting that the split was not just along party lines, but that the issues raised produced splits within the main parties of the left. While PUM dissidents, led by Carlos Tapia, had formed a close association with Barrantes, a further much more serious schism occurred at the time of the PUM's 2nd Congress in July 1988, when top leaders including Santiago Pedraglio and Agustín Haya de la Torre broke away from the leadership of Javier Diez Canseco. Similarly, there were splits in Patria Roja, with the so-called 'bol-sheviks' attacking the party leadership for their support for Barrantes, and within the PCR, one of whose leaders Manuel Dammert became a key player in Convergencia Socialista. Even within the traditionally monolithic structure of the Communist Party there was evidence of sharp differences of opinion.

The political gymnastics of the Communist Party at the Congress of the Izquiera Unida,[16] in themselves a reflection of ambiguities and divisions within the party, in no way resolved the difficulties within the left, though they did serve to cement links between the Communist leadership and the radicals within Izquierda Unida. The strategy of Convergencia Socialista, later renamed Acuerdo Socialista, to swing the Communist Party firmly into the Barrantes camp had failed. As leaders of Convergencia sought to question the legitimacy of the national executive committee and its decisions, it increasingly differentiated itself from the major bloc of the Izquierda Unida and made it more difficult for itself to lay claim to its political identity. As 1989 progressed attempts to bridge the divide proved fruitless, particularly as the deadline approached for the Izquierda Unida to define its candidates both for the municipal elections in November 1989 and for the presidential and congressional elections in April 1990. In the event, two factions of the left entered both electoral contests each with their own separate candidates. The Izquierda Unida had finally split apart.

THE RIGHT RESURGENT

The night of 21 August 1987 was a milestone for the Peruvian right. A demonstration against President García's recent bank nationalisation announcement, organised by a new group – the so-called Movimiento Libertad – filled Lima's Plaza San Martín.

It was probably the biggest ever political demonstration by the right in Peru, which is not accustomed to taking its politics out into the streets. And even though many of those who congregated in the Plaza San Martín were conspicuously upper or middle class in social origin, it showed a newly regained capacity to mobilise public opinion. It was all the more striking coming only nine months after the right had done so disappointingly in the previous year's municipal elections. It revealed not just a new political dynamic at work, but also a rejuvenated leadership in the form of Mario Vargas Llosa.

The demonstration was also significant from another point of view. Not only were there present those prominent in the strictly political sphere, but also notable figures from the business élite which had become accustomed to stay out of the political limelight. It represented an important 'coming together' of the political right and the economic élite in defence of private property and private enterprise.

The relationship between the economic élite and the political parties of the right had never been very tight ever since the 1930s. Up until the 1950s the old oligarchy had tended to work through military governments such as those of Sánchez Cerro, Benavides and Odría. The new political parties that emerged in the 1950s, Acción Popular and the Christian Democrats, were more middle-class parties with a reformist ideology. Though the Velasco regime had not been fundamentally antagonistic to the private sector, the social reforms it introduced and its statist ideology rankled with business interests. Even the return of Belaúnde and Acción Popular in 1980 with a much more conservative ideology failed to produce a close working relationship, with business interests resisting the programme of economic liberalisation. And, though financed by some business groups in 1985, Alan García's APRA government was also feared by many for its populist leanings. However, with the drawn-out campaign to stop Alan García's bank nationalisation plans in 1987, there seemed to be a new basis for a resurgent right with much closer ties to the private sector and capable of expanding on the traditionally narrow social base of Acción Popular and the PPC.

The damage done to the personal standing of Alan García by the frustrated nationalisation opened up for the opposition parties, both left and right, a political space just at a moment in the electoral cycle – nearly halfway into García's five-year term of office – when the attention of the political parties would in any case have been turning once again to planning and organising for the next presidential elections. But the right, taking the offensive against what was essentially a left-wing measure, was much better placed to exploit the advantage. It was helped by a unity of purpose and the emergence of Vargas Llosa whose nominal independence of the two main parties made him more acceptable to each, and helped project a broader, less partisan image.

Despite left-wing sympathies in his youth, Vargas Llosa had become a trusted and valued collaborator of Belaúnde during his 1980–5 term of office. He had headed the commission of enquiry into the killing of the eight journalists in Uchuruccay in 1983, whose findings – though widely criticised – had helped Belaúnde avoid a clash with the military by exonerating the army of blame. In 1984 he nearly became

Belaúnde's prime minister, though he turned the offer down. Not only was his international reputation as a writer an asset in enhancing his political prestige within Peru and abroad, but he was also a figure who, in the public mind, was not personally associated too closely with the cut and thrust of the Lima business world.

Perhaps most important of all was Vargas Llosa's role in the reformulation of right-wing ideology in Peru. Since its establishment in 1981 he had been closely associated with the Instituto Libertad y Democracia (ILD), headed by Hernando de Soto. In his preface to Hernando de Soto's *El Otro Sendero*, Vargas Llosa cogently developed the notion that a large and inefficient state was one of the main reasons for Peru's economic backwardness and poverty. The political importance of *El Otro Sendero* was that it entered a terrain which in intellectual circles had previously been virtually a monopoly of the left: the problems of urban poverty and marginality. These were sectors of society to which right-wing parties had to appeal if ever they were to achieve power through elections, as an ever larger percentage of the electorate was both urban and poor. The attack on the state, of course, also went to the heart of left-wing development strategies which had been so influential in Peru since the time of Velasco. As Hernando de Soto put it in September 1987: 'If only the businessmen of the formal sector could unite with those of the informal sector, they could change the direction of the country's history, since they would defend their interests against a state which now prejudices them'.[17] *El Otro Sendero* finds in the 'informal sector' a business culture, stultified by petty state regulations and a suffocating bureaucracy, which would flourish if only the shackles of the state were lifted. The importance of radical change in the government bureaucracy and that of the public sector, coupled to the promotion of free enterprise, are themes which Vargas Llosa came to reiterate repeatedly, trying to challenge the notion that he was a conservative and to portray himself as a 'radical' instead.

The new ideology of the Peruvian right thus took international neo-liberal thinking and sought to adapt it to specifically Peruvian circumstances. In its origins, it represented a departure from the ideology of parties like Acción Popular which sought its inspiration in Peruvian history and which afforded the state an important role in the strategy of economic development. Though perhaps closer to the PPC's 'social Christian' philosophy with its private sector bias, it involved ideas which were very different from those often espoused by a business community mostly nurtured on import substitution and the protected local market. The beauty of *El Otro Sendero* was that it embodied a set of ideas, though arguably erroneous and a-historical[18] which were simple, easily assimilated and grounded in a reality with which any Peruvian who had had dealings with the official bureaucracy could readily identify.

While much of his public utterances relayed the message implicit in *El Otro Sendero*, the main thrust of Vargas Llosa's speech in the Plaza San Martín, and those elsewhere in the weeks that followed, was the more specifically political message that democracy was threatened by an increasingly authoritarian government. The bank nationalisation measure was portrayed as an arbitrary act by an unbalanced and despotic ruler. García became known as '*caballo loco*' (mad horse), and the state of the president's mental health became the subject of widespread political gossip. In opposing the nationalisation as unconstitutional (even after Congress approved the law), the Movimento Libertad tried to appear as the standard-bearer of both political and economic 'liberty'. A key argument was that a country can only be free when its economy is free and when the rights of property are respected.

The row over the nationalisation of the banks represented a golden opportunity for the Peruvian business *gremios*, previously marginalised by Alan García's 'special relationship' with the biggest business groups, to put themselves back on the map. Confiep, the umbrella organisation representing the whole range of private sector organisations and pressure groups, emerged as a much more important political actor after 1987, and played a leading role in mobilising public opinion against the government. The vehemence of the business reaction against the government owed something to the feeling of having been double-crossed by García. Francisco Pardo Mesones, for instance, the banker who became a figurehead by personally defying intervention in the Banco Mercantil, had previously been a sympathiser and collaborator with APRA. Most important, though, in explaining this reaction is the key role played by banks, *financieras* and insurance companies with which, often through cross-shareholdings and family ties, the main firms were intimately linked.[19] The nationalisation move therefore posed a direct threat to the time-honoured practice in Peruvian banking, whereby companies can borrow (often excessively and on preferential terms) from financial institutions controlled by the same families or groups. Moreover, despite the country's recurrent economic problems, banking in Peru remained a highly profitable business, particularly as a result of the 1985–87 economic reactivation when strong performance enabled them to reduce their own bad debts significantly.[20]

The conversion of the protest movement of 1987 into a major force in Peruvian politics was not a straightforward process. Even in 1987 when there was talk and speculation about the formation of an electoral alliance between Acción Popular, the PPC and the Movimiento Libertad plus other interested individuals and groups, the initiative was slow to get off the ground. The Frente Democrático (Fredemo) was formally established between the three main component groups in February 1988, but it was not until well into the second half of 1988 that it emerged as a strong political force, over a year after the nationalisation fracas.

Part of the problem in launching Fredemo was the difficulty of getting two well-established parties and a loose, and unstructured 'movement' like Libertad to agree on the basic political ground-rules. The formation of an alliance such as Fredemo inevitably meant shelving old mutual recriminations, agreeing on a programme of government, and – by no means least contentious – agreeing on formulae to select candidacies for future office.

Initially, Vargas Llosa's Movimiento Libertad was rather closer to Acción Popular than to the PPC. Vargas Llosa's right-hand man in organising the banks protest, for instance, was Miguel Cruchaga, Belaúnde's nephew and a long-time political organiser in Acción Popular. Another close collaborator was Roberto Dañino, a lawyer who had served from 1980 to 1982 as an adviser to Manuel Ulloa. Vargas Llosa also enjoyed good relations with *Expreso*, Ulloa's daily newspaper. The main danger for the PPC was the risk of losing its identity by being swallowed up in what could easily become an enlarged Acción Popular. The PPC was also conscious of ceding too much to a newly established group of independents with relatively little political experience, who lacked a party organisation in the capital or elsewhere. Nor was Acción Popular happy to cede too much to Vargas Llosa or to compromise its historic position as the senior partner in alliance with the PPC. Indeed, for much of the two years following the bank nationalisation there were persistent rumours that Belaúnde himself intended to displace Vargas Llosa as presidential candidate at the eleventh hour, and run for a third term on the basis of his (remarkably) strong standing with public opinion.

These party conflicts became particularly evident when in mid-1989 it came to the difficult process of choosing Fredemo candidates both for the November municipal elections (especially for the most important post of mayor of Lima), the slate for the president and vice-presidents in the 1990 presidential elections, and, of course, the order of candidates in the lists for senators and deputies. It took Vargas Llosa's 'irrevocable' decision not to stand as presidential candidate to force the other members of the Fredemo alliance to sink their differences and reach agreements which avoided the whole project falling apart. The arrangement that emerged in the end involved recognition of Acción Popular as senior partner, but not to such an extent as to alienate the PPC and Movimiento Libertad.[21]

Beyond these battles over quotas of power in a future administration, there were also important disagreements on policy and general outlook. Indeed the tensions within Fredemo over the distribution of power, reminiscent of disputes within Izquierda Unida, were accentuated by lack of unanimity over what Fredemo's priorities should be once it was in office. Such disputes were not new, having surfaced in the past during the previous Belaúnde government, but they were given greater poignancy by Fredemo's uncompromisingly neo-liberal message with its accent on deregulation, market economics and the abandonment of the old import-substitution model in favour of export-led growth.

Ideological differences came out in a number of ways as Fredemo grew in popularity during 1988 and 1989, emerging as front runner for the 1990 elections in the opinion polls. One contentious issue was the role of the state. Belaúnde and the Acción Popular party faithful made it clear at the party's congress in April 1989 that they did not believe that Peru was prepared for a sudden or radical weakening of the state apparatus. Vargas Llosa subsequently modified his public discourse and argued the need for an 'efficient' state. Closely connected with the role of the state, Fredemo embodied differences of opinion over such issues as the use of subsidies to the private sector. While Vargas Llosa argued that subsidies rendered the producer inefficient, business interests clearly had much to lose if the various subsidies extended to producers were to be suddenly removed. Another connected issue was that of trade protection on which many Peruvian industrialists depended, but which ran counter to the tenets of liberalisation.[22] This issue came to the surface during 1989 when Hernando de Soto raised the polemic of the inefficiency of importing expensive inputs to produce tyres in Peru, when arguably it would be much cheaper (and to the direct benefit of the Peruvian consumer) if tyres were imported direct from the United States. A fourth divisive issue was more in the realm of cultural than economic ideology. This was the divide between the more nationalist vision of some sectors of the right and the new 'internationalist' perspective of the neo-liberals. This came to light, for instance, as a result of comments made by Vargas Llosa in a French newspaper that Peru should aspire to become more like a European country.

Despite such rivalries and different visions of Peru and its future, the pressures towards unity of action on the right – unlike the left – were stronger than those leading towards fragmentation. And, as Fredemo's position in the opinion polls improved to the detriment of its rivals during the course of 1989 – as the prospect of winning power in 1990 became clearer – the factors pushing towards unity tended to predominate.

The electoral chances of Fredemo depended crucially on the ability to appeal not just to the committed voter but to a much wider public. The bedrock of Fredemo's support was the middle and upper class in urban areas, the traditional constituency of Acción Popular and especially the PPC. A Fredemo victory could virtually be taken for granted in middle-class districts of Lima like Lince, Jesús María and Pueblo Libre, and the more elegant residential districts of San Isidro, San Borja, Miraflores and La Molina. But to win Fredemo had to swing over large sectors of the electorate which voted for APRA or the left in 1985: it had to win over both the rural and urban poor.

This, in part, turned on Fredemo's own capacity in building party organisation, getting its ideological message across and projecting the image of its candidate. Fredemo started off with a great disadvantage in terms of party organisation. The only party within Fredemo with a tight organisation was the PPC, but it was strong only in Lima, and then mainly in the sort of districts mentioned above. Party organisation in Acción Popular was more diffuse. In the two years in which it was actively campaigning – years of unprecedented hardship among the poor – Fredemo was able to widen the scope of its political organisation, benefiting to some extent from the weakness of its rivals in APRA and on the left. Despite the disadvantage of an upper-class image, it proved capable of making inroads in poor districts. It put its economic weight, for example, behind 'self-help' construction campaigns in the *pueblos jovenes* of Lima, sponsoring women's organisations and food distribution programmes.[23]

Perhaps more important in projecting its presence, Fredemo's access to the media provided a crucial advantage over the other parties, in particular the television. Even a year before the presidential elections there was a clear bias on most television stations towards Vargas Llosa and Fredemo. The extension of access to television, as in other Latin American countries, has effectively changed some of the rules of the game in electioneering. In 1989, there were estimated to be just under a million TV sets in Lima, with four and a half million people (out of a total of around six million) living in homes with televisions. About the same number of people outside Lima watch television, making a combined viewing public of around 9 million out of a total population of around 21 million. The most important TV channel was Channel 5, Panamericana, the only private station with a truly national network.[24] In 1985, García had benefited from a basically pro-APRA stance at Panamericana – one of its co-directors, Héctor Delgado Parker, was García's close friend and godfather to his daughter. But in the 1989-90 election campaign there was little hiding Channel 5's pro-Fredemo sympathies. Among newspapers, *Expreso*, one of Peru's best-selling papers from 1987 onwards, became the mouthpiece of Fredemo thinking. This growing importance of the media in electioneering was particularly important for a candidate like Vargas Llosa who did not slot so naturally into traditional tub-thumping politics with its street rallies, razzmatazz and populist imagery. Indeed, one of Vargas Llosa's defects – one that his campaign tried to correct – was the image of an intellectual removed from the realities of politics and the everyday problems facing ordinary people.

But if the advances made by Fredemo in the opinion polls owed something to its own campaigning efforts, they also depended in large measure on peculiarly favourable political circumstances. The scale of the economic crisis was such that it did not lead most people to favour further adventures in radical politics. On the contrary, it tended to favour conservatism. The size of the crisis and its social cost were also damaging to APRA and the left-wing parties. For APRA it was impossible to absolve itself from responsibility for what had gone wrong. Unlike Acción Popular in 1985 there were no natural disasters to blame, such as those of 1983. Nor could foreign bankers be held responsible. APRA's presidential candidate, Luis Alva Castro, could not entirely dissociate himself from the economic difficulties encountered from 1988 onwards. But the widespread public identification that the García government was a left-wing government which had failed, made it extraordinarily difficult for the parties and groupings further to the left to present the public with a political message that was convincing or different.

Fredemo, therefore, had much more scope to articulate disillusionment with the APRA government than the left. At the same time, the evident disunity on the left, disorientation in terms of programme and policy, and the lack of decisive leadership, all helped to reinforce that advantage. Once it had sorted out its own internal problems (or at least agreed to shelve the differences) Fredemo appeared to be on a winning ticket, united behind a candidate with a clear message, with strong financial backing and support from much of the media. For a full year before the 1990 election Fredemo was well ahead of its rivals in the opinion polls, making its leaders confident, perhaps over-confident, that they would succeed APRA in government. In the event, however, it was not to be so easy or straightforward.

THE FUJIMORI PHENOMENON

The seven days before the first round of presidential elections, on 8 April 1990, proved a disconcerting time for political analysts and pundits in Peru. By this time the previously unthinkable was beginning to be perceived. A complete political outsider, a virtual unknown without a proper party or a programme, looked like overtaking both APRA and the Izquierda Unida to challenge Fredemo and Mario Vargas Llosa in a second round. Up to two or three weeks before the first round, the Fujimori 'phenomenon' had gone virtually undetected. It must be one of the very few instances in which a serious electoral candidate – subsequently a president – went unnoticed by the opinion polls until the very last minute.[25] But in those two weeks the name of Alberto Fujimori and that of his campaign organisation, Cambio-90, spread like wildfire, reflecting an extraordinary political vacuum. A new political star was born.

Up until the last two weeks most commentators assumed that APRA's candidate, Luis Alva Castro, would be the person to go forward to face almost certain defeat from Vargas Llosa in a second round. At the beginning of the electoral campaign, Vargas Llosa had been pinning his hopes on getting an absolute majority and thereby winning on the first round. However, the chances of this happening started to fade after February 1990 when his lead in the polls started to slip.

One of the first people to take full cognisance of the potential of Fujimori to upset Fredemo's campaign strategy was Alan García. With his finger as usual on the political pulse, García's own polling contractors were picking up Fujimori's growing popularity, especially among lower income groups both in Lima and elsewhere. According to one of García's closest political advisers, Fujimori had already over-taken APRA by the last week in March. García may not have been altogether displeased by the prospect of Alva Castro's relatively poor performance. Indeed, many saw the hand of the president at work in the way in which a new daily newspaper, *Páginas Libres*, with apparently close links to the palace, took up the Fujimori story during the last week, running it on its front page every day.

But the scale of the Fujimori vote on 8 April took everyone by surprise. Excluding null and void votes, he got 24 per cent of the vote to Vargas Llosa's 29 per cent. In contrast, APRA got 20 per cent and the left – its two factions combined – a meagre 11 per cent. Though he came first, the results were a humiliating blow for Vargas Llosa, from which he was unable to recover fully in the second round. Not only had he failed to get anywhere near his '50 per cent-plus-one' objective, but also he was suddenly faced by an opponent who could almost automatically count on support from APRA and the left to form a broad anti-Fredemo coalition. The 'unbeatable' Fredemo bandwagon, which had started to roll two years earlier, and which had seemed unstoppable, was suddenly halted in its tracks.

How do we explain the emergence of this outsider, who managed to swing nearly a quarter of the vote behind him in the first round, and nearly 60 per cent in the second? The result was more the consequence of very exceptional political circumstances than of Fujimori's own qualities, strong though these may have been. No one in Cambio-90 entered the election thinking that their representatives would form the second biggest block in the new Congress or that their leader would be Peru's next president. In fact Fujimori had considerable difficulty in persuading people to run with him.[26] What, therefore, were the circumstances?

In first place, Mario Vargas Llosa – despite having supposedly expert advice from the US marketing agency Sawyer and Miller – proved to be remarkably inept politically. His first major blunder was to announce in December the details of the short-term economic strategy he would employ on reaching office. The Fredemo 'shock treatment', which made no attempt to disguise its expected recessionary impact or its social cost, was hardly welcome news – even for the business groups which supported the Fredemo ticket. In the build up to the elections Fredemo's opponents concentrated their fire on the proffered 'shock' and its social consequences. The anti-Fredemo press, for instance, dwelt in lurid detail on the ransacking of Brazilian supermarkets in Rio de Janeiro in the wake of the Collor Plan (announced on 16 March), portraying it as the shape of things to come in Peru if Vargas Llosa won the elections. Fredemo's announcement of an emergency social programme to help the poorest survive the 'shock' did little to repair the political damage.

A second major error in the campaign was to give free rein to Fredemo's candidates for Congress to develop their own political campaigns. Not only did this produce a massive and uncontrolled propaganda war between candidates, further confusing Fredemo's political message, but it confirmed the widespread suspicion in an extremely visible way that Fredemo was little more than the political instrument of Peru's socio-economic élite, anxious to regain the political influence it had lost in 1985. This impression severely under- mined Vargas Llosa in his attempt to build broadly based electoral support, especially among the urban poor. Vargas Llosa's own political style did not help win the sympathy of the common voter. Coming across as self-satisfied and at times arrogant, he failed to generate the kind of support achieved by Alan García in 1985, whose charisma attracted the independent voter to the APRA cause.

As we have seen, Fredemo was able to make the political running from 1987 onwards, reflecting the collapse in APRA's popularity and the debilitating effects of divisions within the left.

However, Fredemo's advance was based neither on taking up popular issues (like opposition to the return to orthodoxy in economic policy), nor on a strong organised presence in the popular movement. The lack of such organisation was a crucial weakness, but one which Fredemo's campaign organisers hoped would not matter given the weakness of the political parties standing against it. The public which Fredemo had hoped to win over to its side was primarily the urban informal sector, swollen in numbers as a result of the 1988–9 recession, which was one of the less organised sectors politically. But the massive propaganda campaign was not complemented by a strong organisa- tional presence among the mass of the population, especially outside Lima. Indeed the expense of the advertising *blitz* at a time of such widespread popular suffering may even have had a perverse effect, alienating a large number of potential voters.

Another key element in the political situation in 1990 was the weakness of both APRA and the left. The drop in APRA's popularity coincided with the return to recession in 1988. Despite the attempts to revive the economy in 1989 and the relaunch of public works programmes halted for lack of cash in 1987 and 1988, APRA fought the 1990 elections with obvious disadvantages. Its bid was not helped by the candidacy of Alva Castro, who lacked García's political flair. Still, it was remarkable that APRA got nearly 20 per cent of the vote in the first round, confirming that it was a party with lasting levels of discipline and internal organisation and with a strong loyal following, especially in the north.[27]

For the left the 1990 election results were a humiliating setback. Compared with 25 per cent of the vote in 1985 and 30 per cent in the 1986 municipal elections, the 11 per cent it received in 1990 was its lowest level since the Izquierda Unida came into existence in 1980. The poverty of the left-wing vote was partly due to its failure to distinguish itself as a credible alternative to the APRA government since 1985, and to give leadership to popular resentment against the government from 1988 onwards. The splitting of the Izquierda Unida in 1989, had a devastating effect in further undermining public confidence in the left as a credible alternative to APRA and the right. Even militants of the Izquierda Unida felt disheartened and disoriented by the split in the leadership. In both the municipal elections and subsequently in the first round, the splinter group Acuerdo Socialista (later renamed Izquierda Socialista) got only a small vote compared with the Izquierda Unida itself, but the left-wing vote as a whole was much reduced.

In 1990, therefore, there was a sort of political vacuum in which it was possible for a person from outside the traditional political parties and groupings to enter and win. The success of Ricardo Belmont in the elections for mayor of Lima, in November 1989, was a pointer to the potential for an 'independent' candidate. Belmont, a well-known television personality and owner of one of Lima's more recently established television channels, won 45 per cent of the vote against candidates from all the main political groupings, including Fredemo. Basing his campaign on the need to 'depoliticise' municipal government, his victory was also paralleled by that of other 'independents' in other cities, notably in Arequipa and Tacna. In fact this dissatisfaction with traditional parties and their leaders had been noticed well before Belmont entered politics. It was precisely this that had favoured the emergence of that other 'independent', non-professional politician, Mario Vargas Llosa, in 1987. The problem with Vargas Llosa was that two and a half years later he had already become a figure of the political establishment. By 1990, there was a crisis in the representativeness of the established political parties; a rejection of what they offered by way of alternatives and a search for new political messages and figures; there was a deep fatigue with the *políticos de siempre*.

It was in such circumstances that Fujimori entered the scene. Who voted for Fujimori and why? Cambio-90 had its roots in the world of the small-scale business, largely in the informal sector of the economy. Despite Hernando de Soto's appeals for unity among entrepreneurs, formal and informal, this was a world far removed from that of the country's business élite. Indeed, the social groups to which Cambio-90 initially sought to appeal were *microempresarios* whose economic and social advance into the fully fledged private sector seemed to be blocked more by social, cultural and even ethnic barriers than by de Soto's interventionist state. Also, interestingly, Cambio-90 became a political expression of the protestant and evangelical churches. As in other countries of Latin America, these churches had grown rapidly in terms of adherents in Peru in the 1970s and 1980s both in rural and urban areas. Cambio-90 therefore articulated a sort of Peruvian non-conformism.

It is difficult to estimate the size of the class of informal *microempresarios* in relation to the total economically active work-force with any precision, but according to most estimates it accounts for between 35 per cent and half. Fernando Villarán, an expert on the *microempresa* as well as adviser to Fujimori in the campaign, believes that it is a sector which politically has always been underestimated by both political analysts in Peru and by the political parties themselves.[28] Certainly it is a social sector whose political preferences have not been the subject of extensive or systematic study. While it is clear that in the 1983 and 1986 municipal elections the Izquierda Unida drew support from the informal sector and from the *pueblos jovenes*, it also appears as a sector whose political preferences tended to be highly volatile. Though the available evidence at the time of writing was not well systematised, it seems that Fujimori drew a substantial amount of his support from the world of the informal worker, both in Lima and elsewhere.[29] The main reason for this appears to be the lack of alternatives. On the right, Fredemo came over as apologist for another even bigger recessionary shock and as representative of an élite that was socially and ethnically distinct. The left, at the same time, was divided and APRA, inevitably, stood for 'more of the same'.

Cambio-90's support outside Lima was a particularly notable feature of his campaign. In fact Fujimori enjoyed more support in the provinces than in Lima, often in places where his Cambio-90 had little or no organisation and where the candidate had never even visited during the campaign. In Tacna, Cambio-90 topped the poll with 47 per cent of the vote, even though Fujimori had to call off his only scheduled public meeting there. He did exceptionally well in a number of other departments in the south.[30] Fujimori seems to have managed to articulate the spirit of regionalism and the identification of Fredemo and Vargas Llosa not just with the élite but with Lima. The great majority of the voters cannot have known much about who they were voting for, but only that Fujimori was the man to stop Vargas Llosa.

The point at which Cambio-90 reached its 'take-off' stage – at which tactical voting took over is hard to gauge. Fujimori's success in the first round undoubtedly hinged on Cambio-90's breaking through an initial credibility barrier. Once the possibility of his getting into the second round turned into a probability during those two crucial weeks before voting on 8 April then Fujimori emerged as the only candidate capable of creating a coalition to rob Fredemo of victory. As well as attracting the floating voter, the size of Fujimori's vote was the result of Apristas and supporters of the left switching their preferences for tactial reasons to Cambio-90. The migration of left-wing supporters appears particularly significant, given Fujimori's strong support in formerly left-wing strongholds, especially in Lima and the south. In the second round nearly all Apristas gave Fujimori their backing, as well as those who had voted for the two left candidates in the first round. As such, Fujimori, like García in 1985, came to represent a majority of Peruvians. Unlike García, though, he had no real political party behind him.

7 Spiral of Violence

SOCIAL VIOLENCE

The last three years of the García government saw a notable increase in the threshold of violence, which the government, the police, the military and even the formally constituted political parties were ill-equipped to detain. Violence was both political and social, afflicting all parts of the country both urban and rural, and creating a climate of fear not just among the wealthy and the middle class, but also among wide sectors of the poor.

The most overt form of violence was the struggle between guerrillas and the security forces. In 1987 and 1988 in particular, Sendero Luminoso expanded its sphere of influence considerably, while other guerrilla organisations like the MRTA also initiated armed actions. These guerrilla groups, along with the *narcotraficantes*, managed to establish their authority over important areas of the country, areas where effectively the writ of the Peruvian government no longer ran, or where at least its control was only intermittent. In response, counter-insurgency operations became more extensive with new Emergency Zones being declared and a growing number of provinces being placed under direct military jurisdiction. In their attempt to quash the insurgents, the military resorted increasingly to forming armed para-militaries and 'civil defence' patrols. In the cities, too, paramilitary death squads began to operate for the first time, threatening not just guerrilla sympathisers, but community leaders, political figures (especially on the left), human rights activists and journalists (Table 7.1).

This climate of violence was also enhanced by social as well as explicitly political forms of violence and was especially evident in the cities, though it affected rural life too. The distinction lies more in the motives behind acts of violence rather than the form they took: kidnappings and killings, for instance, took place for both political and economic reasons. Criminal violence, especially armed assault and robbery, became particularly common as a result of the fall in living standards in the late 1980s. On the one hand, the economic crisis accentuated the inequalities in Peruvian society, increased the degree of

Table 7.1   Political violence (number of deaths, 1985–9)

	1980–4 (annual average)	1985	1986	1987	1988	1989
Police	29	42	90	95	110	187
Military	7	16	23	34	105	95
Local authorities	15	20	44	37	79	116
Civilians	493	439	385	444	665	1017
Others	—	—	—	1	—	1
Presumed subversives	627	627	403	234	220	553
Total	1171	1144	945	845	1179	1969

Source: Interior Ministry/DESCO, in *Que Hacer* No 64, May-June 1990.
According to this estimate, there were a total of 12 055 deaths between 1980 and 1990.

social dislocation, and contributed to ever greater economic frustration especially among the young. On the other hand, it weakened the capacity of the state to respond effectively, and by increasing the level of corruption in public life, it further eroded public confidence in politicians, bureaucrats and those charged with public order.

It was in this grim situation, unmitigated by the prospect of better things to come, that some Peruvian political analysts came round to contemplating the possibility of the country being torn apart in bloody civil conflict, or atomised into a collection of violent local and regional struggles akin to those of the Lebanon.[1]

The prevalence of social and political unrest during these years prompted a good deal of study as to the origins of violent behaviour, its characteristics and likely future directions. A number of writers sought to emphasise the links between acts of violence and the 'structure of violence' arising from the long historical tradition of racial, economic and social inequality and discrimination. Probably the most influential study was the work of a Special Commission of the Senate, chaired by Senator Enrique Bernales.[2] The Bernales Report sought to widen the terms of reference in the debate over violence at the official level by going beyond the issues of insurgency, counter-insurgency and human rights, by pointing to the social conditions generating acts of violence of all types. As well as identifying the causes

of violence in poverty, social margination and discrimination, it sought
to highlight how these affected specific social groups such as youth,
groups in which Sendero had had conspicuous success in cultivating
support.

In describing the problem of growing violence in contemporary
Peru, the report paid attention to the issue of violent crime, especially
in the cities. According to its findings, in 1987 the city dweller was
three times more likely to be the victim of robbery than the inhabitant
of rural areas; and twice as likely to be wounded or killed. The
Commission was mindful of the inadequacy of official statistics on
violent crime, since many of those affected probably saw little point in
reporting the matter to the police; and the figures almost certainty do
not do justice to the problem of crime in rural areas. Still, the official
figures offer a comparative yardstick, albeit an imperfect one, and
point to a sharp increase in reported criminal behaviour during the
1980s. They also suggest that some correlation existed between
criminal behaviour and variations in the economic cycle. Table 7.2
sets out the total number of recorded crimes in relation to the growth
in population, and the variation from year to year.

The prevalence of fear also arose from the common perception that
the authorities no longer acted as effective guarantors of law and order
or personal security. On the one hand, there was the problem of
corruption in the police force and the extent of abusive and arbitrary
behaviour towards the public. This was also true of the military in
those parts of the country under military jurisdiction. In these areas
there was even less room for any investigation into excesses, unless
specific cases were taken up at the highest level by the Congress. Both
in the Emergency Zones and elsewhere public confidence in the
authorities' ability to enforce justice sunk to new lows.

On the other hand, there were problems which arose from the
deficiencies of the judicial system itself. The long delays in hearing
cases meant that it could often take years for them to be dealt with by
the courts, and for those wrongfully arrested on terrorist charges to
establish their innocence. Intimidation of judges became common, as
did the use of bribery to secure favourable judgements. Meanwhile, it
sometimes proved impossible to get convictions for known Senderistas
on account of legal loopholes. A notable case of this was that of
Osman Morote – reputedly number two after Abimael Guzmán in
Sendero Luminoso – who was aquitted of charges against him in July
1988. Though Morote continued in prison on other charges, such
judgements eroded confidence in the legal system, further convinced

Table 7.2   Criminality: crimes reported to the Guardia Civil, 1974–88

Year	Number of crimes	Crimes per 100 inhabitants	Annual variation %
1974	48 494	3.27	– 0.26
1975	50 517	3.32	4.17
1976	64 185	4.12	27.06
1977	75 552	4.73	17.71
1978	76 097	4.65	0.72
1979	88 784	5.29	16.67
.980	123 230	7.13	38.80
1981	117 383	6.61	– 4.74
1982	113 755	6.24	– 3.09
1983	118 529	6.34	4.20
1984	134 292	7.00	13.30
1985	152 561	7.75	13.60
1986	158 619	7.85	3.97
1987	156 060	7.53	– 1.61
1988	172 121	8.10	10.29

Figures based on data from the National Statistics Institute (INE). The crimes include crimes against the person, those against property, immorality, crimes within the family and against public order.
Source: Comisión Especial del Senado, *Violencia y Pacificación*. DESCO/ Comisión Andina de Juristas, Lima, 1989.

the anti-terrorist police of the need to use torture to extract confessions, and prompted the police to demand further exceptional powers to deal with terrorist cases.

The recommendations of Senator Bernales' commission on violence were reminiscent of the type of policies envisaged by the García government at the outset, but which – largely under pressure from the military – were swiftly abandoned. The commission called for the establishment of a national peace accord; the adoption of an 'integrated' approach to counter-insurgency which paid attention to economic, social and cultural margination in places like Ayacucho; and for full respect for human rights. It also stressed the need for judicial and educational reform, special employment programmes for youth, more social provision for the family, better access to family planning, greater incentives for coca substitution, the encouragement of democratic and popular organisation as the best bulwark against Sendero, and for steps to be taken to reduce corruption in the state.

But in the context of the political and economic crisis at the beginning of 1989 when the report was published, a time when the APRA government was struggling for its own survival, such long-term, overarching objectives seemed little more than high-minded, good intentions, with little immediate applicability.

SENDERO ON THE MARCH

On Sunday 24 July 1988, *El Diario*, the pro-Sendero Lima newspaper published what it called 'the interview of the century'. In forty-eight pages it reproduced a twelve-hour interview which purported to be with Abimael Guzmán, 'President Gonzalo', from his hideaway in a remote part of the country some eighteen hours distant from Lima.[3] In it Guzmán talked widely about his conception of the party, the popular war, military strategy and Sendero's place in the world struggle towards socialist revolution. Assuming it was indeed Guzmán talking, it was the first time he had made any sort of public pronouncement since Sendero began its armed offensive. And, whether or not they were his words, the interview represented a milestone in Sendero's shift towards a more communicative style of politics, pitching its appeal to a wider urban public. For the first time 'Gonzalo thought' (*Pensamiento Gonzalo*) was given a truly massive diffusion, producing perhaps rather more interest and comment than Alan García's annual Independence Day speech to Congress four days later.

One of the key problems facing Sendero in its development was to establish the means of making a transition from a tight-knit, hermetic and highly clandestine organisation to one capable of capturing and directing mass support. By the middle of 1986 there was evidently a growing discussion going on within Sendero as to how this was to proceed. Fragmentary evidence of this is to be found in the minutes of Sendero meetings captured by the security forces and discussed in the Lima press.[4] The reappearance of *El Diario* (previously a paper which supported the Izquierda Unida) as an unmistakably pro-Senderista paper in the second half of 1986 was also indicative; so too was the marked increase in Sendero's political activity in university circles in Lima, especially in San Marcos University. Those within Sendero who favoured a more open approach and saw the need to develop an urban as well as a rural presence seemed to have won the day. The whole issue caused considerable upset within Sendero: it was one of the key points of discussion at the party's 4th National Conference in the middle of 1986 which took place shortly after the massacre in the Lima jails. Adopting a more communicative style, however, did not mean any change in Sendero's refusal to collaborate with other groups on the left. Indeed one of the points of issue within Sendero at this time was official condemnation of members of the Metropolitan Lima Committee for their supposedly 'Cubanist' tendencies – in other words, an overfriendly attitude towards the rival MRTA.

Sendero's strategic thinking was revealed in a 110-page document published in August 1986, called 'Develop the Popular War Serving the World Revolution'. In it Sendero pointed clearly to the need to develop urban work as a necessary complement to the rural guerrilla movement, even though the latter would continue as the main theatre of armed action. It underlined the need to 'give a great deal of attention to the workers' movement in the building of the (Senderista) army; and to bear in mind the huge number of (potential) combatants for the war'. The document emphasises the strategic importance of Lima 'for its role as the capital, its concentration of population and its having the majority of the Peruvian proletariat as well as large numbers of poor people in the suburbs and shanty towns'. The document also admits the shortcomings of Sendero's own popular organisation or support groups, which worked as an adjunct to the party and its army, but which had failed up to this point to make inroads into the cities.

This 'opening up', this development of a more communicative political style, coupled to a new concentration on urban work, may have arisen from looking afresh at the dwindling importance of the rural peasantry as part of the workforce. It may also reflect concern about the development of the MRTA's potential as an alternative pole of attraction, with its finely tuned sense of publicity and propaganda, its nationalist ideology and its less esoteric choice of political symbols. At the same time, the decision to work in an urban context also posed problems in terms of Sendero's own security. It made successful infiltration more likely.[5] So as to reduce any threat from this quarter, what seems to have been decided was that a growing separation was required between the Senderista 'old guard' and the party as such on the one hand, and those who formed part of the various ancillary support and promotion organisations on the other. The party itself was to remain wholly underground at the centre of a system of 'concentric' circles of differing degrees of clandestinity.

Sendero's 1st Congress, held sometime in the middle of 1988, appears to have set the seal in confirming the strategy to be followed. Documents which came to light in the course of 1987 saw the Congress as 'laying the bases for the conquest of power', and resolving discrepancies which had cropped up in the past over strategy. The exact timing of the Congress was supposed to coincide with the climax of the second campaign within the Great Plan to Develop Bases. Coming in the wake of the 1st Congress, Abimael Guzmán's interview in *El Diario* takes on added significance as a statement of the 'true' position of the party.

In terms of concrete activity, Sendero signalled its intention to involve itself in urban politics at the time of the first CGTP-sponsored national one-day strike against the APRA government in January 1987. As scuffles broke out between Senderista supporters and those of the Izquierda Unida at a demonstration in Lima's Plaza Dos de Mayo outside the CGTP headquarters, the former lobbed sticks of dynamite at their adversaries. The veteran Communist Party leader, Jorge del Prado, only narrowly escaped serious injury.

Following up this appearance, Sendero began to make concerted efforts during the rest of 1987 to infiltrate and take over labour unions in some of the large factories in the east of the city along the Carretera Central, and to a lesser extent along the Avenida Argentina in the centre. Typically, the Senderistas' strategy was to get a foothold in a specific union by winning over a few *dirigentes* and thus to make their presence felt in the union's assembly. While their aggressive attitude and threats of violence frightened off other leaders at the plant level, making it easier for them to take over the union by default, what Sendero tended to inherit was just the shell of the union. In most cases, though acting in the name of the union and that of the '*Comité de lucha*' of the area concerned, Sendero conspicuously failed to win over most workers to its point of view. Indeed their refusal to entertain any sort of dialogue with employers rendered normal collective bargaining largely redundant. Meanwhile, their radicalism, their lack of success in conducting factory occupations (where such were attempted) and the youth and lack of experience of most of their cadres meant that they tended to be out of step with most grass roots union members. Despite the severity of the recession of 1988 and 1989, Sendero failed to gain a genuine foothold in the urban factory-based labour movement.[6]

The tactic that became a hallmark of Sendero's attempts to mobilise in urban areas was the *paro armado*, the strike called under threat of violence against those who ignored it. Though first applied in Ayacucho, by 1987 and 1988 Sendero began to declare *paros armados* in other urban centres: Huancayo, Huancavelica, Pasco,

Huánuco and in Lima itself. The success of the *paro armado* depended crucially on the degree of credibility in the threat of violence: it proved easier for Sendero to produce such stoppages in smaller provincial towns than in Lima. In the capital, the *paro armado* depended mainly on intimidating bus drivers into staying at home for fear of their lives or the security of their vehicles, thus making it impossible for others to get to work. But as it evolved, the *paro armado* became increasingly significant for Sendero as a tactic in the cities, in that it put the onus on the security forces to protect the lives and property of very large numbers of people.

Also with the *paro armado*, as with the takeover of factories, selective assassinations and sabotage of industrial plant, Sendero further distinguished itself from the rest of the left for its military approach to politics and the use of terror for political purposes. It proved itself contemptuous of all other sorts of political organisation and determined physically to eliminate groups, institutions and parties which stood in the way of its own relationship with the people. The sublimation of political to military considerations is indicated by the statement in the Bases for Discussion (*Bases de Discusión*) document issued in September 1987. The document, a rallying call for Sendero's 1st Congress, argued that strikes should be developed 'like a guerrilla war' serving to 'educate' those involved. Strikes should go hand in hand with 'armed actions', in that they gave them 'enhanced quality'. Sendero also claimed that those involved in 'mass work' in urban areas would be members of the guerrilla army. So, despite the emphasis placed on the need to develop 'mass work' in the urban context, the methods which Sendero chose to use to conduct its urban politics tended to be as uncompromisingly authoritarian as its earlier practice in rural areas. The result was that its degree of acceptance, particularly among urban workers in Lima and elsewhere, tended to be limited.

In the rural sphere, apart from its hold on the Alto Huallaga, the most important development during the second half of the García administration was the consolidation of Sendero's strength in the central *sierra*: in Pasco and, of particular importance, in Junín. Some of the initial groundwork in Junín had been the work of Osman Morote, who developed Sendero's presence among university and secondary school students in Huancayo and elsewhere between 1984 and 1986.

The central *sierra* was potentially of much greater strategic importance than Ayacucho. It was an important source of Lima's food supply and the route by which food from the *ceja de selva* had to pass.

It was the source of most of Lima's electricity supply from the Mantaro river hydroelectric system. The mines of the central *sierra* also provided Peru with the bulk of its mineral exports, which came mostly from the large state company, Centromin. Finally, it provided a key link in any strategy to encircle Lima.[7]

Apart from constant attacks on the electricity supply grid by blowing up pylons – a feature of Sendero's activities from as early as 1980 and 1981 – the main emphasis of Sendero's activities in Junín and Pasco by 1988 and 1989 were twofold: the development of an organised presence in rural areas and attempts to move in on the mining camps.

The development of Sendero's presence in rural areas of the Mantaro Valley is illustrative of its tactics elsewhere. From 1986 onwards Senderistas started appearing with greater regularity in Junín, spreading in from the neighbouring department of Huancavelica. They moved in on an area plagued, like Puno in the south, by the unresolved problems arising from the 1970s agrarian reform. The large units of landholding created under the agrarian reform, the SAIS, failed to satisfy the needs of most peasant communities. They were also superimposed on old conflicts between the communities and the old *haciendas*. These conflicts had given rise to many bloody skirmishes in the past. One of the biggest SAIS created under the agrarian reform was the SAIS Cahuide (270 000 hectares in area). Communities in its sphere of influence had long been pushing for the SAIS to be restructured so as to benefit them, but maintaining its technical advances and its position in the market as an important supplier of dairy products and wool to Lima. In doing so they were supported by the CCP, with its close ties to the Izquierda Unida and to the PUM. Sendero, however, sought to destroy the SAIS. In January 1989, it moved in on and destroyed Laive, one of the biggest agroindustrial plants in the *sierra*, setting loose or killing its specially bred Holstein cattle, burning down the buildings and smashing machinery.

In the surrounding communities Sendero established its presence by getting rid of unpopular local officials, cracking down on cattle rustlers and imposing its strong moral discipline on community life. To all intents and purposes the communities formed part of Sendero's 'new republic', their members subjects of a highly authoritarian but not altogether malevolent rule. Once again, as in Ayacucho earlier, what was to create bitter friction was Sendero's attempt to force the communities to revert to subsistence agriculture and to stop them selling their produce in local markets. Sendero also failed to resolve intercommunual rivalries. It was these problems which prompted the *comuneros* of one community, Chongos Alto, in April 1989 to seize three known Senderistas and to hand them over to the police in Huancayo. But the police failed to see what was at stake. Considering it a simple conflict between communities, they released the Senderistas. Within a few days Sendero was back in Chongos Alto, assassinating twelve village leaders in reprisal. The Chongos Alto episode serves to reinforce the point that peasant communities were prepared to accept, even welcome, Sendero in that Sendero brought tangible benefits. In instances where this was not the case, where Sendero brought problems on balance rather than benefits, the communal organisation would come to the fore to resist. But as elsewhere, the stronger the level of autonomous organisation, the stronger the resistance and the more bloody the outcome.[8]

Sendero's attempts to infiltrate the mines and to disrupt production had other characteristics, since the miners and other surface workers formed part of a strong, self-conscious union organisation with a long history of conflict with their employers, first with the US-owned Cerro de Pasco Corporation, and after nationalisation, with Centromin. Up until 1988 Sendero's main line of attack was sabotage. Given the problems of replacing broken machinery, the economic·costs of sabotage attacks were often very high, both in terms of the value of parts and the dislocation of production. But by 1989 two further types of action became common: the *paro armado* and assassinations of union leaders who refused to obey Sendero's strike calls. In 1989, there were two *paros armados* decreed by Sendero in the mining districts, one in May and the other in late July. In each case they were successful in partially closing down the mines. Miners' leaders received threatening messages to obey the strike order, while some leaders who opposed the strike call or argued for moderation in labour disputes (of which there were plenty in late 1988 and 1989) were assassinated. Such assassinations undoubtedly had a cautionary effect.

The difficulties for the miners, their leaders and the unions were also compounded by the growing militarisation of the main mining encampments, especially at the time of the two lengthy mining strikes in 1988 and that of 1989. The military, however, tended to overlook the differences between the miners' union and Sendero, seeing the miners as fellow travellers of Sendero, whose strike activity over such issues as national collective bargaining agreements was but a subterfuge for Sendero's subversive designs. Like the campesinos of Ayacucho, the miners found themselves in the uncomfortable position of being caught in the cross-fire, their autonomy under attack from both sides.

Though their presence in the central *sierra* was of crucial importance in terms of the fulfilment of the Senderistas' military strategy – it caused considerable alarm among senior officers in the armed forces – it was part of a generalised expansion and intensification of Sendero's activities in these years along the whole length of the *sierra*. Another area which was considered to be of priority to Sendero was the highlands of La Libertad, Ancash and southern Cajamarca, to the west of the River Marañon and in the hinterland of Trujillo. It was there that Osman Morote was involved, having moved northwards from Huancayo and the Mantaro valley, when he fell prisoner in 1989. But the period also saw the reconstruction of Sendero's presence in Ayacucho where in 1983–5 it suffered serious military reverses, in areas such as La Mar (along the River Apurímac), around Huanta and in Cangallo/Vilcashuamán. Sendero also managed to reconsolidate in the University in Ayacucho itself.

As in the past, one of the principle characteristics of the pattern of rural violence perpetrated by Sendero was its attempt to destroy the formal political *status quo* by getting rid of both elected and appointed officials. By killing, or threatening to kill local officials and representatives, Sendero sought to drive out the 'old order' and to consolidate its own political control. The extent of its activities is indicated by the figures in Table 7.3 which almost certainly under-estimate the scale of the problem. These figures do not include non-elected officials like governors, prefects, subprefects, judges and state attorneys (*fiscales*). According to figures produced by DESCO, the social science centre in Lima, from official data, the total number of local authorities killed by Sendero rose from 37 in 1987 to 79 in 1988 to 116 in 1989.

Table 7.3   Elected local authorities killed or forced to resign, 1986–9

	Mayors	Regidores
Abandoned	13	91
Resigned	86	259
Killed	17	2
Total	116	352

Source: National Electoral Committee (JNE). See *Resumen Semanal* No 521, May 1989

Thus throughout the country Sendero was able to expand its activities in 1988 and 1989, taking advantage of the extent of the economic crisis and its severe impact on rural areas. It was also able to exploit disillusionment with APRA and the signal failure of the Izquierda Unida (or the parties of the left individually) to put themselves at the head of popular mobilisation. However, though it undoubtedly found it easier to win over new people, Sendero came up against a series of political problems which impeded its expansion. In the cities, as we have seen, it found it difficult to infiltrate and take control of urban labour unions. Even within the *pueblos jovenes*, where it managed to build a presence, it had to compete with other political forces, especially on the left, to gain a foothold in the leadership of the popular movement. In rural areas, where it benefited from the weakness of the state at the local level, it failed to win the full confidence of *campesino* communities, let alone more organised sectors of the workforce like the miners of Centromin. The scope for expansion, therefore, for an organisation whose main political weapon was the threat of violence and which did not offer a solution to long-standing social problems, was to prove limited. The area in which Sendero did succeed in implanting itself with greater success than anywhere else, albeit temporarily, was the Alto Huallaga, an area with very different characteristics from those of the *sierra*.

COCA, NARCOS AND GUERRILLAS

While Sendero Luminoso in 1987 and 1988 was taking the building of an urban presence more seriously and seeming to make advances in its strategy of surrounding Lima, it managed to consolidate its control over much of the Huallaga valley, from the outskirts of Tingo María to Tarapoto some 250 miles downstream to the north. Though challenged intermittently by the MRTA, the police and army, Sendero converted itself into the *de facto* protector of the coca farmer, and as such into the virtual guarantor of the regional economy.

Reliable figures on the extent of coca agriculture are not easy to find, yet according to police estimates the total area planted with coca bushes by 1988 was somewhere in the region of 250 000 hectares, and growing at a rate of between 5 per cent and 10 per cent a year. By 1988 the Alto Huallaga is believed to have overtaken the Bolivian Chapare region as the single most important world source of coca. Of Peru's total estimated annual production of around 10 000 tonnes, the Alto

Huallaga accounted for around 90 per cent. The rest came from much smaller, though economically significant, plantations further south along the Apurímac valley and in La Convención in Cuzco. All in all, by 1988 some 250 000 people were thought to be involved in and dependent on the coca economy. The Huallaga valley became an important focus for internal migration as a result. As time went on the expansion of the area planted was mostly northwards where the eradicators found it more difficult to penetrate (or at least do their job in relative safety) and where the police and army also ventured at their peril. By the beginning of 1989, at least, coca plantations stretched north from the Alto Huallaga itself into the Central Huallaga (around Picota, Juanjui and Bellavista), Bajo Mayo (Tarapoto, Sisa, Lamas) and even Alto Mayo valleys (Moyobamba and towards Rioja).

The fall in the world price of cocaine on account of the saturation of the US market and the development of cheaper substitutes like crack did not to lead to any reduction in production of coca. Even at lower prices, coca remained the most profitable form of agriculture to the farmers of the Huallaga valley, providing better incomes than rice and maize, or tropical products like cacao, coffee or fruit. The growth in the area of coca plantings suggests that producers may have compensated for lower margins by producing more. But rather than substitute coca for crops like coffee (which the substitution programmes sought to encourage), farmers preferred to substitute other crops for coca. At the beginning of 1989, for instance, a hectare of coffee would provide the farmer with less than a quarter of the income that a hectare of coca would, even though prices were far lower than they had been at the beginning of the 1980s.

The collapse in agricultural prices as a result of the 1988–9 recession, coupled to the difficulties in getting credit or fertiliser, further encouraged the spread of coca agriculture. Increasingly, there was a scarcity of rice, maize and other locally grown foods in the markets of Tingo María and other towns. One of the effects of *narcotráfico*, indeed, was to make for extremely high prices in the urban economy, since – unlike other parts of Peru – there was no shortage of money in circulation (both dollars and intis) but only a limited range of goods to spend it on.

An important development in Peruvian narco-business during these years was the technification of processing. More sophisticated laboratories began to appear, generally run by the Colombian mafias, transforming cocaine paste into cocaine base or sulphate. Originally most of this processing, producing what is one stage short of the final end-product, had been conducted in Colombia, points in north-western Brazil and along the Peruvian–Colombian border, well to the north of the main coca producing areas. In the late 1980s, laboratories began to grow up nearer to the coca-producing areas, with cocaine paste being flown from the sixty-odd airstrips dotting the Alto Huallaga to Colombia for the final stages of processing.

The annual value of the drugs trade to the Peruvian economy is uncertain, and estimates vary considerably. But even fairly conservative estimates indicate that by 1987 at least, coca exports were worth in the region of $1 billion dollars annually, discounting the value of sales which in effect were creamed off by non-Peruvians and never entered the economy. If this is so, it was nearly twice the value of copper exports. Cuanto SA, the Lima-based econometric agency, run by former Central Bank president Richard Webb and the former head of INE, Graciela Fernández Baca, reckoned that in 1987 coca accounted for nearly 40 per cent of exports, 20 per cent of the country's agricultural GDP and 53 per cent of the GDP of Peruvian Amazonia. Their figures (see Table 7.4 on page 198) represent a useful guide and the basis for some sort of comparisons over time. Official central bank and INE calculations make no proper allowance for coca and cocaine.

With the development of *narcotráfico* in Peru a substantial banking business grew up through which dollars were converted into intis, thereby entering the local financial system. From the early 1980s – until Sendero's operations disrupted banking activities – the most important commercial banks all did a brisk business through a fairly extensive network of branches within the Huallaga region. Light aircraft were used to ferry in the intis, returning to Lima and other centres along the coast with dollars. As we have seen, the local supply of 'coca-dollars' could have a significant – sometimes a crucial impact – on the prevalent street exchange rate in Lima.

It was in this milieu of fast expanding illegal agriculture/processing, far from the world of government control, that Sendero Luminoso came to assert its presence, providing the coca farmers with protection from both the authorities and from the *narcotraficantes*. Though the Alto Huallaga was not quite 'the new republic' which Abimael Guzmán must have had in mind – it was capitalist Peru's most dynamic enclave – it became an area of key importance to the development of Sendero's military activities elsewhere in the country in 1988 and 1989: a source of manpower, arms and cash. It was Sendero's dominance of the Alto Huallaga which made the notion of

Table 7.4 Macroeconomic significance of coca and derivatives, 1979–7
(US$ millions)

	1979	1981	1983	1985	1987
GDP					
without coca	15 531	25 238	19 996	18 204	36 078
with coca	16 614	26 641	21 594	19 404	37 797
difference (%)	7.0	5.6	8.0	6.6	4.8
Exports					
without coca	3676	3249	3015	2978	2605
with coca	4391	4175	4214	3855	3616
difference (%)	19.5	28.5	39.8	29.4	38.8
Agricultural GDP					
without coca	1714	2466	2012	1588	3598
with coca	2082	2944	2412	1911	4306
difference (%)	21.5	19.4	19.9	20.3	19.7
Amazonia GDP					
without coca	1998	3400	2758	2203	3267
with coca	3081	4803	4356	3403	4986
difference (%)	54.2	41.3	57.9	54.5	52.6

Source: Cuanto SA. *Estadísticas para CADE 1988*, IPAE, Lima, 1988.

'strategic equilibrium' with Peru's armed forces something slightly more than just revolutionary fantasy.[9]

In seeking to consolidate its power in the Alto Huallaga, Sendero first sought to get rid of its rivals. Though the MRTA had on occasions expressed admiration for Sendero, Sendero did not reciprocate. When it launched its own guerrilla offensive at the beginning of 1987, the MRTA chose the area around Tarapoto in the north of San Martín to do so. In January 1987, it attacked the township of San José de Sisa in that region. Perhaps overestimating the efficacy of preliminary political work it had undertaken in 1986, the MRTA took the bold step of attacking the town of Tocache. But in Tocache the spheres of interest of the two guerrilla organisations – the MRTA in northern San Martín and Sendero to the south – collided, Sendero did not hesitate to counterattack. Having deftly entered into an alliance of convenience with the *narcotraficantes* of the area, together they inflicted a severe military defeat on the '*tupacamarus*', as they became known. By the end of May 1987, Sendero further reinforced its primacy when it overran the police headquarters in Uchiza after an attack involving some 200 combatants. In Alto Huallaga, it rapidly converted itself into a formidable fighting force. The government responded to the Uchiza attack by declaring the region to be in a state of emergency – a standard reaction – though putting the police, not the military, in charge. With police reinforcements the government managed to regain the main urban centres, but not the rural areas. The MRTA found itself relegated to the sidelines.

The relationship between Sendero and the *narcotraficantes* was neither straightforward nor constant. Initially the '*narcos*' resisted Sendero's intrusion, particularly as Sendero sought to disactivate their own armed bands which had helped protect their interests both in relation to the state authorities and the coca growers. But Sendero's military prowess forced most to submit to it. Nor did the *narcotraficantes* welcome a group whose main achievement was to put themselves at the head of the coca growers, or which forced them to pay 'contributions' (or *cupos*) as well as better prices for the raw material. In other respects, however, Sendero's presence was to prove very valuable. It made repression of their activities increasingly difficult, provided them with effective military support and exacerbated friction between the police and army over what each were supposed to do. The government had tended to use the police against the *narcotraficantes*, and the army against the insurgents. But as the two started to collaborate in the same areas the distinctions between their respective functions became blurred. So, while the *narcotraficantes* ended up paying a price for accepting Sendero, they could in effect leave military responsibilities in Sendero's hands, in the knowledge that Sendero would provide a valuable distraction for the authorities. When the police and army together managed to regain a presence in the Alto Huallaga during the course of 1988 and 1989, the challenge was again something which reinforced the community of interest between Sendero and the *narcotraficantes*. At no point did that community of interest become stronger than when the government appeared to be entertaining the idea of using aerial herbicide spraying to speed up coca eradication.

The fall of Tocache and Uchiza to Sendero came as a particularly sobering reminder of the government's loss of effective control over the whole region, just as the drugs issue was surfacing as a major international problem. Even as late as 1985 and 1986 the methods at the government's disposal to deal with the *narcotraficantes* proved hopelessly inadequate given the dimensions of the problem. Despite financial aid from the United States, the coca eradication programmes had failed to keep abreast of ever increasing acreages. The crop substitution programme had even less to show for it by way of positive results. With the consolidation of Sendero's presence in the Alto Huallaga, police activities against the *narcotraficantes* through the mobile police unit, Umopar, almost came to a standstill. It was in this context of failure, that attention turned to new ways of dealing with the problem.

One possibility was the use of tebuthiuron, more commonly known as 'spike', to destroy the coca plantations through aerial spraying. The advantages of 'spike' was that it would be far quicker and more effective than rooting up the bushes one by one, or at least chopping them down at the stems. Also it meant that eradication could be carried out from the air, without the same sort of risks of attack from the coca growers and Sendero. The disadvantages, however, were that it was indiscriminate, affecting food crops and potentially destroying farmers' legal livelihoods as well as the illegal. Nor were its longer term ecological effects properly understood, and its use threatened to raise a polemic among environmentalists worldwide. Finally, and perhaps most importantly, in seeking to eliminate the Alto Huallaga's staple crop it threatened the economic well-being of the majority of the population. There was therefore a risk of prompting popular mobilisation on a huge scale, which would potentially further play into the hands of Sendero.

The other, less dramatic alternative was to rebuild conditions of minimum security in the Alto Huallaga, and to use this as the basis for military strikes, not so much at the coca growers but at the processors and *narcotraficantes*. The Condor programme of joint US–Peruvian operations had evolved with the use of strikes on processing centres generally identifiable from the air from the airstrips nearby. Condor 7 in 1989, operating out of the newly constructed and heavily fortified Santa Lucía base near Uchiza, was reported to have knocked out ten laboratories, netting some 5 tons of cocaine equivalent. By 1988 and 1989 police operations could at least count on a minimum of air power. Whereas previously the anti-drug police had to plead with the army to borrow helicopters, in 1988 it had at least five ageing helicopters on loan from the United States at its disposal. In 1989, the government had sought to improve this inadequate air transport provision by placing orders in West Germany and the Soviet Union for a fleet of new helicopters, while at the same time trying to develop an effective rapid deployment commando force along the lines of Britain's Special Air Services (SAS), for use in the Alto Huallaga as well as other trouble spots in the Andes.

Despite these developments to improve the effectiveness of both the army and the police, there was still a long way to go before the government could claim that it had Alto Huallaga back under its total control. Sendero's second major attack on Uchiza in March 1989 – following shortly after the reported use of 'spike' on an experimental basis – was further reminder of Sendero's military capability, the support it enjoyed in the Alto Huallaga and the lack of coordination between the police and army in their response to emergencies.

RETHINKING COUNTER-INSURGENCY

'Give me 500 men and I will liberate Ayacucho in one year,' the self-styled 'Comandate Huayhuaco' was quoted as saying in a banner headline on 25 March 1989 in the daily newspaper *Expreso*. Huay-huaco, chief of one of the military controlled civil defence patrols in the Apurímac valley on the borders of Ayacucho department, thus pitched himself into the debate on how most effectively to counteract the influence of Sendero Luminoso, just when all other approaches seemed to be failing. His suggestion was to push ahead with the practice of civil defence patrols, originally used in 1982 and 1983, and to give free rein to local militias to kill suspected Senderistas wherever and whenever they could find them.

The prominence given to Huayhuaco's remarks in the media and in public debate underlined the deficiencies of the more traditional methods of counter-insurgency employed hitherto and the failure of the APRA government to develop an effective new strategy. On the one hand, it was clear that Sendero would not be beaten by military repression alone. Most military strategists argued in favour of an 'integral' approach by which they meant challenging Sendero politic-ally as well as militarily. On the other hand, the *desarrollista* strategy which the García government sought to implement so as to improve social and economic conditions had not produced results, and had been largely abandoned. The permanent threat of Senderista violence had made it almost impossible to get new rural development pro-grammes off the ground, especially if they involved technical staff working in the field. The programmes that were begun had also met with a lukewarm response from a population unwilling to participate for similar reasons. In practice, much of the money which was supposed to be channelled to peasant communities in the Emergency Zone ended up being spent in the city of Ayacucho and other towns, often on urban infrastructure.[10] There was thus a vacuum in thinking on what to do about fighting subversion. There was also a growing sense of frustration within the military on the issue: while the government's own preferred strategy had not worked, García continued to insist publicly that the military respect human rights and resist the temptation to embark on an all-out, indiscriminate 'dirty war'.

It was in this context that the military in Ayacucho and elsewhere in 1987 and 1988 opted for a more defensive rather than offensive strategy, one which emphasised containment of Sendero's activities rather than the pursuit of all out military victory. In September 1986, Alan García had issued a twenty-page directive to the armed forces, urging them to eliminate the terrorist threat, but to respect human rights in doing so. The directive, widely viewed in military circles as being contradictory, further encouraged the 'defensive' attitude. Increasingly, junior officers came to demand written instructions before going out on patrol. Patrols would act to defend themselves from attack, but were reluctant to root out and engage Sendero. Police and military garrisons in smaller towns and villages were withdrawn, and manpower concentrated in fewer but larger urban centres. Demoralisation among troops stationed in Ayacucho became a serious problem, exacerbated by low pay (real terms military pay fell sharply in 1988) and the sullen hostility of much of the local population to what was widely viewed as an 'invasion force'. With the failure to create a rapport with the local population, troops distrusted the people, finding it almost impossible to distinguish between Senderistas and non-Senderistas. They therefore treated all with equal suspicion.

Given these difficulties, the civil defence patrols, armed and supplied by the military, had obvious advantages. Being local people they knew the terrain and its inhabitants. To the troops it passed the onus of much of the killing on to civilians, reducing the possibility that they might be held accountable. But strengthening the system of civil defence patrols also involved certain risks. The loyalty of these peasant militias was difficult to guarantee, and it was by no means impossible that they might turn their arms on the military itself, or alternatively sell them to Sendero, and then ask for more. Evidence came to light, for instance, of grenades given to civil defence patrols by the marines in Ayacucho being subsequently used in terrorist attacks in Lima. Furthermore, there was the danger – possibly perceived with greater clarity by outside observers than by the military itself – that arming peasant groups to fight other peasant groups was simply accelerating a spiral of violence. Given the legacy of long and bitter disputes among different peasant communities, once in motion this spiral would be very hard to restrain.[11]

In fighting back against Sendero the military was also beset by the problem of the dispersion of guerrilla activities. By 1987 the focus of Sendero's activity ranged far from its original concentration in and around Ayacucho. It spread almost the whole length of the *sierra*, penetrating also jungle areas like Huánuco and San Martín as well as parts of Junín and Ayacucho, and the cities and towns of the coast. And with the development of the MRTA's rural guerrilla activities, Sendero was not the sole enemy.

The immediate response of the government to the spread of insurgent activities was to declare new Emergency Zones, akin to the original Ayacucho zone. As in Ayacucho, political as well as military responsibilities were vested in specially appointed military commanders, while civil rights and constitutional guarantees were generally curtailed. Consequently, as guerrilla violence spread, so did the area of the country under direct military jurisdiction. Whereas the original Ayacucho Emergency Zone, set up in December 1982, had consisted of nine provinces, by 1984 fourteen provinces were under military command, and by mid-1989 fifty-six provinces. The declaration of Emergency Zones was not so much the result of a carefully worked out counter-insurgency plan, but more a knee-jerk response to guerrilla initiatives: the government had to be seen to be doing something. In most cases such declarations involved the dispatch of reinforcements of both police and troops, the introduction of controls such as curfews and restrictions on travel, and the marginalisation of many existing civilian authorities.

The scale of human rights violation in military controlled areas is amply documented elsewhere.[12] Problems like extra-judicial killings, 'disappearances', arbitrary arrests and the use of torture remained commonplace, as the security forces sought to suppress Sendero. The violation of human rights remained a constant problem in the Ayacucho Emergency Zone, though of course is was not infrequent elsewhere. Killings tended not to be very selective and most of the victims appear to have had little or nothing to do with Sendero. Military attempts to conceal the problem of human rights violation made it more difficult for members of the press, representatives of human rights organisations and even employees of the attorney-general's office, to visit and travel freely in the Ayacucho Emergency Zone. Members of the military meanwhile remained largely unaccountable for human rights violations. As a special United Nations rapporteur on torture put it: 'The main problem . . . is that . . . the [legal] machinery provided has ground to a halt . . . Legal provisions are seen by those who are directly responsible for the restoration of law and stability as too burdensome in the fight against a ruthless enemy'.[13]

The whole issue of human rights surfaced again in the middle of 1988, when once again a massacre in a peasant community shook public opinion. But the response of the APRA government to the Cayara massacre in May stands in sharp contrast to that of Accomarca two and a half years earlier. The killing of some thirty villagers, witnessed by surviviors, was at first officially denied by the military. Even though opposition congressmen travelled to Cayara and were present at the identification of the bodies, and irrespective of the testimony of the attorney-general's representative that the bodies had been disinterred and disposed of, an official commission led by Carlos Enrique Melgar, an Aprista senator, reported three weeks afterwards that 'no human remains were to be found, and therefore no massacre took place'. The discovery of a number of bodies nearby three months later was downplayed by the defence minister, who said that the whole affair had been deliberately exaggerated so as to sway public opinion against the military and to 'question the action of the forces of order in their fight against subversion'.

The government's response to Cayara was an indication of its weakness *vis-à-vis* the military establishment, and in particular the diminished political standing of the president. García was no longer able to set the terms of his relationship with the military as he had done in 1985. As we have seen, he was forced to backtrack in 1987 on his attempt to consolidate civilian control over the military by accepting a general as head of the new Defence Ministry.[14] The bank nationalisation débâcle and the economic crisis of 1988 further reduced the standing of the president, especially as by the time of the Cayara affair, social tensions threatened to explode into violent conflict, with the country appearing increasingly 'ungovernable'.[15]

Shortly after the events at Cayara became public, officials from the Defence Ministry prevailed on the then prime minister, Armando Villanueva, to grant the military greater autonomy in the conduct of counter-insurgency operations. Following a sequence of meetings of the Inter-ministerial Counter-insurgency Coordinating Committee (CICLAS), the government agreed to a number of points to make counter-insurgency more effective.[16] These included allowing the military to intervene in parts of the country not formally under states of emergency; a promised review of the legal framework to facilitate counter-insurgency; a unification of command of all those involved; centralisation of all intelligence; and the establishment of an (extra-budget) national defence fund. In his annual 1988 Independence Day speech, four days after the Guzmán interview in *El Diario*, García's central theme was the need for unity against terrorism, and for a national crusade against Sendero Luminoso.

While inter-institutional rivalries continued to dog counter-insurgency efforts, the call for unity of command and the pooling of intelligence once again drew attention to the deficiencies of counter-insurgency policy. The poor coordination between police and the military in the Alto Huallaga was illustrative of wider problems of rivalries and distrust between the agencies most closely involved. Even the creation of the single Defence Ministry in 1987 and a single police force in 1988 did not solve the problem on the ground.

Another old problem which it took a long time to address was the lack of adequate military equipment. Military budgets were not allocated according to the spending priorities required to fight an internal guerrilla war. It was only by 1989 and 1990 that the army was able to acquire helicopters in sufficient quantities, and that rapid deployment of well-trained troops became possible. The effectiveness of counter-insurgency suffered from the impact of inflation on military budgets. Indeed the shift to a more defensive military strategy in 1987 and 1988 was in part due to the lack of financial resources.[17]

Fears that the difficulties faced by the authorities in conducting an effective counter-insurgency strategy were forcing them to turn to more desperate tactics were raised by the appearance of death squads in the latter part of 1988. The first killing by the so-called Comando Rodrigo Franco (CRF), took place within a few hours of García's 1988 Independence Day speech, when the lawyer acting for Osman Morote was gunned down in Lima.[18] Other killings followed in the name of the CRF.

From the start it was widely believed that CRF had close links with the military, the Interior Ministry, and APRA. The pattern of its activities, however, suggests that the name became a useful flag of convenience for a number of groups involved in paramilitary activity. In Ayacucho, the CRF appeared to act in conjunction with the military, if not directly under its aegis. Elsewhere, in Puno and Arequipa, for instance, murders carried out in the name of CRF bore the hallmarks more of Aprista armed gangs, while in Lima – where a great many prominent leaders on the left received various types of death threat in the first half of 1989 – it was believed that CRF was more closely linked with the Interior Ministry and the specialist anti-terrorist police, Dircote. Probably one of CRF's most prominent victims was Saúl Cantoral, general secretary of the Peruvian miners' federation, who was assassinated in March 1989. The figure constantly rumoured to be the mastermind behind the CRF was Agustín Mantilla, vice-minister of the interior since 1985, who became minister in May 1989. The political significance of Mantilla's possible role in the CRF gains weight, given his particularly close relationship with Alan García. If it was true that he was involved in the CRF, then it seemed possible that knowledge of the death squads and their activities went right to the very top.

TESTING TIME FOR SENDERO

For Sendero Luminoso the end of 1989 and the year 1990 was a period of key importance in the strategic advance of the *guerra de guerrillas*. According to Sendero's own plans, the organisation should have been well on its way towards 'strategic equilibrium' by 1990, the point at which it could fight the armed forces on more or less equal terms. The electoral calendar provided a special challenge. Given Sendero's commitment to disrupting elections wherever and whenever, the concentration of three elections in seven months – the November 1989 municipal elections and the two rounds of presidential elections in April and June 1990 – provided an obvious challenge. Moreover, Sendero's ability to disrupt electoral activity over substantial areas of the country came to be seen as a key test of the organisation's real military and political strength. Another date, too, had special signif-icance. On 17 May 1990, Sendero's armed uprising was ten years old. It was widely expected, especially given Sendero's penchant for celebrating anniversaries, that this would have been the opportunity for some bold new initiative.

However, in practice the apprehensions of the authorities were misplaced. The November elections went off fairly smoothly, even though Sendero had threatened many candidates and declared a *paro armado* in Ayacucho. In most parts of the country voting took place without violent incidents, after a massive security operation, although non-voting and null-or-void voting was very high in Ayacucho and other parts of the *sierra*. The first round of presidential elections the following April, preceded by a number of armed actions, took place normally almost everywhere. Similarly, though accompanied by bombings and blackouts in Lima, the second round also took place in relative peace and tranquillity. Sendero thus showed itself unable seriously to interrupt the electoral process. Even more surprisingly, 17 May and 18 May came and went with no major show of force, except a bombing attack on the campaign headquarters of Cambio-90 in the city of Ayacucho.

How do we explain the lull in Senderista activity, just at the moment when one would expect the opposite? Three explanations are possible: that Sendero had never been as powerful in military terms that the build-up in 1988 had suggested; that the organisation had been weakened during this period by both the effects of counter-insurgency operations or internal division (or both); or that it was biding its time and waiting for a more propitious moment to return to the offensive.

It is not easy to establish with any precision which of these was nearer the truth. However, it is clear that during 1989 and 1990 Sendero faced some major military reverses. Nowhere was this more obvious and more damaging than in the Alto Huallaga.

Following the Uchiza raid, the government had responded by giving effective power to the military throughout the whole region. A new commander was appointed, General Alberto Arciniega. Under Arciniega and the army, the main thrust of policy shifted away from coca eradication and drug control, towards confronting Sendero. The only way to establish military control, argued Arciniega, was to separate Sendero from its social base. That meant winning over the coca producers, convincing them that they would no longer be the main target of repression. During his period as commander in the Alto Huallaga, Arciniega had considerable success in winning over the local people, convincing them that they need not fear the immediate threat of eradication, still less aerial spraying with 'spike'. At the same time, from the new military base at Santa Lucía, Arciniega dealt Sendero a number of serious military defeats. The problem with Arciniega's approach was that it attracted furious criticism from Washington to the effect that he was in the pay of the *narcotraficantes*, while it also led to further recriminations between the army and the police.

The success of counter-insurgency in the Alto Huallaga was not mirrored by any immediate shifts in policy elsewhere. However, there is little doubt that it had a significant effect in weakening Sendero's overall military capacity. No longer was relatively sophisticated weaponry so easy to acquire. At the same time, the authorities were able to pull off operations which reduced Sendero's operational capacity.

During late 1989 and early 1990 it became evident that Sendero was having difficulty in continuing to expand at the rate at which it had grown in the two previous years. We have already noted how even in the more remote Andean communities, *comuneros* did not necessarily accept Sendero with open arms. They might welcome some of Sendero's activities, but they tended not to go along with other demands that opposed their interests. Since Sendero generally imposed itself by force, it commanded respect for that reason. It did not necessarily command much loyalty. Sendero thus found it difficult to build up a real and durable political support which went beyond obedience for fear of reprisals.[19]

Sendero's ability to interpose itself among more organised sectors of the workforce – the miners of the central *sierra* or factory workers in Lima – also proved to be very limited. Once again the power it wielded tended to be derived more from fear than from committed support. Sendero found it difficult to provide what such sectors – often with long traditions of union militancy behind them – wanted: better wages and better living conditions. For such workers, the destruction of their factory, the machinery in it, or the interrupting of power supplies was not the answer to their problems. Moreover, it was wholly alien to their political traditions. Thus, as Raúl González a leading *Senderologo*, has noted, the advance of Sendero was blocked by its failure to develop political and military cadres among those whom it sought to win over. It proved unable to create 'popular committees' in the peasant communities, or to build the Popular Guerrilla Army (EGP) in such a way as to get anywhere near 'strategic equilibrium'.[20] Perhaps it is in recognition of this that the 1986 document 'Develop the Popular War Serving the World Revolution' put such emphasis on recruiting for the EGP in the city.

It was in this context that there was persistent speculation by the beginning of 1990 of serious divisions in Sendero, in particular between the leadership and the various organisations within Sendero's orbit charged with carrying out specific duties. The existence or not of such divisions is hard to prove, though in the circumstances of an unfulfilled revolutionary timetable and important reverses on the military front, it is not difficult to imagine. Rumours of Guzmán's death added further to the speculation about splits. The most direct evidence of an internal rupture was the appearance of leaflets in May 1990 arguing in favour of abandoning armed struggle. Some Senderistas even handed themselves over to the armed peasant patrols. But while the leaflets showed signs of being produced by hands of others than Sendero,[21] the 'surrenders' too could have been staged to give the impression of advances in counter-insurgency strategy.

While leading '*senderologos*' differed on how much to read into the various accounts of internal divisions and rejection of the leadership,[22] they concurred that, as a new government took office, these problems were not such as to disarticulate Sendero. Even under the hypothesis that a Fujimori government was conspicuously more successful than its two predecessors in conducting counter-insurgency operations, Senderismo would take a long time to quell.

Conclusions

The objective of this book has been to attempt an assessment of the performance of the García administration in the light of the problems facing Peru. The extremes of wealth and poverty, the lack of political and economic integration between regions, the relatively strong articulation of social demands, and the weakness of the state in mediating them and spearheading reform, all helped to make Peru a peculiarly difficult country to govern. This was even more the case in the unfavourable external economic climate of the 1980s. It was likely that any president in these circumstances would have suffered '*desgaste*' as a result of five years in office.

But at the same time, when he became president in 1985, the political circumstances facing Alan García were not entirely unfavourable. He had come to office with a landslide election victory in reaction to the conservatism of his predecessor. This allowed him to legitimately claim strong popular backing for a leftward leaning, reforming programme. On the basis of the elections, his party won a majority of seats in both houses of Congress, a party with a strong tradition of discipline and loyalty towards the leadership. The opposition forces in Congress were also divided and dispirited. Furthermore – for good or for bad – the political system in Peru gave considerable leeway for the executive to govern by administrative fiat. García, therefore, was not without power.

Also, there was widespread recognition – even among opponents of APRA – that the time had finally come for Peru's oldest mass-based party to be given a chance to govern the country and to put its ideas into practice. Throughout the country people were attracted by the force and dynamism of the young man who, in the space of five years had come from relative obscurity to the very centre of the political limelight, picking up the mantle of perhaps Peru's greatest political leader of the century, Víctor Raúl Haya de la Torre, and legacy of social reform initiated by General Juan Velasco. In 1985 there was great hope that García was the man who could help steer his country towards a better future with greater prosperity, less social inequality, and more balanced regional development. García therefore also enjoyed considerable political authority as well as power.

This sense of optimism was given added force by the successes of the first two years: inflation was reduced, growth was attained, constitutional authority was seemingly established over the military, and a degree of national pride restored in Peru's standing, especially in relation to foreign creditors. Public support for the government remained strong right through to the second half of 1987, and García maintained his political preeminence. The opportunity therefore existed for García to make use of his powers and his political authority and to capitalise on the degree of economic stabilisation achieved to push ahead with more fundamental reforms.

But this optimism proved to be misplaced; the opportunity was in large measure dissipated, perhaps in the erroneous belief that the economic upturn since 1985 – and with it García's political supremacy – could be maintained for longer than proved to be the case. Though it was true that the heterodox experiment in Peru lasted significantly longer than its contemporary variants in Argentina and Brazil, it was not long enough for the necessary headway to be made in a number of areas indispensable if longer-term goals were to be achieved. Seen in retrospect, there were a number of crucial errors and omissions, some of which were recognised by the administration, others less so.

First, it was essential to have a medium- and long-term economic strategy as well as a short-term stabilisation plan. If short-term policy did not fit into a wider and more comprehensive strategy, it was almost bound to run into incoherence, contradictions and ultimate failure. As we have seen, the García government came to office without having a carefully prepared strategic game-plan. Though initiatives emerged (and some proved very innovative and successful) overall policy tended to be improvised – reacting to circumstances rather than shaping them. Not only did the lack of a blueprint lead to incoherencies in decision-making, it also meant that it took much longer than otherwise would have been the case to get policies and programmes under way. Time was thus wasted when otherwise things were going García's way. The need for a carefully crafted short-, medium- and long-term plan was, of course, all the greater given the innovative and unorthodox nature of the sort of economic policies which were employed.

Second, APRA did not come into office disposed to share power with other political forces. The importance of having a policy of alliances only became clear during the second half of the García administration; in 1985 it seemed there was no reason to seek such collaboration. APRA's strong showing in the 1985 elections was therefore possibly a weakness in that it lured the party into believing it could rule the country on its own. Also, the party's traditional ideological ambivalence – its leftish origins but its subsequent practice of striking deals with the right – made it harder to establish political alliances. Both the right and the left tended to regard APRA with a good deal of suspicion. Indeed, while García sought to build links with the left, much of his party were basically conservative in outlook. At no time was this lack of a strategy of alliances clearer than at the time of the bank nationalisation in 1987. García at that point suddenly found himself dependent on the left without first having created the conditions for such an understanding. Meanwhile his government's attitude towards private business was equally ambivalent. The logic of its heterodox experiment was to forge close links with the private sector since the pursuit of growth implied large-scale private invest- ment. Yet this relationship was not built up on the basis of defined institutional structures or agreed rules of the game. Rather, typically, García sought to conduct these relations in a very personalist manner. His government was also capricious and inconsistent towards the private sector, sowing doubts as to its longer-term intentions particu- larly in relation to the intended balance between private enterprise and state intervention. Having decided to build the alliance with the 'twelve apostles', the government signally failed to generate the necessary confidence even before García tempestuously ordered the nationalisa- tion of private financial institutions.

Third, García has to do something to pacify the country. This was possibly the biggest challenge of all, given the deep social, ethnic and regional divides which Sendero helped expose. The experience of Belaúnde had shown the limitations of the military approach to counter-insurgency. At the outset, García rightly stressed the need to combat Sendero not just by military means, but by spearheading a development strategy for Peru's poorest departments to benefit the peasant producer. He also rightly stressed the centrality of agriculture in any such strategy. The problem was to make a programme to dynamise peasant agriculture effective, especially in the adverse conditions created by Sendero's presence. The heterodox reactiva- tion, as we have seen, had a significant impact on agricultural incomes by increasing the demand for food. But the government ran into enormous difficulties in building on this and ensuring that the poor received the benefits. While the improvement hinged mainly on macroeconomic considerations, the government's plans to target rural poverty were often poorly planned, wasteful or too late. The introduc- tion of the Plan Sierra, unveiled only in 1988, was symptomatic of the delay in introducing plans geared towards benefiting peasant agriculture. Meanwhile, Sendero was able to grow, feeding of rural discontent and disillusionment about the inadequacies of state provision over a range of issues. The *rimanacuys* provided a good opportunity, not just to build up García's profile in rural areas but to provide a forum for discussion and confidence-building between government and peasant communities. But this idea was dropped in the wake of the November 1986 municipal elections, and indeed was never tried in Ayacucho. Equally, Sendero's entry into the Alto Huallaga owed much to the lack of confidence between producers and state institutions, especially with regard to coca eradication and crop substitution. Despite the rhetoric, the achievements in social communication with rural Peru were very limited.

Fourth, García failed to use the 1985–7 breathing-space to strengthen the economic foundations of the state. The calculation that the heterodox experiment would improve the government's tax revenue proved erroneous, and little was done to raise new taxes or to make the existing tax system work better. Without an effective overhaul of the tax system, it was inappropriate to think that the government would be able to intervene more in pursuit of economic development or greater social equity. At the same time, parallel to this, little was done to improve training or working conditions within the public administration, and especially in central government. Without a substantial improvement in training, pay and morale within the state bureaucracy, it was again inappropriate to think in terms of improving the *quality* of state intervention.

Finally, little was done at the outset to push ahead with programmes for political, administrative and economic decentralisation. It was only in the last two years that the García government took up the issue of regionalisation, and pursued it with energy. Of course, the pattern of Peru's economic and political development makes it difficult to promote decentralisation, and it remains to be seen whether the regional governments elected in 1989 and 1990 will enjoy real autonomy from Lima in decision-making and use of resources. But, unless the central government is prepared to make genuine concessions in devolving power, it is likely to continue to run into radical, and sometimes violent, challenges from the regions. The creation of a more agile institutional structure to link government and the governed in Peru is a fundamental requisite for the establishment of a stronger democracy capable of drawing on the energy of popular organisation rather than suppressing it.

These are some of the more general areas in which the shortcomings of the García government were, in retrospect, most evident. They all, to varying degrees, reflected the lack of a clear strategy from the outset to link the main points of a short- and longer-term economic reactivation strategy to institutional change. The pattern of decision-making was thus not guided by strategic planning but by knee-jerk responses, a situation made worse by García's highly personalist, anti-institutional style of government.

García's guiding instincts were those of a politician rather than a technocrat. Political rather than economic considerations were his main points of reference. Economics, ultimately, had to fit into political constraints, rather than the other way round. The key imperative was the need to extend the social base of support for the government and enhance its legitimacy in the eyes of the population. For García, popularity was one of his most important political assets, providing the basis of his authority in dealing with other political actors. In this sense his government fits into a populist tradition which flourished in countries like Brazil and Argentina in the 1930s and 1940s, and more recently in Venezuela in the 1970s, but which with APRA's suppression had never fully developed in Peru.

The problem for this sort of government is that popularity is a volatile commodity, closely tied to a government's ability to meet expectations by sustaining economic growth and by distributing its fruits as widely as possible. A fast-growing economy makes it easier to satisfy different interest groups and reconcile conflicts between them. It also makes it easier to hold together a political coalition through the distribution of material inducements and favours.

The degree to which the sort of economic reactivation strategy adopted by García would *inevitably* lead to disaster is, of course, a controversial point. There were always constraints to growth, especially in a country so dependent on imports to sustain it. However, we have sought to argue that the collapse which took place in 1988 was not entirely a forgone conclusion, and that the failure to anticipate its effects and to take evasive action was an act of irresponsibility which was not justified by the political circumstances. In particular, if the government had gone for a more modest rhythm of growth than the 10 per cent attained in 1986 and the nearly 8 per cent in 1987, the domestic investment and foreign exchange constraints would have been considerably less, and the model would probably have lasted longer. Also, had the García government followed through with its debt policy, having already alienated the international financial community, valuable foreign exchange might have been saved. As it was, despite the posture of limiting debt repayment to 10 per cent of exports, more went out in debt payment than came back in new loans. Finally, it is hard to avoid the conclusion that the attempted bank nationalisation, whatever the reason for it, was an act of folly which wrecked relations with the private sector for no real gain, and which exposed García's lack of judgement on a crucial issue just when the opposition was looking for an issue to challenge his authority.

When the 'down-turn' came, though, the government's agenda for structural reform was rendered virtually meaningless. Heterodoxy itself, premised on an improvement in popular levels of consumption, was abandoned in favour of a return to orthodox formulae and the easing of external constraints through another massive contraction in domestic demand. Extreme economic and political instability meant that longer-term goals of structural reform were forgotten in face of the exigencies of crisis management, while the government's effective timescale was one of day-to-day survival. The only area in which advances were made was in that of regionalisation. The scale of the 1988–9 economic crisis was such as not only to discredit García's leadership, but also many of the objectives which (albeit rhetorically) he had initially stood for. The economic crisis, meanwhile, further weakened the state as an instrument of possible change. The political reaction, as shown by the election results in 1989 and 1990, was a sharp shift to the right: APRA's interventionist proposals were rejected in favour of the virtues of 'minimal' government. This was evident not just in the political platform of Mario Vargas Llosa, but also in that of Alberto Fujimori, whose appeal also had to do with a low-key, pragmatic political style – the opposite of García's in 1985 – and his avoidance of making exaggerated commitments.

But despite the political reaction in 1990 caused by disillusion at the gap between García's promises and his achievements, many of the same issues seemed likely to persist to haunt his successor. Would Fujimori be able to stabilise the economy and pave the way to a return to sustainable growth? Would he be able to revive the apparatus of government so at least to administer the country? Would he be able to preserve the necessary political balance in face of continuing social polarisation without becoming the plaything of any one interest group? Would he be able to deal with the problem of insurgency and social violence without succumbing entirely to the armed forces? Would he be able to tap the creative energies of the mass of the population to their full potential? And, perhaps most important of all, would he be able to do anything about the daunting problem of rebuilding confidence between government and the governed – between the 'official' Peru and the 'real' Peru beyond the limits of an enclave of businessmen, politicians and bureaucrats in the capital city? Or was Peru to hobble from one crisis to another, ungovernable, without sense of direction, with the underlying problems becoming ever more acute. Though the agenda in many ways was not that different from when García assumed power five years before, the urgency of finding solutions was even more pressing.

Notes and References

1 Introduction

1. See R. Thorp and G. Bertram, *Peru 1890–1977: Growth and Policy in an Open Economy* (London: Macmillan, 1978,) on which many of the following views on Peru's economic development are based.
2. This was the case during the guano boom and the early twentieth century boom in mineral exports. An interesting exception to the rule was the 1890s when Peru's currency was tied to silver and the international market for silver collapsed. In these circumstances, despite buoyant world markets for other export commodities, Peru lacked the foreign exchange to import. Domestic industries blossomed as a result.
3. E. V. K. FitzGerald, *The Political Economy of Peru 1956–78: Economic Development and the Restructuring of Capital* (Cambridge: Cambridge University Press, 1979).
4. See the *Financial Times*, for instance, 30 August 1989. This quotes Inter-American Development Bank figures which show Lima to have a higher percentage of its workforce in the informal sector than any other major city in Latin America.
5. Joel Jurado, *Protagonismo de Clases Populares: Límites y Potencialidades en la Crisis*, (Lima, IDS, January 1989).
6. Oscar Altimir, *La Dimensión de la Pobreza en América Latina* (Santiago: ECLA, 1978).
7. Adolfo Figueroa, 'Integración de las Políticas de Corto y Largo Plazo', in *Economía*, no. 23, June 1989.
8. Central Bank (BCRP), *Mapa de la Extrema Pobreza* (Lima, 1982).
9. José Matos Mar, *Desborde Popular y Crisis del Estado. El Nuevo Rostro del Perú en la Década de 1980* (Lima, IEP, 1984).
10. Carlos Franco, 'Nación, Estado y Clases: Debate en los 80' in *Socialismo y Participación* no. 29, March 1985.
11. Imelda Vega Centeno, 'Ser Joven y Mestizo: Crisis Social y Crisis Cultural en el Peru', *Márgenes* year II. no. 3.
12. On the early history of APRA, see Steve Stein, *Populism in Peru: The Emergence of the Masses and the Politics of Social Control*, (Madison, 1980). Also Peter Klaren, *Modernization, Dislocation, and Aprismo* (Austin: University of Texas, 1973).
13. See also Julio Cotler, *Los Partidos Políticos y la Democracia en el Perú* (Buenos Aires: CLACSO, 1988).
14. The exception to this rule was the government of Bustamante y Rivero in the immediate post-war period (1945–8) in which Apristas participated in the cabinet, but in which the party's inflexibility (especially Haya's) was a major factor in that government's final collapse.

15. Imelda Vega-Centeno, *Aprisimo Popular: Cultura, Religión y Politica* (Lima: Cisepa – PUC/Tarea, 1991).
16. See John Crabtree, 'From Belaúnde to García', *Bulletin of Latin American Research*, vol.4, no.2, 1985.

2 Economic Policy: Playing by New Rules

1. For the social effects of Belaúnde's economic policies see Leonel Figueroa, 'Economic Adjustment and Development in Peru: Towards an Alternative Policy', in Cornia, Francis and Jolly (eds), *Adjustment with a Human Face*, vol II (Oxford: Oxford University Press, 1987). Figueroa was president of the central bank under García (1985–87).
2. For a comparison of heterodox measures in Argentina, Brazil and Peru see John Crabtree, 'Let's Do It Our Way', *Third World Affairs*, July 1987.
3. Daniel Carbonetto (ed.), *El Perú Heterodoxo* (Lima: INP, 1986).
4. This argument is mentioned, for instance in, Rosemary Thorp, 'Peruvian Adjustment Policies, 1978–85: The Effects of a Prolonged Crisis', in Thorp and Whitehead (eds), *Latin American Debt and the Adjustment Crisis* (London: Macmillan/St Antony's, 1987).
5. For García's position on this and other issues, see Alan García, *A La Inmensa Mayoría*: Discursos, 1985–8 (2 vols) (Lima, 1987).
6. *The Peru Report*, May 1987.
7. Alan García, *A La Inmensa Mayoría*.
8. Instituto Nacional de Planificación (INP), 'La Distribución del Ingreso en el Perú' (mimeo), 1986.
9. Adolfo Figueroa, 'Integración de las Políticas de Corto y Largo Plazo', *Economía* no. 23, June 1989.
10. Centro de Estudios para el Desarrollo y la Participación (CEDEP), *Lima Informal*, Lima, 1988.
11. This is one of the tentative conclusions of the Labour Ministry's 1986 Household Survey, *Encuesta de Hogares no. 18*.
12. COINCIDE 'Como Usan las Comunidades del Cusco el Fondo de Apoyo al Desarrollo Comunal' in *El Problema Agrario en Debate* Lima: SEPIA II, 1987.
13. *The Andean Report*, January 1987: from 480 tractors to 1500. From 173,000 tonnes to 376,000 of fertiliser according to INE; *Compendio Estadístico* 1987.
14. Hernando de Soto, *El Otro Sendero* (Lima: Ed. El Barranco 1986); published in English as *The Other Path: The Invisible Revolution in the Third World* (London: Tauris, 1989).
15. All three preoccupations, for instance, emerged from answers to a questionnaire to party leaders in the book *Decidamos Nuestro Futuro* (1985), edited by the Universidad del Pacífico and the Friedrich Ebert Foundation, Lima 1988.
16. Outlined in Margarita Trillo and Jorge Vega, 'Gasto Público, Tributación, Déficit Fiscal e Inflación en el Perú (1970–88)', in *Economía*, no. 23, June, 1989.
17. Jorge Vega, 'El Sistema Tributario Peruano', Lima, 1988 (mimeo) on which much of this section is based.

18. See Alberto Giesecke (ed.), *Burocracia, Democratización y Sociedad*: Lima: Fomciencias, Concytec, Lima, 1989, for an account of the problems facing the Peruvian public administration at various levels.
19. Narda Henríquez, *Decentralización y Poder* (Lima: Universidad Católica, 1987).
20. Under the regionalisation proposals, they were eventually placed under control from elected regional assemblies.
21. Lewis Taylor, 'Agrarian Unrest and Political Conflict in Puno 1985–87', *Bulletin of Latin American Research*, vol.6 no. 2, 1987.
22. Carol Graham, 'APRA 1968–1988: From Evolution to Government – the Elusive Search for Political Integration in Peru', D.Phil Thesis, Oxford, 1989.

3 APRA's Political Triumph

1. For voting patterns see the various works of Fernando Tuesta, especially *Perú Política en Cifras* (Lima: Friedrich Ebert Foundation, 1987). The figures quoted here (and in Tuesta) are percentages of valid votes. They are not percentages of the total vote including null and void votes. As of 1985 the system used in presidential elections was that to win outright a candidate had to win 50 per cent plus one of the *total* vote including null and void votes. So, though García got 53.1 per cent of the valid vote he still theoretically did not win an absolute majority in terms of the total vote. In the event, a second round was avoided because Alfonso Barrantes who was the runner-up declined to stand for a second round.
2. See Peri Paredes and Griselda Tello, *Pobreza Urbana y Trabajo Femenino*, Lima: ADEC, 1988. Also interviews by the author with Cooperación Popular leaders in 1986 confirmed the overtly partisan purposes of PAIT.
3. *Comedores populares* expanded rapidly in the early 1980s, and provided community-run feeding facilities to families in the neighbourhood. From 1984 onwards the municipality of Lima organised a mass programme to provide milk to school children, the *Vaso de Leche* Programme.
4. Tuesta, *Perú Política en Cifras.*
5. The best and most detailed account of what happened and who was responsible is the Senate Commission's report researched and written by senator Rolando Ames, '*Informe al Congreso sobre los Sucesos de los Penales*' (Lima: OCISA, 1988). The massacre caused a particularly bad impression among European social democrats, though some Latin American leaders, notably Carlos Andrés Pérez of Venezuela, sought to back García up.
6. *The Andean Report*, January 1986.
7. *The Andean Report*. April 1986.
8. Tuesta, *Perú Política en Cifras.*
9. Survey conducted by the author in February 1987.
10. See Fernando Rospigliosi, 'Perú: Entre el Acuerdo y la Libanización', *Pensamiento Iberamericano*, no.14, July–December 1988. Rospigliosi's interpretation is that the entry of the parties of the left into formal politics in the 1977–80 period aided the democratic transition. This point of view has been challenged by Luis Pásara in an unpublished article,

'Perú: La Izquierda Legal en la Precariedad Democrática'. Pásara draws attention to the reiterated call by important parties within Izquierda Unida to armed struggle. On balance it seems safer to base a judgement on what the left-wing parties did rather than what they said.

11. *The Peru Report*, June 1987.

4 Sendero Luminso and the Guerrilla Challenge

1. A separate group, Puka Llajta had an organised presence in Junín and Puno, and the MIR Cuarta Etapa in the highlands of Cajamarca and La Libertad. By 1980 Sendero had absorbed Vanguardia Revolucionaria – Proletario-Comunista (VR-PC) with its foothold in Andahuaylas in Apurímac.

2. In January 1983, the role of the military was given major publicity when eight journalists were killed in mysterious circumstances at the village of Uchuruccay in Ayacucho. The government was obliged to appoint an investigating commission, headed by novelist Mario Vargas Llosa, which blamed local peasants for the killings. These findings failed to dispel a widespread belief, subsequently partly substantiated, that military-organised peasant patrols were to blame.

3. Central Bank (BCRP), *Mapa de la Extrema Pobreza* (Lima: 1982).

4. For the early history of Sendero Luminoso, see Carlos I. Degregori, *Ayacucho 1969–79 – El Surgimiento de Sendero Luminoso* (Lima: IEP 1990).

5. See Alan Angell, 'Classroom Maoists: The Politics of the Peruvian Schoolteachers under Military Government', *Bulletin of Latin American Research*, vol. 2 no. 1. Peru is exceptional in Latin America for the strength of Maoism. When the PCP split in 1964 just over half the party's militants associated themselves with the Maoist fraction, and nearly all those involved in peasant work.

6. In 1990 the security forces discovered a house in Lima in which apparently Guzmán had been living until fairly recently.

7. Philip Mauceri, *Los Militares en el Perú: Su Política en el Contexto de la Insurgencia y Democratización (1980–9)* (Lima: IEP, 1989).

8. For instance, *Actualidad Militar* (Mar–June 1983), cited in Mauceri, *Los Militares en el Peru*.

9. Raúl González, 'MRTA – La Historia Desconocida', *Que Hacer*, no. 51, March–April 1988.

10. Mauceri, *Los Militares en el Peru*.

11. Within the military, the Centro de Altos Estudios Militares (CAEM) exercised an important role in the elaboration of a developmental approach. See, for instance, CAEM, 'Proyecto de Gobierno en Defensa Nacional', August 1986.

12. *The Peru Report*, April 1987.

13. See Rolando Ames, *Informe al Congreso Sobre los Sucesos de los Penales*.

14. García took the coup threat very seriously, ordering artillery to shoot down any further plane which should fly low over the palace. For a graphic account see G. Thorndike, *La Revolución Imposible* (Lima: EMISA, 1988).

15. López Albújar was not sworn in until October 1987.
16. *The Peru Report*, January 1987.
17. See Lewis Taylor, 'Agrarian Unrest and Political Conflict in Puno (1985–87)', *Bulletin of Latin American Research*, vol. 6, no. 2, 1987.
18. Qué Hacer no. Puno – El Corredor Senderista, *Qué Hacer* no. 39, February–March 1986.
19. Raúl González, 'Los Mineros de Pasco – El Talon de Aquiles de Sendero', *Qué Hacer* no. 40, April–May 1986.
20. Raúl González, 'Coca y Subversión en el Huallaga', *Qué Hacer*, no. 48, September–October 1987.

5 The Economy from Boom to Bust and Beyond

1. Guillermo Wiese, head of Peru's second largest privately owned bank, the Banco Wiese, heard the news on the radio while holidaying at Paracas.
2. *The Peru Report*, August 1987.
3. Alan García, *El Futuro Diferente. La Tarea Histórica del APRA*. Especially chapter VII (Lima: JALSA 1982).
4. *The Peru Report*, August 1987.
5. Banks in cocaine towns like Uchiza exchanged dollars for intis, flying the dollars out of the jungle to Lima and coastal towns.
6. Quoted in *The Peru Report*, October 1987.
7. *The Peru Report*, August 1987.
8. *The Andean Report*, October 1987.
9. *Peru: The Top 1500 (1988 edition)*, (Lima: Peru Reporting EIRL, 1988).
10. This was a particularly strong line of argument in the political propaganda of Mario Vargas Llosa's Movimiento Libertad, which was born as a response to the nationalisation move.
11. *The Peru Report*, February 1988.
12. The World Bank, *Peru: Policies to Stop Hyperinflation and Initiate Economic Recovery* (2 vols) (Washington, 1988).
13. *The Peru Report*, April 1988.
14. For dollarisation and its bearing on hyperinflation in Peru, see Oscar Dancourt and Ivory Yong, 'Sobre la Hiperinflación Peruana', *Economía* no. 23, June 1989. Also on hyperinflation see Jurgen Schuldt, *Hacia la Hiperinflación en el Perú* (Lima: Universidad del Pacífico, 1988).
15. *Caretas* 1024, 19 September 1988.
16. Labour Ministry, *Encuesta de Hogares*, nos 19 and 20, February 1990.
17. Javier Abugattás, 'Un Programa Social Transitorio (1990–92)', in the Central Bank's monthly review *Moneda*, vol 2, no. 20, February 1990.
18. AB Prisma/UPCH Working Group, *The Probable Effects of the Present Economic Crisis on the Status of Young Children in a Peri-urban Population*, report presented to UNICEF, September 1989. The project was financed partly by USAID.
19. For instance, Provida, an NGO working in several poor districts, reports on the falling calorific content of food provided by *comedores populares* between 1987 and 1989 as the price of the food purchased rose faster than the purchasing power of beneficiaries. As the economic crisis worsened, *comedores populares* tended to become more important as a source of

food in poor neighbourhoods as more people made use of them, while the quality of food provided tended to decline.

6 The Political Response to the Crisis

1. José Matos Mar, *Desborde Popular y Crisis del Estado. El nuevo Rostro del Perú en la Década de 1980* (Lima: IEP, 1984).
2. Carmen Rosa Balbi, 'La Recesión Silenciosa', in *Que Hacer*, no. 59, June–July 1989.
3. Victor Robles Sosa, 'La Batalla de los Trabajadores', *Que Hacer*, no. 56, December 1988–January 1989.
4. Jackeline Velazco, Movilizaciones Agrarias, 1985–89: Un Analisis Económico', CISEPA, no.89 (Catholic University, July 1990).
5. See Raúl González, 'Los Olvidados', in *Que Hacer*, no. 47, June–July 1987.
6. An account of the various pressure groups which developed within APRA at this time is to be found in *The Peru Report*, June 1988, on which this is based.
7. *Que Hacer*, no. 47, June–July 1987. Cusco: APRA o Muerte.
8. *The Peru Report*, June 1988.
9. See, for instance, *Caretas* 1013, 4 July 1988.
10. 'Por una Alternativa Revolucionaria de Poder'; 9th Congress of the PCP, 27–31 May 1987, Political Theses.
11. *Estatizar para Democratisar. La IU responde a la Derecha y al APRA*, Izquierda Unida, (Lima: 1987) The book includes speeches by Enrique Bernales, Jorge del Prado, Javier Diez Canseco, Carlos Malpica and Gustavo Mohme. The quote is from Javier Diez Canseco.
12. 'El Pueblo Construye su Futuro'. Asamblea Nacional Popular. Editora Humbolt, p. 16. This leaflet contains the main resolutions agreed by the ANP and was edited by the event's organisers. Since the agreements remained unpublished this is the only text available. It accurately captures the political mood of the ANP.
13. Unpublished survey conducted by the team from the magazine *El Zorro de Abajo*.
14. Mario Zolezzi, 'Parto en el Arenal', *Que Hacer*, no. 50, January–February 1988.
15. *The Andean Report*, March 1988, points to the CGTP's decision to accept application by the CCP and oil workers (FENATRAPP). By 1988 the CGTP accounted for around 95 per cent of the labour movement.
16. See José María Salcedo, 'IU: El Drama Recién Comienza?' *Que Hacer*, no. 57, February–March 1989.
17. Quoted in *El Nacional* 21 September 1987.
18. See, for instance, Rosemary Thorp, 'Los Caminos del Capitalismo en el Peru', *Páginas*, 102, April 1990. In fact Hernando de Soto parted political company with Vargas Llosa in 1988, acting at various points as consultant for the García government.
19. For a critical description of the role of banks in the economic power groups, recently updated (1989), see Carlos Malpica, *El Poder Económico en el Perú* (2 vols), (Lima: Mosca Azul, 1989).

20. See *The Peruvian Financial System at the Time of the Expropriation* (Lima: Peru Reporting EIRL 1987).
21. The formula finally adopted for the 1989 municipal election was that Acción Popular would provide the candidate for Lima, and the PPC the candidate for Callao. For the presidential election Acción Popular provided a candidate for first vice-president, and the PPC for the second vice-president. An equal number of candidates were to stand from all three political forces in the elections for Congress.
22. See *Que Hacer*, no. 61, October–November 1989. Letter from the textile industrialist Gian Flavio Gerbolini in response to an earlier interview with one of Fredemo's ideologues, Jaime de Althaus, chief editorial writer on *Expreso*.
23. See Víctor Robles, 'Los Jovenes de Fredemo' in *Que Hacer*, no. 60, August–September 1989. This also shows how Fredemo was able to build up a presence in the student movement.
24. For a thorough article on the television business in Peru, see *The Peru Report*, March 1989.
25. Peruvian electoral law prohibits the publication of opinion polls in the last week before an election, so the last minute rush of support towards Fujimori went largely undetected.
26. *Caretas* 1104, 16 April 1990.
27. APRA won more votes than any other party in the first round in Amazonas, Ancash, Cajamarca, La Libertad, Lambayeque and Piura.
28. Fernando Villarán, 'El Fenómeno Fujimori o Crisis de las Ideas Convencionales', *Que Hacer*, no. 64, May–June 1990. He quotes various estimates as to the size of the informal *microempresariado*.
29. Evidence from questionnaires on political attitudes among informal sector workers conducted by Eliana Chávez, *Que Hacer*, no. 64 May–June 1990.
30. Cambio-90 also came top in Ayacucho, Cuzco, Huancavelica, Junín, Pasco and Puno.

7 Spiral of Violence

1. For instance Fernando Rospigliosi, 'El Riesgo de la Libanización', *La República*, April 1989.
2. Comisión Especial del Senado sobre las Causas de la Violencia y Alternativas de Pacificación en el Perú, *Violencia y Pacificación* (Lima: DESCO and Comisión Andina de Juristas, February 1989.)
3. 'La Entrevista del Siglo: Presidente Gonzalo Rompe el Silencio', interview by Luis Arce Borja, *El Diario*, July 24 1988. Subsequent information suggested, however, that the interview took place in Lima. See Caretas 1112, 12 June 1990.
4. See, for instance, the minutes of the 4th Plenary in April 1986 and the 4th National Conference in July 1986.
5. Intelligence officials in Lima in early 1987 thought that Sendero's move towards more urban work would make infiltration much easier. Interviews with the author.

6. Carmen Rosa Balbi, 'Senderos Minados', in *Que Hacer*, no. 61, October–November 1989.
7. Between 1986 and 1989 Sendero managed to use its presence in the *sierra central* to increase its influence in the southern part of Lima department (around Cañete) as well as to the north of Lima (around Barranca and Huarmey).
8. Nelson Manrique, 'La Década de la Violencia', *Márgenes*, no. 5–6, December 1989.
9. 'Strategic equilibrium' for Sendero was the phase between 'strategic defence' and the 'strategic offensive' in which the armed forces and the Popular Guerrilla Army (EGP) confronted one another on more or less even terms.
10. *The Peru Report*, April 1987.
11. Carlos Ivan Degregori, 'Sendas Peligrosas: La Guerra del Comandante Huayhuaco', *Que Hacer* no. 58, April–May 1989.
12. See, for instance, Amnesty International Peru Briefing, *Caught Between Two Fires*, November 1989; US State Department Human Rights Reports; Americas Watch Reports.
13. Quoted in Ammesty International, ibid.
14. Philip Mauceri, *Los Militares en el Perú*.
15. There were frequent rumours of a pending coup in the months following the September *paquetazo*. These became so intense by January 1989 that the US ambassador in Lima felt obliged to make a public statement expressing his government's opposition to any disruption of constitutional rule in Peru.
16. *The Peru Report*, July 1988.
17. General López Albújar, Defence Minister (1987–9). Interviewed in *Que Hacer*, no. 57, February–March 1989.
18. Rodrigo Franco was a prominent Aprista who had been assassinated by Sendero in the suburbs of Lima earlier in 1988.
19. This comes over strongly in Sendero's dealings with communities in the highlands of Junín. See Nelson Manrique, 'La Década de la Violencia',
20. Raúl González, 'Sendero: Duro Desgaste y Crisis Estratégica', in *Que Hacer*, no. 64, May–June 1990.
21. *Caretas* 1109, 21 May 1990.
22. While for González it was 'clear that problems in Sendero exist, basically between the party leadership and the *organismos generados*, for Gustavo Gorriti, author of a book on Sendero, the evidence for the division was 'pretty weak' (interview in *La República Dominical*, 13 May 1990. Carlos Ivan Degregori argued that despite possible 'internal contradictions' it was 'premature' to say that this constituted a 'division' (interview *La República Dominical*, 20 May 1990.

Bibliography

The APRA Government, 1985–90

Abugattás, Javier, *Estabilización y Crecimiento Económico en el Perú* (Lima: Fundación F. Ebert, GRADE and Brookings Institution, 1990).

Adrianzén, Alberto *et al.*, *Democracia: Realidades y Perspectivas* (Lima: Instituto Bartolomé de las Casas Rímac, 1988).

Alarco, Germán and Del Hierro, Patricia. *Algunas Enseñanzas sobre el Manejo en la Política Económica para un Nuevo Gobierno* (Lima: Fundación F. Ebert, 1990).

Alarco, Germán, *et al.* *Empleo, Salarios y Distribución del Ingreso: Márgenes de Política* (Lima: Fundación E. Ebert, 1986).

————*La Inversión en el Perú: Determinantes, Financiamiento y Requerimientos Futuros* (Lima: Fundación F. Ebert, 1989).

————*Economía Peruana 1985–1990: Enseñanzas de la Expansión y del Colapso* (Lima: Fundación F. Ebert, 1990).

Alcorta, Ludovico, *Concentración y Centralización de Capital en el Perú* (Lima: Fundación F. Ebert, Lima 1987).

Amat y León, Carlos et al., *Los Hogares Rurales en el Perú: Importancia y Articulación con el Desarrollo Agrario* (Lima: Fundación F. Ebert, 1987).

Americas Watch, 'Derechos Humanos en el Perú: Primer Año del Presidente García', Comisión Andina de Juristas, Lima, 1986.

————'A Certain Passivity: Failing to Curb Human Rights Abuses in Peru', New York, (1987).

Ames, Rolando (ed.), *Informe al Congreso Sobre los Sucesos de los Penales* (Lima: Ocisa, 1988).

Amnesty International, *Perú: Desapariciones, Torturas y Ejecuciones Sumarias* (London, 1987).

————*Caught Between Two Fires* (Peru Briefing) (London, 1989).

Anderson, James, *Terrorism in Peru: Sendero Luminoso – A New Revolutionary Model?* (London: Institute for the Study of Terrorism, 1987).

Asamblea Nacional Popular (ANP), *El Pueblo Construye su Futuro* (Lima, 1988).

Balbi, Carmen Rosa, *Identidad Clasista en el Sindicalismo. Su Impacto en las Fábricas* (Lima: DESCO, 1989).

————*Las Relaciones Estado-Sindicalismo en el Perú, 1985–87* (Lima: Fundación F. Ebert, 1988).

————'Sindicalismo y Caminos de Concertación', in *Socialismo y Participación*, no. 38, June 1987.

Ballón, Eduardo, *Democracia y Sistema Político a Nivel Local: El Caso de Villa El Salvador* (Lima: CLACSO-DESCO, 1986).

————(ed.), *Los Movimientos Sociales en la Crisis: El Caso Peruano* (Lima: DESCO, 1986).

Banco Central de Reserva del Perú (BCRP), *Memoria 1988* (Lima, 1988).

225

Bernales Enrique (ed.), *Violencia y Pacificación*, report of the Special Senate Commission on Violence and Pacification (Lima: DESCO, 1989).

Bonilla, Heraclio *et al.*, 'La Crisis de Qué Crisis?' *Economía*, no. 23, June 1989.

Bonilla, Heraclio and Drake, Paul (eds) *El Apra: De la Ideología a la Praxis* (Lima: Nuevo Mundo, 1989).

Burga, Jorge B. and Delpech, Claire, *Villa El Salvador. La Ciudad y su Desarrollo Realidad y Propuestas* (Lima, CIED, 1988).

Burga, Manuel, *Nacimiento de una Utopia* (Lima: Instituto de Apoyo Agraria (IAA), 1988).

Cáceres, Armando. *El Ajuste Forzado: La Economía Peruana durante 1988* (Diagnóstico y Debate series) (Lima: Fundación F. Ebert 1989).

Caravedo, Báltazar, *Región Urbana y Estratégia Decentralista* (Diagnóstico y Debate series) (Lima: Fundación F. Ebert, 1988).

Carbonetto, Daniel *et al.*, *El Perú Heterodoxo* (Lima: INP, 1987).

Centro de Estudios para el Desarrollo y la Participación (CEDEP), *Lima Informal* (Lima, 1988).

Chávez, Eliana, *El Sector Informal Urbano: De Reproducción de la Fuerza de Trabajo a Posibilidades de Producción* (Lima: Fundación F. Ebert, 1988).

Chávez, Jorge, 'The Failure of Orthodoxy and Heterodoxy: An Outdated Trade-off for Less Developed Economies (mimeo), Oxford, 1989.

Cotler, Julio, 'La Radicalización Política de la Juventud Popular en el Perú', *Revista de la CEPAL*, no. 29, Santiago, 1986.

———(ed.), *Para afirmar la Democracia* (Lima: IEP, 1987).

Crabtree, John, 'From Belaúnde to García', *Bulletin of Latin American Research*, vol. 4, no. 2, 1985.

———'Alan García's Government', *Third World Quarterly*, July 1987.

———'Let's Do it Our Way: Heterodoxy in Brazil, Argentina and Peru', *Third World Affairs*, 1988.

Dancourt, Oscar *et al*, *Inflación y Redistribución en el Perú* (Lima: Fundación F. Ebert, 1985).

———*Hiperinflación y Política Económica en el Perú: Una Interpretación* (Lima: Universidad Católica, 1989).

Degregori, Carlos Iván *et al*, *Conquistadores de un Nuevo Mundo, de Invasores a Ciudadanos*, (Lima: IEP, 1986).

———'Sendero Luminoso: I, Los Hondos y Mortales Desencuentros. II, Lucha Armada y Utopía Autoritaria', IEP Working paper (Lima, 1986).

———*Qué difícil es ser Dios. Ideología y Violencia Política en Sendero Luminoso* (Lima: El Zorro de Abajo, 1989).

DESCO, *Violencia Política en el Perú* (Lima, 1989).

De Soto, Hernando, *El Otro Sendero. La Revolución Informal* (Lima: Editorial El Barranco, 1986).

Dornbusch, Rudiger, 'From Stabilization to Growth', *The Peru Report*, Lima, November 1989.

Durand, Francisco, *Los Empresarios y la Concertación* (Diagnóstico y Debate series) (Lima: Fundación F. Ebert 1987).

———*La Burguesía: Los Primeros Industriales; Alan García y Los Empresarios* (Lima: DESCO, 1988).

Eguren, Fernando, Hopkins, Raúl, Kervyn, Bruno and Montoya, Rodrigo (eds), *Perú: El Problema Agrario en Debate* (SEPIA II) (Lima: SEPIA, 1988).

Escobal, Javier *et al.*, *Precios, Costos y Desequilibrio Monetario: La Experiencia Peruana 1981–88* (Lima: GRADE, 1989).

————*Políticas de Precios y Subsidios Agrícolas: Impacto Macroeconómico y Sectorial. Perú 1985–88* (Lima: GRADE, 1989).

Favre, Henri, *Perú: Sendero Luminoso y Horizontes Ocultos* (Mexico: UNAM, 1987) (Cuadernos Americanos, no. 4).

Figueroa, Adolfo, 'Integración de las Políticas de Corto y Largo Plazo', *Economía*, no. 23, Lima, 1989.

Figueroa, Leonel, 'Economic Adjustment and Development in Peru: Towards an Alternative Policy', in Cornia, Stewart and Jolly (eds), *Adjustment with a Human Face* (Oxford: Oxford University Press, 1987).

Flores Galindo, Alberto and Manrique, Nelson, *Violencia y Campesinado* (Lima: Institute de Apoyo Agrario, 1986).

Franco, Carlos, 'Nación, Estado y Clases', in *Socialismo y Participación*, no. 29, Lima, March 1985.

————*Deuda y Dependencia: Diálogo con el Enfoque y Propuestas de Alan García* (Lima: Editores EMI, 1989).

————*El Perú de los 90: Un Camino Posible* (Lima: CEDEP, 1989).

Fundación Ebert-APEP, *Siete Ensayos sobre la Violencia en el Perú* (Lima, 1985).

Galin, Pedro *et al.*, *Asalariados y Clases Populares en Lima Metropolitana* (Lima: IEP, 1986).

García, Alan *Un Futuro Diferente: La Tarea Histórica del APRA* (Lima: JALSA, 1985).

————*A la Inmensa Mayoría, Discursos (1985–8)* (Lima: EMI Editores, 1988).

Giesecke, Alberto and Hurtado, Isabel. *Cómo Funciona la Administración Pública Peruana* (Lima: Fundación F. Ebert, 1987).

Giesecke, Alberto (ed.), *Burocracia, Democratización y Sociedad* (Lima: Fomciencias and Concytec, 1989).

Glewwe Paul and De Tray, Dennis, *The Poor in Latin America during Adjustment: A Case Study of Peru*, LSMS Working Paper (Washington: World Bank, 1989).

Golte, Jurgen and Adams, Norma. *Los Caballos de Troya de los Invasores: Estratégias Campesinas en la Conquista de la Gran Lima* (Lima: IEP, 1987).

Gonzáles de Olarte, Efraín. *Crisis y Democracia: El Perú en Busca de un Nuevo Paradigma de Desarrollo* (Lima: IEP, 1987).

————(ed.) *Economía para la Democracia* (Lima: IEP, 1989).

González Raúl, 'Coca's Shining Path' in *The Real Green Revolution*, NACLA 22 (6), March 1989.

Graham, Carol, 'APRA 1968–88: From Evolution to Government: The Elusive Search for Political Integration in Peru', D.Phil thesis, Oxford, 1989

Grompone, Romeo, *Talleristas y Vendedores Ambulantes en Lima* (Lima: DESCO, 1985).

Guzmán, Abimael, 'La Entrevista del Siglo', *El Diario*, 24 July 1988, Lima.

Hauser, Heinz-Michael *et al.*, *La Política Económica Heterodoxa: Entre Imperativos, Tácticas y Alianzas Sociales: Perú 1985–89* (Diagnóstico y Debate Series) (Lima: Fundación F. Ebert 1989).

Henríquez, Narda, *Decentralización y Poder* (Lima: Universidad Católica, 1987).

Herrera, César, 'Restricción de Divisas. Efecto Macroeconómico y Alternativas de Política' Lima: IEP (Working Papers), 1989.

Herrera, César *et al.*, *Reactivación y Política Económica Heterodoxa 1985–86*, (Lima: Fundación F. Ebert, 1987).

Hertogne, Alain and Labrousse, Alain, *Le Sentier Lumineux de Pérou. Un Nouvel Integrisme dans le Tiers Monde* (Paris: Editions La Découverte, 1989).

Iguíñiz, Javier, *Política Económica 1985–86 Deslindes Mirando al Futuro,* (Lima: DESCO, 1986).

————'Proyecto Nacional, Situación Económica y Política de Ingresos en el Perú, in *Política Económica y Actores Sociales* (Santiago: PREALC, 1988).

————(ed.), *La Cuestión Rural en el Perú*, (Lima: Universidad Católica, 1986).

Instituto Nacional de Estadística (INE), *Encuesta Nacional sobre Medición de Niveles de Vida 1985/86* (Lima: INE, 1986).

Instituto Nacional de Planificación (INP), 'La Distribución del Ingreso en el Perú' (mimeo), Lima, 1986.

Jiménez, Félix, 'Conflicto, Precios Relativos e Inflación en una Economia Estancada. El Caso del Perú', *Socialismo y Participación*, no. 44, Lima, December 1988.

Jurado, Joel, 'Protagonismo de Clases Populares: Límites y Potencialidades en la Crisis' (mimeo), IDS, Lima, 1989.

Kisic, Drago, *De la Corresponsabilidad a la Moratoria: El Caso de la Deuda Externa Peruana 1978–86*, (Lima: Fundación F. Ebert, 1987).

Lauer, Mirko, 'La Nueva Derecha en el Perú', in *Nueva Sociedad*, no. 98, Caracas, 1988.

León, Janina, *Del Crecimiento Generalizado a la Crisis de la Economía* (Lima: GRADE, 1988).

Malpica, Carlos, *El Poder Económico en el Perú* (2 vols) (Lima: Mosca Azul, 1989).

Manrique, 'Nelson, La Década de la Violencia', in *Márgenes* nos 5 and 6, SUR, Lima 1989.

Matos Mar, José, *Desborde Popular y Crisis del Estado. El Nuevo Rostro del Perú en la Década de 1980* (Lima: IEP, 1984).

Mauceri, Philip, *Los Militares en el Perú: Su Política en la Insurgencia y Democratización (1980–89)* (Lima: IEP, 1989).

Morales, Edmundo, *Cocaine: White Gold Rush in Peru* (Tucson: University of Arizona Press, 1989).

Palma, Diego, *La Informalidad, Lo Popular y El Cambio Social* (Lima: DESCO, 1987).

Paredes, Peri and Tello, Griselda, *Pobreza Urbana y Trabajo Femenino*, (Lima: ADEC-ATC, 1988).

Paredes, Peri, *Las Estratégias de Contratación Laboral: La Experiencia del PROEM y sus Alternativas* (Lima: Fundación F. Ebert, 1988).

Parodi, Jorge: '*Ser Obrero es Algo Relativo*' (Lima: IEP, 1986).

Pásara, Luis and Parodi, Jorge (eds), *Democrácia, Sociedad y Gobierno en el Perú* (Lima: Cedys, 1988).

Pease, Henry, *Democracia y Precariedad bajo el Populismo Aprista* (Lima: DESCO, 1988).

Peru Reporting, *The Top 1500, 1988 edition* (Lima, 1988).

————*The Peruvian Financial System at the Time of the Expropriation,* (Lima 1987).

Plaza, Orlando and Francke, Marfil, *Formas de Dominio: Economía y Comunidades Campesinas* (Lima: DESCO, 1986).

Portocarrero, Gonzalo and Oliart, Patricia, *El Perú desde la Escuela* (Lima: Instituto de Apoyo Agrario (IAA), 1989).

Prisma/Universidad Cayetano Heredia, 'The Probable Effects of the Present Economic Crisis on the Status of Young Children in a Peri-urban Population' (Lima, 1989).

Rochabrun, Guillermo, 'Crisis, Democracy and the Left in Peru', in *Latin American Perspectives,* vol 15, no. 3 (California: Sage Publications, 1988).

Rospigliosi, Fernando, 'Los Jóvenes Obreros de los 80. Inseguridad, Eventualidad y Radicalismo' (Lima: IEP, Working Papers, 1987).

————'Perú: Entre el Acuerdo y la Libanización', in *Pensamiento Iberamericano,* no. 14, 1988.

————'Comisión Ames: Escrupulosa Investigación, Contundentes Acusaciones. Nulos Resultados?' In *Márgenes,* no.3, 1988.

Salcedo, José María, 'Tsunami Fujimori', *La República,* Lima, 1990.

Sánchez, Luis, 'La Política del Gobierno para Comunidades Campesinas', in Cueva (ed.) *Sierra Central: Comunidad Campesina, Problemas y Alternativas* (Lima: Fundación F. Ebert, 1987).

Sulmont, Denis et al., *Violencia y Movimiento Sindical* (Lima: CEAAL, 1989).

Sulmont, Denis, *Cuestionamiento y Posibilidades de Renovación en el Movimiento Sindical* (Lima: Cuadernos Laborales 57, ADEC-ATC, 1990).

Taylor, Lewis, 'Agrarian Unrest and Political Conflict in Puno (1985–87)', in *Bulletin of Latin American Research,* vol. 6, no. 2, 1987.

Thorndike, Guillermo, *La Revolución Imposible,* (Lima: EMISA, 1988).

Thorne, Alfredo et al., *Financiamiento e Informalidad. Mercado Financiero Noorganizado y Financiamiento de la Actividad Informal* (Lima: Fundación F. Ebert, 1988).

Thorp, Rosemary, '"Structuralist" Attempts at Short-term Management in the 1980s: The Case of Peru under Alan García', *European Journal of Development Research,* vol. 1, no. 2, December 1989.

————'Evaluación de la Administración Económica en el Perú durante el Período 1985–88', in Toledo (ed.) *Perú y América Latina en Crisis: Cómo Financiar el Crecimiento,* (Lima: ESAN/IDE, 1990).

Toledo, Alejandro, *Perú: Hacia un Programa Económico de Ajuste*: Simulación Econométrica 1988–1992 (Lima: ESAN, 1989).

————*Perú y América Latina en Crisis: Cómo Financier el Crecimiento* (Lima: ESAN/IDE, 1990).

Torres, Victor and O'Phelan, Fernando, *Inversión Extranjera Directa en el Perú. Década del 80: Balance y Perspectivas* (Lima: IPRI and PNUD, 1990).

Trillo, Margarita and Vega, Jorge, 'Gasto Público, Tributación, Déficit Fiscal e Inflación en el Perú (1970–88), *Economía* no. 23, Lima, 1989.

Tuesta, Fernando, *Perú Política en Cifras* (Lima: Fundación F. Ebert, 1987).
————*Pobreza Urbana y Cambios Electorales en Lima* (Lima: DESCO, 1989).
Ugarteche, Oscar, 'Peru: The Foreign Debt and Heterodox Adjustment Policy under Alan García', in Griffith-Jones (ed.), *Managing World Debt* (London: Harvester, 1988).
————'Perú y el 10%. La Política de Deuda Bajo Presión', *Nueva Sociedad*, no. 98, Caracas 1988.
Vega-Centeno, Imelda, 'Ser Joven y Mestizo. Crisis Social y Crisis Cultural en el Perú de Hoy', *Márgenes*, no. 3, SUR, Lima, 1988.
————*Aprismo Popular: Cultura Religión y Política* (Lima: Cisepa–PUC/ Tarea 1991).
Vega-Centeno, Máximo *et al.*, *La Violencia Estructural en el Perú. Causas, Mecanismos y Manifestaciones Económicas* (Lima: Asociación Peruana de Estudios para la Paz, 1990).
Velarde, Julio, *Impacto Macroeconómico de los Gastos Militares en el Perú 1960–87* (Lima: Universidad del Pacífico, 1990).
Velazco, Jackeline, *Crisis y Movilización Popular*, (Lima: Catholic University, 1989).
Vigier, María Elena and Paredes, Peri, *Los Trabajadores del Programa Nacional de Apoyo de Ingreso Temporal de Lima Metropolitana* (Lima: OIT-INP, 1986).
Wise, Carol, 'Economía Política del Perú: Rechazo a la Receta Ortodoxa' (Lima: IEP Working Papers, 1987).
World Bank, *Peru: Policies to Stop Hyperinflation and Initiate Economic Recovery* (Washington, DC: World Bank, 1988).

Magazines and Other Publications

Actualidad Económica
Actualidad Militar
Allpanchis
Analisis Laboral
Andean Report
Caretas
Coyuntura Laboral
Cuadernos Laborales
Cuadernos Urbanos
Debate
Debate Agrario
Márgenes
Moneda

Nota Semanal (BCRP)
Oiga
Páginas
Perú Económico
Peru Report
Proceso Económico
Que Hacer
Resumen Semanal
Sí
Socialismo y Participación
Sur
Tipo de Cambio
Zorro de Abajo

Index